After the Death of God

After the Death of God

SECULARIZATION AS A
PHILOSOPHICAL CHALLENGE
FROM KANT TO NIETZSCHE

Espen Hammer

THE UNIVERSITY OF CHICAGO PRESS
CHICAGO AND LONDON

The University of Chicago Press, Chicago 60637
The University of Chicago Press, Ltd., London
© 2025 by The University of Chicago
All rights reserved. No part of this book may be used or reproduced in any manner whatsoever without written permission, except in the case of brief quotations in critical articles and reviews. For more information, contact the University of Chicago Press, 1427 E. 60th St., Chicago, IL 60637.
Published 2025

34 33 32 31 30 29 28 27 26 25   1 2 3 4 5

ISBN-13: 978-0-226-83849-6 (cloth)
ISBN-13: 978-0-226-83850-2 (paper)
ISBN-13: 978-0-226-83851-9 (e-book)
DOI: https://doi.org/10.7208/chicago/9780226838519.001.0001

Library of Congress Cataloging-in-Publication Data

Names: Hammer, Espen, author.
Title: After the death of God : secularization as a philosophical challenge from Kant to Nietzsche / Espen Hammer.
Description: Chicago : The University of Chicago Press, 2025. | Includes bibliographical references and index.
Identifiers: LCCN 2024033885 | ISBN 9780226838496 (cloth) | ISBN 9780226838502 (paperback) | ISBN 9780226838519 (e-book)
Subjects: LCSH: Secularization—Philosophy. | Death of God—Philosophy. | Belief and doubt. | Modernism (Christian theology). | Philosophy, German—19th century. | Religion—Philosophy.
Classification: LCC BL2747.8.H3244 2025 | DDC 211/.8—dc23/eng20240927
LC record available at https://lccn.loc.gov/2024033885

After the Death of God

SECULARIZATION AS A
PHILOSOPHICAL CHALLENGE
FROM KANT TO NIETZSCHE

Espen Hammer

THE UNIVERSITY OF CHICAGO PRESS
CHICAGO AND LONDON

The University of Chicago Press, Chicago 60637
The University of Chicago Press, Ltd., London
© 2025 by The University of Chicago
All rights reserved. No part of this book may be used or reproduced in any manner whatsoever without written permission, except in the case of brief quotations in critical articles and reviews. For more information, contact the University of Chicago Press, 1427 E. 60th St., Chicago, IL 60637.
Published 2025

34 33 32 31 30 29 28 27 26 25   1 2 3 4 5

ISBN-13: 978-0-226-83849-6 (cloth)
ISBN-13: 978-0-226-83850-2 (paper)
ISBN-13: 978-0-226-83851-9 (e-book)
DOI: https://doi.org/10.7208/chicago/9780226838519.001.0001

Library of Congress Cataloging-in-Publication Data

Names: Hammer, Espen, author.
Title: After the death of God : secularization as a philosophical challenge from Kant to Nietzsche / Espen Hammer.
Description: Chicago : The University of Chicago Press, 2025. | Includes bibliographical references and index.
Identifiers: LCCN 2024033885 | ISBN 9780226838496 (cloth) | ISBN 9780226838502 (paperback) | ISBN 9780226838519 (e-book)
Subjects: LCSH: Secularization—Philosophy. | Death of God—Philosophy. | Belief and doubt. | Modernism (Christian theology). | Philosophy, German—19th century. | Religion—Philosophy.
Classification: LCC BL2747.8.H3244 2025 | DDC 211/.8—dc23/eng20240927
LC record available at https://lccn.loc.gov/2024033885

Contents

Preface vii

Introductory Remarks · 1

CHAPTER ONE
Secularization and Modernity · 8

CHAPTER TWO
The Kantian Compromise · 47

CHAPTER THREE
Hegel's Rescue Mission · 80

CHAPTER FOUR
A Social Critique of Religion: Feuerbach and Marx · 112

CHAPTER FIVE
Nietzsche and the Overcoming of Christianity · 150

Concluding Remarks · 188

Bibliography 197
Index 205

Preface

When I was growing up in Norway during the seventies and eighties, religious practice, whether in the form of pietism or as more official versions of Protestantism in the public churches, was rapidly becoming marginalized. Its erstwhile authority and spellbinding capacity, its ability to sway minds, shape lives, and even give people something to die for, was now—as Kierkegaard had already predicted it would do—taking refuge in small communities, with little or no influence on society at large. While a certain percentage of the older population still went to church and at times showed signs of religious fervor, the rest of society viewed religious services merely as occasions to celebrate important holidays such as Christmas (which had long since become a consumerist family event) or Easter, or to conduct marriage and funeral ceremonies. As Ingmar Bergman memorably illustrated in his 1963 movie *Winter Light*, what went on inside churches—the complete liturgy—most laypeople considered unengaging, alienating, and even crushingly boring: in some sense unavoidable but with no meaning of its own and without any future. You would not want to spend a minute longer than needed in those dark, tomblike structures where people spoke sanctimoniously, but with their eyes glazing over at the pages of a text, most of which more than 2,500 years old, dealing with piousness, suffering, and death.

Although it was not until 2008 that the Norwegian government put an end to compulsory Christian education with a confessional element in its primary school system—no doubt very late given the inroads liberalism had made in Europe over the previous decades—the values embedded in the reigning social democratic consensus were decidedly progressive, emphasizing equality and social welfare, the right to pursue happiness and pleasure, and a technoscientific and essentially naturalistic view of human reality. Thus, it was felt, the great existential contingencies of life that organized religion in its traditional garb had responded to could neither be endowed with religious significance nor be met with any form of tragic wisdom. They would have to lend themselves to a technological solution, be suffered silently, or become the object of some form of therapy. Apart from its historical, political, and aesthetic role, which no serious student of the humanities could ignore, I should not be taking much interest in religion.

As an adult, however, I have become far more appreciative not only of how religion—and for me Christianity in particular—has affected society (that is, the objective questions the historical sciences will be raising), but also of the complex and often very deep and compelling ways it makes ethical and existential concerns vivid and meaningful at an experiential, first-person level. I strongly sense how my upbringing in a profoundly secular social reality has shaped my response to religion. At the same time, I keep discovering that the claims religion raises are neither intellectually nor existentially disrespectable. Indeed, many of them keep impressing themselves on me.

According to the classical secularization thesis, which emerged during the European Enlightenment and found proponents well into the twentieth century, religion should long since have been consigned to the dustheap of history. All expressions of belief, ranging from faith in the form of piousness and devotion to organized liturgical activity and the formation of political will, would gradually yet persistently weaken and finally disappear under the pressure of modernization and, in particular, scientific and technological rationality. Thus social and cultural modernization would be predicated on secularization, and in some cases be deemed identical with it.

The secularization thesis has long been under attack, however, and today, as it has become abundantly evident that religion may not only persist but thrive under conditions that are decidedly modern, it finds few supporters. While in modernity religion *changes*, often profoundly, the claim that it is destined to disappear has simply become impossible to square with the available evidence. In the United States, for example, though hardly in Europe, adherence to a religious creed is just as widespread today as it was fifty or a hundred years ago. Moreover, an enormous variety of spiritual orientations have sprung up, making the number of individuals who say they believe in something binding and transcendent greater than at any other time in late modern history. At the same time, however, there are few historians who would deny that secularization has occurred and profoundly changed us and our societies.

In spite of the empirical implausibility of the secularization thesis, certain contemporary thinkers, most famously biologist Richard Dawkins and cultural historian Christopher Hitchens, have continued to approach religion with the intellectual resources of classical enlightenment thought.[1] Opposing religion directly to natural science while assuming compatibility, they have argued that, as opposed to what is going on in science, religious believers quite recklessly make claims for which there can be no acceptable and rationally binding evidence. Religion therefore is bound to be irrational—its claims to truth can never be properly warranted. And if that is not enough, considered as a system of belief it not only is irrational and most likely false, but is detrimental to fundamental human interests in freedom and moral respect. In Dawkins and Hitchens the concept of secularization becomes not only a framework for theorizing social change but, in definite enlightenment style, a moral imperative: religion, their views imply, signals epistemic and moral immaturity, the unwillingness to be rational, and is ultimately an impediment to human progress.

Yet is the ongoing standoff between faith and knowledge, religion and modernity, that the Enlightenment has bequeathed to us inevitable? Is it even intellectually sound? Might the promises and commitments marking the religious consciousness be more an integral part of a rationally desirable concept of modernity than we often think?

While secularization is most often dealt with in the sociology of religion, this will not be my primary concern. In this book I will be reconstructing and analyzing a discourse of secularization that can be traced back to Kant and to the idealist and anti-idealist aftermath of his thinking in Hegel, Feuerbach, Marx, and Nietzsche, and that has been taken up and continued in the works of Max Weber, Carl Schmitt, Karl Löwith, Hans Blumenberg, and, after the turn of the millennium, by thinkers such as Charles Taylor and Jürgen Habermas. In the development of this tradition, which I will focus on from Kant to Nietzsche, the assessment of religion and its fate in modernity has been considerably more complex and dialectical than what one will find in the accounts of secularization that come directly out of the Enlightenment. Rather than searching for reasons to reject religion outright, these thinkers have called for a diagnostic and interpretive account of its ultimate significance and role *within the context of modernity*. Is religious belief fundamentally antimodern? Or might we grant that religion feeds into and, indeed, informs modernity and what one could loosely call the modern project? Could it be that commitments, ideals, and aspirations that have structured the religious mind-set might be granted a certain validity

---

1. Richard Dawkins, *The God Delusion* (London: Bantam, 2006); Christopher Hitchens, *God Is Not Great: How Religion Poisons Everything* (New York: Twelve Books, 2007). See also Sam Harris, *The End of Faith: Religion, Terror, and the Future of Reason* (New York: W. W. Norton, 2004).

even in their secular or postmetaphysical garb? Perhaps secularization, unlike what traditional secularization narratives have made us believe, is more than a zero-sum game.

It is the latter possibility that has intrigued the European thinkers I've mentioned. For Kant and the philosophers following in his footsteps—even hesitantly—the Enlightenment successfully attacked the metaphysical basis of religion. All of them except Kant himself adopt some version of the God is dead formula: that is, they reject, or at least radically reinterpret, the ontotheology that over the centuries had accompanied, and often animated, rational theology. The notion of some *ens realissimum* or *ens originarium* transcending the order of the sensible while serving as its ultimate principle and foundation finds little or no adherence in the post-Kantian tradition of European philosophy. Rather, what marks the development after Kant, making it relevant not only for our understanding of secularization but for the assessment of religion's potential role in modernity itself, is its interest in combining what Theodor W. Adorno has called *critique and rescue* (*Kritik und Rettung*). While subjecting religion to epistemic *critique*, thinkers such as Kant, Hegel, Feuerbach, Marx, and Nietzsche have sought, though in a philosophically reconfigured form and with ongoing attention to the empirical process of secularization, to *rescue* elements of religious commitment. To rescue something may mean to prolong its existence, though without changing its nature. Thus a swimmer might be rescued from drowning yet remain essentially the same person after the incident. However, *Rettung* may also indicate that some phenomenon or commitment is considered and even transformed so as to retain and refine certain key features while dispelling others. Unlike the moment of critique, which centers on a narrow metaphysical understanding of religion, the rescuing that will be in focus throughout this book places religion within a practical framework, suggesting that, if adequately interpreted, religion in its successive form can inform our self-understanding as social beings. When transformed philosophically, what used to be purely religious motifs may appear as necessary supplements to rational behavior, accounting for motivation and meaning.

With Kant and the tradition via Hegel, Feuerbach, Marx, and Nietzsche as its primary historical focus, I will explore and analyze this dual movement. I will not be trying to adjudicate between these philosophers or grade their performance. They all provide original and powerful views of how the process of secularization may be interpreted philosophically. Starting with Kant, who stands as the modern father figure of the "critique and rescue" approach, I will argue that in this tradition religion represents a form of promise or authority that reason cannot easily accommodate but nevertheless finds it depends on. Whereas Kant sees religion as offering a much-needed yet evidence-transcending supplement to the rational requirements of the moral law, Hegel takes the opposite approach. In Hegel the transcendent authority of religion becomes appropriated by the intersubjective and dialectical processes of meaning-making he calls spirit (*Geist*) and is ultimately secularized. Feuerbach and Marx continue Hegel's project while in significant ways radicalizing it. For them, whatever religion once was must be considered in terms of humanity's self-alienation. From now on, they argue, that alienation must be overcome through a complex movement of self-actualization requiring critique and social change. Nietzsche, finally, takes the commitment of critique to the extreme and accuses Christianity of harboring a nihilistic impulse that threatens to destroy European culture. With the dramatic gestures for which he became famous, he invokes the sacred terror and bliss associated with the figure of Dionysus while seeking to rescue a direct sense of prerational religious authority.

The framework for the post-Kantian philosophical discourse of secularization is Christianity, particularly in its Reformist, Protestant forms. While both Hegel and Nietzsche take a strong interest in other religions (especially Judaism and ancient Greek polytheism) and make reflection on them central to their own accounts, Christianity remains the crucial and, in their culture, dominating religious form, serving as their main point of reference. I therefore feel no particular regret at keeping Christianity in focus when discussing these thinkers. While my study thus risks becoming Eurocentric, I do so out of fidelity to the historical facts and not, I hope, from some kind of entrenched bias.

I should also make it clear that I am not calling for a revival of religion in what are predominantly secular Western societies. My interest in this book is primarily diagnostic. As the process of secularization is revisited by sociologists and historians, and as liberal thinkers debate the role of religion in public speech and liberal democracy, I argue that returning to the nineteenth-century philosophical response to secularization may give us a better understanding of the process of modernization, including secularization, than that provided by the narratives shaped directly by the Enlightenment.

Of course, secularization is not dealt with, and responded to, only in philosophy. In German and British Romanticism, for example, it has affected the arts and generated a long-standing preoccupation with artistic expression and its claim to transcend the framework of everyday speech and representation. Much German poetry from Friedrich Hölderlin and Novalis to Stefan George and Georg Trakl cultivated a melancholic longing for a lost, apparently irretrievable yet also indeterminate, presence capable of restoring meaning to an otherwise alienated and overly rationalized existence.

Moreover, in the wake of the French Revolution and the slow but persistent emergence of liberal democracy in Europe, we may witness the ongoing negotiation of the significance of secularization: religion recedes from public life, becoming increasingly a private concern; and as religion is differentiated from the rest of society, the rational bureaucratic rule described by Max Weber, accompanied by a liberal understanding of government in thinkers from Kant and Mill to Rawls, comes to the fore. Simultaneously, we see various conservative and reactive responses ranging from de Maistre and de Bonald to Schmitt and Ratzinger.

Yet even if art and politics provide their own interpretations of secularization, it is philosophy—or so I will argue—that most powerfully brings into view the fate of religion in modernity. Twentieth-century thinkers such as Adorno and Heidegger keep circling the question of some absent source of authority, viewing late modernity as largely under the spell of nihilism while calling for philosophy to perform a radical self-criticism meant to instill a proper sense of what this absence entails.[2] However, the philosophical discourse of secularization was never more fervent and wide-reaching than during the long nineteenth century from Kant to Nietzsche. Hence this book and the quest for a deeper understanding of the options facing us as members of a still secularizing society.

∴

Writing this book has taken longer than I like to admit. While I have been working on it, I have been greatly supported by my colleagues and students in the Philosophy Department at Temple University. I am also grateful to Temple University for offering me leave in 2017 to devote myself to this project. Many audiences have heard some of this material presented, and I thank them for their helpful feedback. In fact, my first ideas in this area of research came to me more than ten years ago during my time as a recurrent visiting professor at the Center for the Study of Cultural Complexity at the University of Oslo. Gratitude is due to Thomas Hylland Eriksen for making that possible and for sharpening my sensitivity to the cultural importance of religion. Among the many good friends who have inspired my work and helped me focus, I would especially like to mention Peter Dews, Richard Eldridge, Peter E. Gordon, Axel Honneth, Reidar Maliks, Fred Rush, Martin Shuster, and my student Mang Su.

---

2. Hent de Vries, *Minimal Theologies: Critiques of Secular Reason in Adorno and Levinas* (Baltimore: Johns Hopkins University Press, 2005).

Introductory Remarks

For at least two centuries, secularization in its various forms and expressions has been a hallmark of modern consciousness and a defining moment of modernity itself. In its self-consciously adopted version as secularism, it found its heroic voice in the Enlightenment call for individual and collective autonomy, the overcoming of illusory and oppressive conceptions of dependence and limitation, and the acceptance of human finitude. As a historical process to be accounted for by historians and sociologists, it has included such developments as the rise of epistemic and social authority assigned to natural science, the ethical and political individualism associated with a liberal rather than a theocratic order, and new consumerist freedoms related to the emergence and consolidation of capitalism. As the catholic *ordo* slowly but persistently—and, as David Martin and others have suggested, often in distinct steps rather than as a seamless continuity—weakened its hold on society and individual minds, institutions increasingly attained rational, self-legislative characteristics, nature lost its erstwhile enchanted veneer of being a repository of divine will and agency while faith, once intimately tied to individuals' communally constituted identity, increasingly became a matter of personal choice or even taste.[1] Any attempt at coming to grips with this sprawling and enormously complex panorama of events—such as most recently Charles Taylor in *A Secular Age*—may from the outset seem seriously challenged.[2]

While tethered to a narrative of secularization, the significantly more modest aim of this book is to examine the *response* to "the death of God" by Kant and the nineteenth-century aftermath of the Kantian revolution in philosophy represented by such thinkers as Hegel, Feuerbach, Marx, and Nietzsche. For these philosophers, while the Enlightenment *critique*

---

1. David Martin, *On Secularization: Toward a Revised General Theory* (Aldershot: Ashgate, 2005), 3–7.

2. Charles Taylor, *A Secular Age* (Cambridge, MA: Harvard University Press, 2007).

of rational metaphysics, and hence of the notion of God as a supersensible agent exceeding standard means of secure epistemic possession, was either articulated (and affirmed) or simply taken for granted, the nonexistence of God, or at least the impossibility of knowing whether a divine power exists, was not a mere given. Unlike generations of both contemporary and later secularists, they saw themselves as adding to the critique of religion a moment of *rescue*.[3]

Of course, the attempt at rescuing something that supposedly has gone lost in what Charles Taylor calls the "immanent frame" has followed modernization like a shadow. It has taken on deeply reactionary hues in Hölderlin and Heidegger and precipitated radical reconceptualizations of metaphysics in Benjamin, Adorno, and Levinas. In art and in ordinary life, it has motivated many generations to find "meaning without God" or even, as Ronald Dworkin calls it, "religion without God."[4] Whether implicit or explicit, its acknowledgment of loss, often expressed in a melancholy register, has rarely been entirely absent. As Judith Shklar points out, the loss of a "secure religious universe" may well have been the defining experience of "the romantic mind": "For them the recognition that 'God is dead' was a tragedy. Their one hope was to find a poetic vision of reality which could fill the emotional emptiness of the world of prose, of political maxims, and of scientific logic. Here the young rebels of the *Sturm und Drang*, even the mature Schiller and Goethe, all the poets of the romantic revival in England, France, and Germany, and such later imaginative thinkers as Kierkegaard and Nietzsche were quite at one."[5]

For Kant and the other members of the post-Kantian tradition of European philosophy I discuss in this book, the question of religion was always

---

3. Theodor W. Adorno, *Metaphysics: Concepts and Problems*, trans. Edmund Jephcott (Stanford, CA: Stanford University Press, 2001), 19: "On one hand metaphysics is always, if you will, rationalistic as a critique of a conception of true, essential being-in-itself which does not justify itself before reason; but, on the other, it is always also an attempt to rescue something which the philosopher's genius feels to be fading and vanishing. There is in fact no metaphysics, or very little, which is not an attempt to save—and to save by means of concepts—what appeared at the time to be threatened precisely by concepts, and was in the process of being disintegrated, or corroded, to use the more affective language of the ancient anti-Sophists. Metaphysics is thus, one might say, something fundamentally modern—if you do not restrict the concept of modernity to our world but extend it to include Greek history."

4. Ronald Dworkin, *Religion without God* (Cambridge, MA: Harvard University Press, 2013).

5. Judith N. Shklar, *After Utopia: The Decline of Political Faith* (Princeton, NJ: Princeton University Press, 2020), 36.

tied to the question of what would count as a satisfying form of modern life.⁶ Under what conditions can modernity find a reasonable legitimation? For contemporary secularists and "New Atheists" such as Richard Dawkins and Christopher Hitchens, such a satisfying form of life will have to be secular *simpliciter* and involve neither any yearning for lost meaning nor any effort to rescue what purportedly went lost in the process of secularization. In the spirit of classical Enlightenment critique, in which religious belief is compared directly with scientific belief, religion emerges as epistemically ungrounded, calling for irrational commitments that in the name of reason should be discarded. Moreover, the New Atheists not only consider religion to be illusory, giving people false hopes. Rather, as a system of ethical beliefs and precepts, most religions, they claim, support and indeed underwrite practices that tend to be at odds with the inherent dignity ascribed to individuals in a modern liberal order.

When Kant and the post-Kantian tradition of European philosophy attempt to rescue elements of religion by transforming them to be not only compatible with, but crucial to, their views of what would count as a satisfying form of modern life, they translate and reconfigure religious aspiration into an ethical framework and an ethical language, and they ask how an ideal form of life may comprise commitments to individuals' freedom both to shape their lives autonomously and to be able to find the kind of depth or meaning in human experience and relations that, with the loss of religion and rapid modernization, has seemed in danger of disintegrating.⁷

In Kant's moral theology that ethical framework takes a decisively moral shape, emphasizing the freedom and dignity of individuals. Thus, on his account, faith in the traditional sense must be interpreted as a complement to morality, postulating a supreme being able to guarantee happiness for those morally worthy of obtaining it. Given Kant's opposition to rationalist metaphysics, the picture he provides of faith is based purely in morality while carrying no cognitive commitment regarding the actual existence of God. The only modality in which notions of God may rationally play a role for the individual is that of hope.

---

6. For a recent and ambitious account of how the structure of religious thought lingers and is transformed in the development from Kant to Hegel and beyond, see Michael Rosen, *The Shadow of God: Kant, Hegel, and the Passage from Heaven to History* (Cambridge, MA: Harvard University Press, 2022).

7. Jürgen Habermas writes that among the modern societies of today "only those that are able to introduce into the secular domain the essential contents of their religious traditions which point beyond the merely human realm will also be able to rescue the substance of the human." See Habermas et al., *An Awareness of What Is Missing: Faith and Reason in a Post-secular Age* (Malden, MA: Polity Press, 2010), 5.

The young Hegel displays a great deal of sympathy for Kant's moral doctrine yet finds that the moral commitments it projects can become genuinely motivating and binding only in a community of mutually recognizing individuals bound together by a common history and shared practices. In complex ways, the later Hegel transforms the early interest in communal life into a rational framework that he labels *Geist* or "spirit," and religion starts figuring as one of spirit's modes in which to obtain self-knowledge. However, as spirit, according to Hegel's view, exhausts itself in human institutions and self-understanding, allowing freedom to emerge in social forms structured in accordance with reason's demands, the content that once was the prerogative of religion—"the absolute"—becomes intellectualized (and a matter exclusively of philosophical understanding), while any vision of the wholly transcendent loses its authority.

Whereas Kant, despite his wholesale rejection of rationalist metaphysics, leaves the door open to meaningful religious piety (albeit in a morally transformed form), Hegel sees the modern world as fundamentally prosaic. All the erstwhile integrating images have lost their legitimacy; and while religion may continue to exist in people's private lives, reason reigns indiscriminately in the public realm. Feuerbach and Marx, moreover, undertake a related critique of religious hypostatization, and like Hegel they seek to transform an erstwhile religious vocabulary into a conception of nonalienated, communal existence. Yet in Feuerbach and Marx, the idealist presuppositions of Hegel's interpretation of spirit, which especially Marx interprets as religious in nature, become subject to critique. For the first time in this unruly philosophical development, religious belief comes to be considered as merely illusory. Where Kant and Hegel, each in his own qualified way, leave some scope for religion in modernity, Feuerbach and Marx, viewing religion as a false projection of human interest, call for its total overcoming. For Marx in particular, the God is dead motif involves social critique, emphasizing agents' material and social conditions. Only by changing those conditions can they hope to overcome their alienation and thereby also overcome religion. Yet in the anticipation of a fully postcapitalistic, communally oriented society, Marx returns to a religious motif while also radically transforming it.

In Nietzsche, finally, the God is dead theme is subjected to an ironic dialectic. On one hand, he provides a critique of Christianity—not just of its metaphysical views but, more important, of its motivating psychological characteristics, which he gathers under the rubric of *ressentiment*, a self-destructive hatred of all that is deemed vital and life-enhancing. With its valorizing of the transcendent over the immanent, soul over body, immutability over change, Christianity has itself been nihilistic. However,

Nietzsche not only criticizes the allegedly nihilistic implications of religion. In writings such as *The Birth of Tragedy* and *Thus Spoke Zarathustra*, he envisions a replacement for the exhausted Christian vision. Nietzsche attempts to return religion from the transcendent heights of metaphysics and ontotheology to the archaic immediacy of pre-Christian experiences of the sacred. As he makes clear, that shift permits the formulation of new and radical ideals of communal self-organization and political action. While Hegel paints a picture of modernity as more or less devoid of authoritative appeals to the sacred—a European modernity devoted to reason in all its manifestations and expressions—Nietzsche promotes a rejection of Western modernity in both its Enlightenment and its Hegelian form. Likewise, Nietzsche at least implicitly rejects Marx's conception of the nonalienated society, claiming that its egalitarian vision of social coexistence without domination is nihilistic and without opportunities for genuine human flourishing.

Kant, Hegel, Feuerbach, Marx, and Nietzsche agree that the conception of the divine familiar from rationalistic metaphysics and Christian ontotheology can no longer be sustained. While differing with regard to the details, they also think of religion in its traditional form—configured as subservience to a transcendental power—as hampering ones potential for leading a satisfying, flourishing, and free life. By deciphering religion's often implicit expression of yearning for a better life, they nevertheless detect a vision of a renewed social bond, calling for some form of reorganized society. When interpreted in the right manner, religion becomes the ladder for reaching a new communal existence—although, as Wittgenstein put it in *Tractatus*, "one must, so to speak, throw away the ladder after one has climbed up it."

We see, then, that the often so unsettling theme of "God is dead" that in some way or the other comes to the fore in the thinkers I have been mentioning (except Kant, who largely retains a philosophical theology of transcendence) is less about God than about us. It generates a claim about what, given our historical circumstances, we should commit ourselves to and thus signals the need to inquire into the implications, both descriptive and normative, of secularization. By viewing religion as a set of cognitive claims, to be treated on a par with scientific propositions, the classical Enlightenment critics of religion such as Hume and Voltaire (as well as their contemporary proponents) did not properly understand its social significance. Their focus was always on its potential for rational justification and, especially in the French Enlightenment, on its role as a mere tool of oppression. Kant and the post-Kantian thinkers, rather than merely scrutinizing religion's cognitive potential or, as in sociological theories of secularization, offering explanations, causal or otherwise, of its purported demise, are engaged in disclosing, highlighting, and justifying authoritative modern aspirations from the vantage point of a reconceptualized and postmetaphysical form of religion.

But the approaches—and models—they bring forward differ considerably. By invoking his postulates of pure reason, Kant appeals to *intelligibility*—the intelligibility of moral life and hence of our most crucial interest as human, rational subjects. Hegel, by contrast, offers a *sublation model*, calling for the content of religious belief to be transformed in a discursive, rational direction. Philosophy, the intellectually transparent and self-consciously rational successor of religion, continues to entertain "the absolute," though in a transformed, sublated form. Feuerbach, moreover, appeals to a *projection model* in which religion becomes an expression of self-alienation. Through criticism and social change, the externalized content is supposed to be reappropriated, thereby eliminating alienation. For the sake of human self-actualization, Feuerbach thus seeks to rescue elements of religion. Marx's *ideology model* builds on Feuerbach's projection view yet situates religion more resolutely within sociohistorical and economic contexts of class-based oppression. He thus calls for a theoretical achievement of finitude in which the promise of religion re-emerges in terms of a conception of reconciled communal life within a naturalist framework. Searching for a sense of the sacred at odds with the rationalist vision of modernity that we see articulated in Kant and Hegel, Nietzsche, finally, formulates a *resurrection model*: religion is supposed to return, though in a completely different garb from that of Christianity.

While a certain narrative of meaningful development can be provided—philosophers responding to their predecessors and striving, within shifting theoretical environments, to both rearticulate the questions and offer new answers—I am not trying to offer anything like a full view of this development, nor am I excluding the possibility that there are thinkers within this tradition who challenge much of what I say. The Christianity of the late Fichte and the middle and late Schelling spring to mind, and so does Kierkegaard, who, although clearly feeling the impact of secularization, strives to rescue a very metaphysical view of religion from its cognitivist, enlightenment critique.[8]

---

8. To many students of nineteenth-century European philosophy, Kierkegaard may seem like an obvious counterexample to my claim about the centrality of the "God is dead" theme. Although I do not discuss Kierkegaard in this book, in response to this point it should be considered that no viable approach to this thinker can afford to overlook his passionate critique not only of cognitivist versions of faith but of the church in

Finally, this book is informed by my conviction that a genuinely successful historical study of philosophical ideas must situate the ideas within their historical contexts. My hypothesis that the many-faceted processes of secularization are the appropriate context for discussing Kant and the post-Kantian debate on religion is a direct expression of this commitment. Without knowledge of the social and historical conditions of human thinking—the tendencies that motivate specific questions as pressing and form the background for their intelligible formulation—the study of philosophy in its historical configuration may easily become sterile and misleading.

---

general. For Kierkegaard, Christianity seems to have found itself in a deep and perhaps intractable crisis. As he abundantly makes clear in such writings as *Fear and Trembling* and *Concluding Unscientific Postscript*, its only prospect for survival consists in stripping faith of all rational dimensions while focusing exclusively on its "decisionistic," "irrational" ones.

[CHAPTER ONE]

Secularization and Modernity

My reconstruction of central positions within the Kantian and post-Kantian nineteenth-century debate about religion is predicated on the notion that they should be viewed as responding in various ways to a process of secularization. Without some deeper understanding of what that process involves, that notion would stand in danger of becoming either indeterminate or vacuous.

The secularization paradigm has been actualized in several theoretical approaches, but its fundamental hypothesis is clear and unequivocal. The engine of all genuine secularization is the spread, in modernity, of attitudes and dispositions informed by reason and rationalization to ever more areas and domains of human engagement. For many adherents of the secularization paradigm, the purported causal relation between the adoption of especially a scientific worldview and the diminishing of religion is linear. Religion may recede entirely, yielding, as in much of contemporary Europe, a fully secular society in which versions of atheism dominate both private and public life. Or, if religious attitudes and practices linger, they may increasingly become viewed as irrelevant to public life. According to Taylor, "aftereffects" of organized religious life tend to take expressivist forms, being confined to the private sphere and demanding greater authenticity within the framework of "liberated" self-expression.

Secularization, however, is a multidimensional concept, referring to far-reaching processes of individual, psychological, social, cultural, intellectual, and political transformation. At a minimum it involves a loss of faith, the diminishing authority of visions and conceptions of the sacred and the divine, and with that of any metaphysically oriented sense of grace, Providence, objective purpose, and indeed of God's very existence. A secular person is someone for whom there is no God and the visible, predominantly material world is all there is. For the fully secular individual, not only have the cognitive commitments associated with religious faith been lost, but the dispositions and affects needed to entertain such a cognitive stance are gone as well. Nonbelievers simply do not have an ear for religious claims; to them the music has become incomprehensible, calling for a quietist interpretation: prayer is just a person talking in a certain way, churches are buildings with a certain history, and so on.

The term secularization, however, also refers to the process whereby religion loses its traditional hold on political imagery, institutionally sanctioned forms of self-representation, and the whole panoply of collectively accepted modes of self-understanding associated with ideas of the sacred. In this second sense, secularization often but not always involves the loss of individual faith. Thus in standard versions of liberalism, for example, from Kant and Mill to Rawls, not only does the proper use of public reason remain independent of any reference to religious authority, but a liberal government itself is supposed to conduct its tasks independent of religious concerns, dogmas, and institutions. Private citizens, by contrast, are considered free to follow whatever inclinations they might have when it comes to religious belief. Following system functionalists such as Talcott Parsons and Niklas Luhmann, this second type of secularization has typically been theorized in terms of social and cultural differentiation. As José Casanova puts it, the "core and the central thesis of the theory of secularization is the conceptualization of the process of societal modernization as a process of functional differentiation and emancipation of the secular spheres—primarily the state, the economy, and science—from the religious sphere and the concomitant differentiation and specialization of religion within its own newly found religious sphere."[1]

Tied up with this process of differentiation there have been highly complex transformations intellectually, politically, socially, and psychologically. *Intellectually*, the concept of reason has been subjected to severe criticism, transforming the classical view of reason as a contemplative faculty, able to ascertain a totality and its ground, into the modern view of reason as a self-reflective, calculative, and inferential faculty. *Politically*, the rise of liberalism deprived citizens of the older understanding of the ontological status of the political community as being sanctioned by a larger authoritative and religious source. After centuries of organically structured feudalism, the French Revolution initiated the rise of liberalism with its wholesale rejection of religious legitimation, rights-based individualism, and, after a while, commitment to popular sovereignty. *Socially*, the process of differentiation has gone hand in hand with pervasive and deep-seated changes in mentalities and ways of life. The latter includes the rise of bourgeois

---

1. José Casanova, *Public Religions in the Modern World* (Chicago: University of Chicago Press, 1994), 19.

individualism, transformed patterns of temporal awareness assigning a priority to the future over traditionally sanctioned validities, and the rise of mass production and scientifically inclined attitudes to nature as well as a greater dynamism and speed at every level of human transaction and interest.[2] *Psychologically*, secularization involved the emergence of what Taylor calls a "buffered self," oriented less toward experiencing continuities between itself and an extended reality and more toward representation and objectification. With these changes followed a more pronounced sense of human finitude (different from the Christian emphasis on corporeality and sinfulness), releasing individual human lives more or less entirely from any larger narrative visions, whether eschatological, mythical, or historical, of the kind found in religion.

My aim in this chapter is threefold. Using Auguste Comte as my test case, I aim to criticize an epistemic, reason-centered secularization theory and understand its limitations. I then turn to a communal, neo-Durkheimian view of religion, offering an account of its key claims and structure. Finally, I draw on this view to obtain a conception of loss associated with secularization that, rather than focusing on the subtraction involved in losing one's faith in some supernatural reality, understands the loss of religion and the "death of God" mainly as a loss of social solidarity and cohesion. It is from this vantage point that I will later conduct my readings of Kant as well as of key figures in the post-Kantian tradition up to Nietzsche.

The Secularization Paradigm: Reason and Modernity

From the French and British Enlightenment to Kant, Hegel, and Habermas, the rule of reason has been viewed as the master trope of modernity and successful modernization. In this strand of Enlightenment thinking, being committed to modernity has been considered to involve subjection to the rule of reason in every aspect of an agent's existence, ranging from individual self-determination to democratic, discursive will formation as well as, of course, knowledge production, most emblematically practiced and employed in the natural sciences and in technology. As a result of its practitioners' commitment to various kinds of verification-transcendent sources of epistemic and moral authority, religion has often been associated with an antimodern stance, predicted to weaken as the process of

---

2. For an account of social acceleration, see Hartmut Rosa, *Social Acceleration: A New Theory of Modernity*, trans. Jonathan Trejo-Mathys (New York: Columbia University Press, 2015).

modernization takes hold of ever more sectors and value spheres in society. The attribution of antimodern features to religion, combined with a view of history as the victory of reason over superstition, becomes a central element of the secularization paradigm. That transforms this fundamentally normative commitment to reason into a causal account, arguing that the elevation of science to become the most authoritative of all forms of epistemic endeavors contributes to undermining the authority of religious belief.

The European Enlightenment, in which the secularization paradigm first came to light, was a highly multifarious movement, and the hypostatizing of reason does not generalize to all its supposed representatives.[3] Indeed, some Enlightenment thinkers, such as David Hume, expressed deep skepticism regarding reason and its role in human life, instead highlighting the importance of habits and feelings, especially within moral life. For Hume, what motivates humans to act is not reason but "passion." And like Edmund Burke, whose 1790 *Reflections on the Revolution in France* pushed back against a rationalist view of politics, he warned against downplaying the authority of custom in favor of rational principles. Likewise, many of the Romantics from the Schlegel brothers and Novalis to Wordsworth and Coleridge subscribed to enlightenment visions of autonomy while viewing sentiment as the central focus of successful self-cultivation. The French Enlightenment, however, including such figures as Voltaire, d'Alembert, Condorcet, Saint-Simon, and Comte, tended to ascribe to reason a foundational role as the ultimate guarantee and guardian of human dignity and freedom. The revolutionaries of 1789 purported to debunk dogmatically authorized rulership, whether in politics or in religion, in favor of a general commitment to reason. It was also in the French context that the secularization paradigm was first articulated.

Possibly the most instructive and exemplary of these early formulations of the secularization paradigm may have been that of Auguste Comte, whose *Cours de philosophie positive*, initiated in 1826 as university lectures and finally published as a complete six-volume work in 1842, outlines and elaborates all its essential features. Of great centrality to the *Cours* is the well-known division between three "theoretical states": the theological, the metaphysical, and the scientific.

Comte's writing throughout the *Cours* expresses a strong predilection for the scientific state, which is regarded as the natural, inevitable, and desirable

---

3. For a recent and powerful emphasis on these points, see Ritchie Robertson, *The Enlightenment: The Pursuit of Happiness, 1680–1790* (New York: Harper, 2021).

end point of both phylogenetic and ontogenetic development.[4] Yet even though the commitment to reason in its scientific form is a constant refrain in this work, placing Comte squarely alongside those who consider the use of reason as the highest goal of human activity and as something that *ought* to figure as the most important and central end of both cultural and individual development, he somewhat paradoxically rejects the objectivity of value (including claims about what *ought* to be) and instead formulates the theory of development (which, after all, is his theory of secularization) in strictly descriptive terms as referring to "law."

> In . . . studying the total development of human intelligence in its different spheres of activity, from its first and simplest beginning up to our own time, I believe that I have discovered a great fundamental law, to which the mind is subjected by an invariable necessity. The truth of this law can, I think, be demonstrated both by reasoned proofs furnished by a knowledge of our mental organization, and by historical verification due to an attentive study of the past. This law consists in the fact that each of our principal conceptions, each branch of our knowledge, passes in succession through three different theoretical states: the theological or fictitious state, the metaphysical or abstract state, and the scientific or positive state. In other words, the human mind—by its very nature—makes use successively in each of its researches of three methods of philosophizing, whose characters are essentially different and even radically opposed to each other.[5]

Comte makes a number of significant claims in this passage. Since he understands history's progressive movement in terms of lawlike relations between sets of historical events, or what is sometimes referred to as the "law of three stages," the development from religion via metaphysics to science constitutes a linear, irreversible, and universal process. Moreover, religion is considered to be incommensurable with any of the two subsequent stages, in particular that of science, which represents the crowning

---

4. Robert C. Scharff, "Why Was Comte an Epistemologist?," in *Debates in Nineteenth Century European Philosophy: Essential Readings and Contemporary Responses*, ed. Kristin Gjesdal (New York: Routledge, 2016), 179: "For [Comte], third-stage life just is our final condition—that is, the successful *ending* of a quest that is now acknowledged to be *endless*. . . . Third-stage life is not just somewhat better than theologically or metaphysically defined life; it is our proper condition and is understood in maturity to be that condition."

5. Auguste Comte, *Introduction to Positive Philosophy*, trans. Frederick Ferré (Indianapolis: Hackett, 1988), 1–2.

achievement of rationalized modernity. Thus, as metaphysics and, in the final instance, scientific orientations attain cognitive dominance, one may infer that in completed historical development, religious sentiments will simply be left behind. In Comte's estimate, religion can neither rationally nor factually coincide with science.

The theological state, he claims, involves a "fictitious" interpretation of phenomena in light of some postulated first cause considered to be supernatural.[6] Thinking and experiencing in images, it is the stage characteristic of children and, more generally, the "primitive mind," searching for a remedy to cope with life's many contingencies. The metaphysical state, he continues, provides what amounts to a rationalized version of the theological state. Rather than supernatural agents created by the imagination, it operates with "abstract forces, real entities or personified abstractions, inherent in the different beings of the world."[7] The positive state, however, in which humankind generates and starts cultivating a scientific stance, involves giving up the search for the origin and hidden causes of the universe. Rather than seeking to obtain absolute truth, the scientific mind restricts itself to dealing with phenomena, what can be observed through the use of scientific instruments and procedure, combining that with fallibilistic and probabilistic reasoning about the lawlike relations between phenomena. Ultimately, the scientific mind aims to formulate natural, causal laws that apply universally. The positive state is thus radically antireligious and antimetaphysical; on the grounds of its commitment to positivism, the idea that the establishment of scientific truth must be based exclusively on observation, it militantly reduces reality to the observable.

I mentioned Comte's equivocation between a descriptive and a normative account of the stages. However, he also equivocates regarding the quest for a highest cause or, as he puts it, "sole source of phenomena." On the one hand, he claims that this quest ends with the disintegration of the metaphysical state. Science just orients itself with reference to the endless plurality of phenomena characterizing the natural world. On the other hand, however, he speculates about how science may in fact both tend toward and rationally need a highest principle under which all other knowledge of natural laws may be subsumed. Gravity, he avers, which plays a foundational role in Newtonian mechanics, may be such a principle.

Indeed, despite his scientific nominalism and antirealism, Comte displays a strong penchant for the universal and the unitary structure. In addition to the notion of the highest principle or phenomenon, he proposes

6. Comte, *Introduction*, 2.
7. Comte, *Introduction*, 2.

that all the positive sciences stand in dependency relations to each other, starting with the most universal and abstract and ending with the most particular and concrete. Thus astronomy is the most general, foundational, and abstract science, followed by physics, chemistry, physiology, and what Comte, last, calls social physics, or the theory of society and psychic life, studying "the most special, complicated, and concrete phenomena—those which most directly concern human interests."[8] Sociology, in other words, presupposes all the other sciences.

Yet another component of the *Cours*, equally central, centers on the application of science to the practical task of rationally organizing society and enhancing industrial growth. To execute these tasks, society will need a class of engineers able to "settle the relation between theory and practice" by mediating between the scientists proper, who are concerned with acquiring knowledge for its own sake, and the "actual directors of industry."[9] Ultimately—and again while purporting to remain in a purely descriptive register—Comte advocates technocracy, the social organization of technocrats applying scientifically informed instrumental reasoning to objective social reality.

Comte's secularization theory is not limited to an account of scientific rationalization as the main engine of modernization. As central to secularization, it also postulates differentiation between value spheres. While the theological level tends to blur distinctions such as those between faith and knowledge and between the inner and the outer, projecting a fictitious vision of an enchanted, teleologically structured universe responsive to divine and quasi-divine purposiveness, in a modern, secular reality not only are the sciences kept rigorously separate from one another, but theory and practice, art and science, the inner and the outer are differentiated, allowing each pursuit to attain maximum autonomy. Comte's nature can be viewed in terms of facts and constellations of facts: wholly disenchanted, it does not speak or in any way address us. The expressive dimension of psychic life, while able to generate artistic counterworlds, has no bearing on the rational interpretation of reality.

Despite the vast scope and extraordinary ambition of the *Cours*, Comte never manages to justify his account of secularization. Nor does he demonstrate that the evolutionary "laws" hold universally and necessarily or provide any a priori account of the inevitable organization, nature, and succession of the various stages. While many societies and cultures—Northern Europe springs to mind—may indeed have been on something like a

---

8. Comte, *Introduction*, 57.
9. Comte, *Introduction*, 41.

Comtean path, from Comte's perspective others have been regressive or prone to achieve highly ambiguous and "mixed" results with, as in the contemporary United States and Russia, a strong scientific orientation existing alongside equally strongly held religious beliefs. However, the most questionable part of Comte's account has to do with religion, which, anticipating Dawkins and Hitchens, he theorizes as mere superstition—a prerational thinking in images, postulating a supersensible "first cause"—different from scientific belief formation yet similar enough to allow for epistemic comparison. In the following discussion I intend to suggest that this conclusion rests on a hopelessly narrow understanding of religion. According to Comte, being religious involves taking up a cognitive stance, ushering in individual belief; it is thus compatible with science yet also deeply opposed to it. Yet what if religion must be viewed in terms that are not cognitivist? If so, a fundamental premise of Comte's whole theoretical edifice must be rejected, calling into question his whole understanding of secularization. In the following material I will develop a view of religion as an authority-bestowing, self-legitimating social practice.

Religion as Social Practice

Visions of secularism and secularization depend on one's account and understanding of religion. In typical formulations of the secularization paradigm, in which religion is analyzed in terms of agents holding irrational beliefs—beliefs that, because they are metaphysical, purporting to refer to supersensible entities and events, cannot be justified—the achievement of secularization centers on substituting faith for reason. However, in the notion of religion that post-Enlightenment thinkers such as Hegel, Feuerbach, Marx, and Nietzsche espouse, the question of secularization, however implicit, does not hinge exclusively on the problem of belief. For these thinkers, while religion involves endorsing a specific set of beliefs about the supersensible, the more central fact is that it projects a vision of ethical and communal life underwritten by a sense of the authority of the sacred. What kind of community, they thus ask, would be a meaningful successor to a religiously structured form of life? In their view, the relevant question is not, Given its cognitive deficits, how can or will religion come to an end? Rather, it must be, How can secularism build on religion, and transform it, to be consistent with defining demands of modernity while also incorporating religion's social significance?

Yet what is religion? What counts or qualifies as religion? What is faith? What is religious practice?

In view of the extraordinary multifariousness of religious practice, asking for a simple definition may seem pointless. William James, in *The Varieties of Religious Experience*, referring to the great variety of views on offer, thus concludes that "the very fact that these definitions are so many and so different from one another is enough to prove that the word 'religion' cannot stand for any single principle or essence."[10] A more recent theorist, Karen Armstrong, likewise claims that "there is no universal way to define religion."[11] And as Tim Crane, a contemporary philosopher writing on religion, points out, "there is no single word in ancient Greek or Latin, nor in the Hebrew Bible, that we can translate as 'religion.'"[12] It is not even clear when the very idea that there is such a phenomenon as religion came into being. Indeed, the notion of religion as it is used today, set in contrast to the particular creeds, is a relatively new invention, having circulated in Western culture only since the seventeenth century.[13]

For the sake of having a concept of religion that makes it possible to frame and analyze the commitments typical of Kant, Hegel, and post-Hegelian writers on European philosophy of religion, I will nevertheless start by considering some stipulations Crane has made. They are simple and transparent, effectively illustrating why the often so exclusive enlightenment focus on belief can be misleading. While Crane, as I just indicated, does not see providing a rigorous definition identifying the "essence" of religion as an exercise worth pursuing, he does, in my view reasonably, subscribe to the possibility of identifying "important" characteristics. (I take it that by "important" Crane has in mind criteria for applying the word "religion" that nontrivially point to features that historically have played a constitutive role in knowing what would count as religious. They are important because of the way we have come to think of religion and what it involves.)

---

10. William James, *The Varieties of Religious Experience* (New York: Longmans, Green, 1902), 26.

11. Karen Armstrong, *Fields of Blood* (London: Bodley Head, 2014), 2.

12. Tim Crane, *The Meaning of Belief: Religion from an Atheist's Point of View* (Cambridge, MA: Harvard University Press, 2017), 5.

13. The ultimate origins of the Latin term *religiō* are obscure. In *On the Nature of the Gods* (*De natura deorum*), trans. H. Rackham (Cambridge, MA: Harvard University Press, 1933), 28, Cicero defines *religiō* as *cultum deorum*, "the proper performance of rites in veneration of the gods." The emphasis on individual virtue, whether in terms of worship or of paying the proper respect to family, rulers, and other authorities, remains crucial as the term continues to be used in medieval culture. It is not until the seventeenth century, after the Reformation, that "religion" starts referring to wider systems of belief and theological systems.

Religion, Crane claims, "is a systematic and practical attempt by human beings to find meaning in the world and their place in it, in terms of their relationship to something transcendent."[14] The claim may be broken down into four key elements:

Systematicity. Many people report having spiritual experiences of various kinds. They may associate some sort of mystery with, say, the ocean, with nature, or with the cosmos as a whole. They may feel in awe of life itself, its complexity and self-organization, and wonder what "stands behind it" or "accounts for it." Or they may feel that forces of good and evil, distinguishable from the empirical agents supposedly embodying them, are locked in some eternal battle. Certain texts may strike them as having authority that cannot have been established purely on human grounds. However, to count as genuinely religious, we would want to know whether these sentiments have a place within, or can meaningfully be inserted into, a larger framework involving ideas and practices that hang together and, in a loose sense of the word, form a systematic whole. A religion is codified. It contains beliefs, metaphors, and narratives—containing both descriptive, evaluative, and normative provisions—forming a unity. There are sacred texts and in most cases a theology, even if rudimentary.

Practicality. In addition to believing certain more or less systematically organized propositions, being religious involves being committed to acting in ways that are considered to be in accord with the religion's official precepts or that express the believer's views about what it is that would count as being aligned with the supposedly fundamental order behind existence. Typically, such actions are codified and regulated, based on repetition of performances like prayer and ritualized actions. Of course, religious orientations may largely be contemplative. However, even in cases that involve monks, for example, withdrawn from the world of practical concern, such believers do take part in rituals involving various activities expressive of faith that ultimately are supposed to bring one closer to the divine.

Meaning. Religions provide meaning to individual lives by allowing believers to identify with a higher purpose, expressive of the transcendent order underlying all things. This is one crucial way, Crane claims, religion is fundamentally different from science. While science is tailored to interpreting and explaining fact, asking questions such as Why does this happen? (and expecting a causal explanation), religion deals with meaning and value, asking questions such as "For what purpose do I exist?" or "How can my suffering find any justification?" "What is the point of all of this?"

14. Crane, *Meaning of Belief*, 6.

Finding meanings entails not only seeing individual actions and events as having a point but finding some structure of intelligibility that may account for a purported totality. Thus the religious quest for meaning typically pertains to a life considered as a whole or, even more commonly, the world itself considered as a whole. Of course, both science and secular philosophy are sometimes said to look for structures of intelligibility. However, religion differs from them in that its structure of intelligibility is believed to be transcendent, or at least to partake in some transcendent order.

Transcendence. The thought here is that religions invite or encourage believers to entertain beliefs in the existence of realms other than ordinary experience. As Crane emphasizes, the point is not that these realms necessarily contain what the rationalists and Kant thought of as "supernatural entities," then the notion of such entities makes sense only when juxtaposed to nature considered as a law-governed whole, a concept that did not emerge until the scientific revolution in the seventeenth century. The point, rather, is that the transcendent lies beyond the world of the ordinary and the everyday, as well as the kinds of experiences we associate with having access to that prosaic world and acting in it. Although sense-transcendent entities—quarks, electrons, and such—are frequently referred to in science, the religiously transcendent cannot in any circumstances be identified with the scientifically transcendent, which, after all, is accounted for within the immanent framework of scientific theorizing in general. Quarks, for example, play a role in accounting for the behavior of atoms, referring to the causal order of nature, or at least to the statistical laws of quantum mechanics. By contrast, the religiously transcendent, while not in principle inaccessible to the senses (sacred objects, for example, can be perceived), refers the believer to an order that transcends both the causal order known to science and the world of everyday experience. The religious believer finds herself able to suspend, and indeed transcend, the grip of the empirical as it is ordinarily known.

If we leave science out of consideration, the standard, adult mode of approaching the world is, as pragmatists argue, in terms of a practical or pragmatic interest. There is always *something that needs to be taken care of*: the world of the everyday is one of planning, activity, and repetition. It is also a world of individuals, faced with existential anxieties related to transience, separation, suffering, and loss, pertaining to them as individuals. Religion permits people to be relieved of their anxieties—or at least to assume a "reconciled" stance toward the challenges it responds to.

As many thinkers have noted, there seems to be an intrinsic human need to escape from the ordinary. As Robert Bellah puts it, "one of the first things to be noticed about the world of daily life is that *nobody can stand to live in it all the time.*"¹⁵ Transcendence may connote *participation*, as, for example, when agents are absorbed in games. As Bellah and others claim, preaxial religions may have offered something of this kind of experience of the transcendent, involving suspension of the individualized, pragmatic, calculating attitude in favor of some sort of submersion into a larger, more authoritative structure. With the rise of axial religions, and especially under the influence of ancient Greek rationalist philosophy, visions of ludic, ecstatic, and enactive identification were gradually replaced by more intellectualist visions of ascent, and the act of identification became a matter of isolating and cultivating capacities believed to accrue exclusively to a nonmaterial entity—the soul—linking humans in some genealogically privileged way to the order of transcendent being. While participation would still be central, it would be given a more metaphysical or idealist interpretation.

Central to the conception of transcendent being is the idea that identification or participation—or perhaps only the very *possibility* of such identification or participation—offers the believer a sense of hope that some larger order, distinguishable from the order of the everyday (and, later, the order of scientific understanding), might provide meaning to one's existence. That larger order, in for example Christianity and Islam, may provide meaning by promising salvation. However, it may also do so by being taken as purposive: the transcendent order is then conceived of as containing a "will," that of "God," whose power, benevolence, and rationality are seen as "unrestricted" and involving "perfection," capable of instilling hope even in the present "vale of tears." Indeed, James claims, the greatest good for the believer is to live in *harmony* with this order.¹⁶ The believer seeks to do so by living a life conforming to religious precepts—essentially a life of piety, faith, or holiness.

Crane's four key points helpfully bring the nature of religion into focus. Most important, they suggest that faith, while involving a commitment to the existence of a transcendent order, is vastly different from the doxastic stances familiar from strictly cognitive pursuits such as science. Despite the well-known charges made by Enlightenment critics of religion such as Hume and by today's so-called New Atheists, who argue that faith is best understood as "a hypothesis" to the effect "that there exists a superhuman, supernatural intelligence,"¹⁷ the fact that one's belief in God cannot be proved,

---

15. Robert N. Bellah, *Religion in Human Evolution: From the Paleolithic to the Axial Age* (Cambridge, MA: Harvard University Press, 2011), 3.

16. James, *Varieties of Religious Experience*, 53.

17. See Richard Dawkins, *The God Delusion*. For other prominent representatives of the New Atheists, see A. C. Grayling, *Against All Gods* (London: Oberon Books, 2007), and Daniel C. Dennett, *Breaking the Spell* (London: Allen Lane, 2006).

while often a cause of great concern or even agony among religiously inclined people, *is not in itself an argument against faith*. Indeed, as Crane puts it, religion is "*essentially* a struggle: to reconcile what can be explicit and what cannot be expressed, between what is mysterious about the world and what is clearly known."[18] For the believer, the world's *ground*—the transcendent order, assumed to be the ultimate explanation of why the world exists and how it is ordered (and will continue to develop until the end of days)—is inherently *mysterious*, calling for figurative, indirect expressions of belief (or sometimes, as in Kierkegaard, explicitly renouncing all aspirations to knowledge and accepting the inherent absurdity of faith), rather than forming propositions purporting to be justified and true of some set of transcendent facts. The scientist seeks to map and track the world in theoretical propositions that are cognitively secured by providing methodologically acceptable forms of evidence. Her aim is predictive and explanatory control formulated in causal terms. The believer, by contrast, aspires to a form of more or less cognitively unassured recognition, sometimes called grace, whereby the transcendent order—and with it the world of immanence as well—is experienced, often "emotionally," as fulfilling or redeeming one's own existence. At the same time, the believer often thinks such experiences of "proximity," of "being touched by something indefinable yet exceedingly powerful," are to be had only in exceptional situations of negativity involving the rejection of worldly attachment, perhaps through suffering or through intense spiritual exercise including prayer or ascesis. As Crane points out, organized religious activity even allows for a great deal of disappointment, as though it is to be expected. Sticking to a worldview can be hard, and just as disbelief is to be expected in other areas of passionate engagement such as love relations, so it is an inevitable part of the life of faith.

Crane provides an extremely useful phenomenology of religious faith. However, except by pointing out that the transcendent ground often appears inscrutable to the believer, he does not directly confront the skeptical enlightenment question regarding its authority. How is that supposed authority constituted? How can religious practice lay claim to any kind of authority? On what basis can it claim allegiance? As Comte and numerous others, including the New Atheists, have argued, a view focused predominantly on belief—that faith is to entertain a consistently oriented belief in the existence of God (and with that, in the implications a transcendent order might have for oneself and the world)—would consider the lack of reliable evidence to be a severe blow to any claim to such authority, and skeptical secularism would emerge as our only rationally defensible stance with regard to religion.

18. Crane, *Meaning of Belief*, 78.

The Problem of Authority

The most promising competitor to the enlightenment vision of rational answerability is the *social model* of authorization, initially developed by sociologist Émile Durkheim. In *The Division of Labor in Society* and especially in *The Elementary Forms of Religious Life*, Durkheim claims that manifestations of religious faith must be interpreted as expressions of the *conscience collective* of a particular community.[19] To be a believer is not primarily, or only, to adopt religious beliefs; it is to *belong* to a church or religious group—a collective, in other words, whose unity follows from the collectivist or communal ideals to which all members of the collective subscribe: "A religion is a unified system of beliefs and practices relative to sacred things, that is to say, things set apart and surrounded by prohibitions—beliefs and practices that unite its adherents in a single moral community called a church."[20] According to Durkheim, the sentiments, norms, and ideals that make up the *conscience collective* are valid or authoritative not because individual members of the collective see ways to justify them. They are neither a product nor a property associated with the activities of any specific individuals. Nor do they lend themselves to rational deliberation. Rather, it is their function to express and be constitutive of social cohesion. What makes them binding is that without them society would not exist—and without society, the individual, being dependent on others to provide everything from material safety and nourishment to moral and legal protection, would in most cases not exist either. A society that never saw itself as such, and that tried to confer all moral authority on individuals, would disintegrate: there would no longer be any social cohesion. Indeed, individuals attempting to transcend the socially constituted moral horizon altogether would appear to be not only "wrong" but without any authority at all. As Durkheim conceives of it, they would seem not quite human and even dangerous.

So society cannot abandon these categories to the free will of particular individuals without abandoning itself. To live, society needs not only a degree of moral conformity but a minimum of logical conformity as well. Therefore, to prevent dissident views it leans on its members with

---

19. Émile Durkheim, *The Division of Labor in Society*, trans. W. D. Halls (New York: Free Press, 2014), and *The Elementary Forms of Religious Life*, trans. Carol Cosman (Oxford: Oxford University Press, 2001), 42: "Religious beliefs proper are always held by a defined collectivity that professes them and practices the rites that go with them."

20. Durkheim, *Elementary Forms of Religious Life*, 46.

all the weight of authority. What happens when a mind openly departs from these norms of all thought? Society no longer considers that mind human in the full sense of the word, and treats it accordingly. This is why when we try, even deep inside ourselves, to shake off these fundamental notions, we feel that we are not completely free, that something resists us, inside and outside. Outside us, it is opinion that judges us; but further, since society is also represented inside us, it sets itself against these revolutionary impulses from within. We have the feeling that if we abandon these constraints, our thought will cease to be truly human. This seems to be the origin of the very special authority inherent in reason that makes us confidently accept its suggestions. This is the authority of society colouring certain ways of thinking that are the indispensable conditions of all common action.[21]

Identification with the community—and with the norms that define the specific nature of the community—takes place, Durkheim argues, through institutionalized practice. Believers take part in shared and rigorously codified rituals that link present activity with past communal activity. However, in interpreting these activities as constitutive of authority, they also experience certain objects, words, and practices as *sacred*. As Rudolf Otto argued, the sacred is both terrifying (or "daunting"), fascinating, and attractive.[22] While pointing to, or manifesting, the "wholly other," it projects a sense of intractable, impenetrable mystery. Simultaneously, it incorporates an absolute and nonrational (nonjustifiable, ungrounded) sense of authority. Faced with the sacred, believers experience the existential weight of a form of normativity that, far from being constituted rationally, is that of an overwhelming power or force, the opposition to which is bound to have devastating consequences. Thus the sacred both admonishes and prohibits; and while

---

21. Durkheim, *Elementary Forms of Religious Life*, 19. For a radically communal interpretation of Christianity, see John Rawls, *A Brief Inquiry into the Meaning of Sin and Faith* (Cambridge, MA: Harvard University Press, 2009). For Rawls (193), sin is quite simply the repudiation of man's communal existence: "Since man is a creature made for community, and since the perfect expression of his being is responding to God's governess, living nourished in divine grace, it seems that sin must be some repudiation of man's true end. Sin, then, must be the abuse, the aberration, and the destruction of community, and that which sunders all responsible relations with one's fellow men. Sin destroys the foundation-ground of community. It throws one into the abyss of isolation and separation in which man ceases to be man."

22. Rudolf Otto, *The Idea of the Holy: An Inquiry into the Non-rational Factor in the Idea of the Divine and Its Relation to the Rational*, trans. John W. Harvey (Oxford: Oxford University Press, 1958), 31.

doing this it instills in the believer an experience of participation, of being "a part of," that Otto characterizes in terms of Schleiermacher's notion of "creature-feeling," that is, a feeling of dependence.[23]

While emphasizing the social aspect of religion, Durkheim's account is a functionalist one: the interest lies in how religions serve the purpose of expressing social solidarity. It is by this approach that religious life may ultimately be explained. However, Durkheim never really considers the impact religion has on society.

Sharing with Durkheim a social approach to religion yet placing even more emphasis on its capacity to bestow meaning and legitimacy on actual social practices, Peter Berger has argued that one should see religion not only as ensuing *from* the social world but as reflecting back on it in highly significant ways.[24] According to Berger, religion is to be viewed as a collectively produced *construction of reality*. The reality Berger has in mind is thus different from nature in the scientific sense. It includes all the ways societies externalize, objectivize, and internalize orders. In social construction theory, money is often used as an example of such production of reality. Money is a human creation. It would not exist had it not been for this "externalization." However, money is also reified to become an objectivated part of human reality. We relate to money not as a human invention but as something we may speak about objectively. Finally, individuals internalize the significance that money has for human interaction, self-interpretation, and their sense of risk and opportunity. According to Berger, owing to the nonspecialized character of the human animal's instinctual structure being radically different from that of the nonhuman animal, which immediately and in a very specialized manner projects a particular environment for it, "man must *make* a world for himself."[25] He cannot simply rely on his instincts but, using both reason and imagination, must shape a world—a meaningful order, or *nomos*—in which to orient himself. Although he does not analyze all the components of such orders, it is evident that with a socially constructed world Berger has in mind not only items (like money) about which factual statements can be made, but also morally and ethically salient meanings that individuals and societies interpret as offering moral

---

23. Otto, *Idea of the Holy*, 19.

24. Peter L. Berger, *The Sacred Canopy: Elements of a Sociological Theory of Religion* (New York: Anchor Books, 1990).

25. Berger, *Sacred Canopy*, 5. The "world-openness" of human existence is a major theme in Arnold Gehlen's philosophical anthropology. See Arnold Gehlen, *Man: His Nature and Place in the World*, trans. C. McMillan and K. Pillemer (New York: Columbia University Press, 1988).

maxims, value hierarchies, and judgments, as well as traditional wisdom in the form of concrete advice and injunctions regarding typically confronted dilemmas in a normally structured human life. Being separated from such orders (and hence separated from the community the orders ultimately flow from), individuals experience what Durkheim called *anomie*: they experience their own existence and actions as having little or no meaning, see their experience as incapable of offering guidance and orientation, and in extreme cases become worldless, experiencing a diminished capacity to get both intellectually and emotionally involved with other people and with the world itself. As Berger puts this profoundly Durkheimian idea, "The ultimate danger of such separation, however, is the danger of meaninglessness. This danger is the nightmare *par excellence*, in which the individual is submerged in a world of disorder, senselessness and madness."[26]

Religion, Berger claims, projects a meaningful order onto the totality of being. It represents the most extensive form of self-externalization available to human beings. In religious self-externalization, nomos and cosmos appear coextensive: the world considered as a totality is imbued with significance, and certain objects of experience—sacred objects—are viewed as possessing a mysterious and awesome power. In response to the question of what it is that makes the religious self-externalization plausible or binding, Berger closely follows Durkheim, arguing that it ultimately comes down to communal assent and acceptance. "The reality of the Christian world depends upon the presence of social structures within which this reality is taken for granted and within which successive generations of individuals are socialized in such a way that this world will be real *to them*."[27] One might object that any "reality" must be objective and thus purport to invite the formation of universally true propositions. However, Berger does not engage with the question of whether religious propositions allow of any truth value in the realist sense. As a sociologist, he restricts himself to analyzing the significance religion has for members of a given community. For those agents, there is little room for skepticism: what they are faced with religiously is absolute reality. When looked at from the outside, however, the relation between believer and object can be objectivized and the claim to truth and experience of absolute reality, characteristic of faith, may yield to a more explanatory account.

---

26. Berger, *Sacred Canopy*, 22.
27. Berger, *Sacred Canopy*, 46.

The point can be rendered in Wittgensteinian terms. Religious practice may be analyzed as a set of interrelated language games.[28] Not only is it communal, projecting intersubjectively sanctioned and structured interpretations onto reality, but it is embedded in broader domains of practices shared by every competent speaker of the community. Religious language games permit participants to acknowledge certain procedures of justification and explanation as being intelligible. From a vantage point outside the community, one may observe but not engage with the processes that establish assent and reality. Cultural atheists, then, whose worldview is informed by science, cannot on this account engage directly with an orthodox Catholic. They may call for a separate way of thinking or, if they can, use force to prevent the believer from worshipping. What they cannot do—since they have not internalized the rules and mastered the practices that inform and shape belief—is present arguments that the believers will see as relevant or serious.

Most important, religions provide authoritative and predominantly prereflective legitimacy to human institutions, which on this basis can be located within a sacred and cosmic frame of reference, and to archetypal human experiences, commitments, and aspirations. Staking out not only what fundamentally *is* but also *what should be and has value* and, in particular, how human lives may attain full self-realization and self-actualization, they effectively respond to the existential and theodicean *why questions*: Why are things the way they are? Why is life so full of suffering and dissatisfaction? Why am I here, and what is the ultimate purpose of life? By submitting to the power of the collectively constituted nomos, the individual escapes the terror of existential loneliness, the sense of being separated from sources of genuine significance, and finds meaning by becoming an integral part of an all-embracing, powerful, and sacred order.

We see, in other words, that for both Durkheim and Berger, there is an intimate relationship between religion and social solidarity. For both thinkers, religion unites the individual to his or her community by way of acts of identification with a self-externalized order or nomos. Identifying with the sacred order—predominantly through action, but also through subjective involvement or belief—may seem to the individual like a leap into a mysterious and transcendent world. What it really amounts to, however, is a return to, or reconciliation with, one's own community, whose sources of social solidarity have been projected beyond the everyday and into a cosmic or transcendent totality.

---

28. The literature on Wittgenstein and religion is considerable. For a good place to start, see D. Z. Phillips, *Wittgenstein and Religion* (London: St. Martin's Press, 1993).

As we saw with Durkheim, to be outside the space of religion, without recourse to the sacred, is thus potentially to experience anomie. While individuals experiencing anomie may typically (but not necessarily) see themselves as exercising their own free will—and hence a capacity or power to *oppose* the sacred order—the accompanying experience is one of chaos, delegitimization, a lack of orientation, and, translated into religious terms, of a destructive, shadowy world of evil threatening to destroy the community. The exercise of free will, as both Genesis 1 and a number of Christian thinkers, including Schelling, have advocated, is therefore intricately linked to evil, interpreted as the rejection of the sacred order and therefore also of community. While in much Christian theology love, including the bestowal of grace by a forgiving God, is what reestablishes the communal bond, freedom is the *other* of God. Although much Christian thinking, including that of Augustine, Milton, and Hegel, has maintained that God could create the world as an other to Himself only by admitting freedom and thus the ability to oppose God's own will (if He didn't, the world would not be created as an other to God but simply, as in Neoplatonism, flow from His being and be an extension of Him), thereby accounting for the centrality of history in Christian soteriology, freedom qua opposing, self-reflective power must be either canceled or sublated for anomie and evil to be overcome.

At this point we should also be prepared to accept that, according to Durkheim's and Berger's view of religion, secularization is likely to involve a loss of social solidarity combined with an increased commitment to, and capacity for, the exercise of individual freedom, whether in thought or in action. This is definitely the case in Durkheim, who relates what he interprets as the weakening of the *conscience collective* to the historical transformation from mechanical to organic solidarity, or from societies whose cohesion is based on a general acceptance of shared values and beliefs to societies organized around more formal and contractual relations between individuals whose goals and self-interpretations are determined independent of their social identity. Defining secularization as "the process by which sectors of society and culture are removed from the domination of religious institutions and symbols," Berger likewise points to such "carriers" as the rise of natural science and industrial capitalism, which, as Weber argued, "disenchants" the world by reducing every major human challenge to the technical and instrumental register.[29] However, he also traces the preparation for this kind of disenchantment in the history of Protestantism, which, attempting to purify faith, divested the material world of sacred spaces and numinous qualities. Rejecting mystery, miracle,

29. Berger, *Sacred Canopy*, 107.

and magic, reality was thus polarized between a radically transcendent divinity and a radically fallen humanity, paving the way for a complete disenchantment of everything in between. Most significant, however, with the rise of modernity, religion lost its erstwhile embeddedness in unreflective social practice, leaving the individual to grapple with religious questions independently, as a matter of consciousness and psychology. What is left of religious experience in much post-Schleiermacherian Protestant thought is simply a feeling—of potential therapeutic value for the individual but devoid of any social sanctioning, and in that sense arbitrary. Unsurprisingly, according to Berger the problem of legitimation returns to haunt the twentieth-century intellectual imagination.

A Neo-Durkheimian Account of Religious Promise

Neo-Durkheimian views of religion sit uneasily with the individualizing and subjectifying of faith that have marked the development of Christianity since the Reformation. However, if the process of individualizing and subjectifying precisely *is* what it is for a religion to undergo secularization, then the neo-Durkheimian view may help us understand what secularization leaves behind and why, in addition to offering numerous ways human subjects may experience greater freedom and satisfaction, it can be experienced as involving a loss.

Losing something is different from liberating oneself from something. A loss is something to be mourned; it may call for a retrieval of what has been lost. On such an interpretation, while the attempt to bring religion back would not necessarily be reactionary, the effort would both fly in the face of the actual and steady process of secularization in most of the Western world *and* raise the question of all the issues that made secularization look like a process of liberation based in a more adequate appreciation of the human condition. Moreover, what one might hope to see returned would depend on one's working definition of what has been lost.

According to a neo-Durkheimian view of religion, such as we find in Berger, the dimensions most central in terms of what secularization effects relate to meaning and the symbolically mediated relationship between the individual and the community. A sacred reality is one in which, while tragic events do occur and human life is exposed to contingency, there is a deep sense of fundamental meaning behind every event. Rather than being exposed to a world of blind causal forces that can be mastered only through technology, the believer in a presecular community sees herself as confronted with a cosmic order in which divine forces can address her as the unique being she is, hold her responsible for her actions, bestow meaning on them, punish her if necessary, and promise grace and salvation. As the individual is confronted with the effects of secularization, she loses that sense of interacting with a greater and caring order—and of having a designated part in it. On the neo-Durkheimian view, religions project a considerable sense of metaphysical confidence, of what Georg Lukács, in *The Theory of the Novel*, thinks of as being settled, "at home," as opposed to what he calls "transcendental homelessness."[30] Ultimately, the experience of deep meaning is related to an unquestioned belief in the legitimacy of the order itself. Its shape and normative configuration can be accounted for as the result of how it is seen as flowing from a sacred, mysterious source.

The uniquely religious experience of meaning affects not only how the individual views the universe at large. It also relates to one's sense of self and selfhood. In the religious dispensation, attaining selfhood is less a matter of searching for ways to view oneself as the source of authority (in the sense of "the pursuit of autonomy," of cultivating an inner self capable of withstanding external pressure) in matters pertaining to one's fundamental commitments and more a matter of seeking out, and obtaining, recognition by one's peers. Acting morally thus takes profoundly conventional forms; it means that agents become initiated in practices of judgment and action that together (and to an extent that may be viewed as satisfying traditional expectations) can be viewed as expressive of a virtuous character.

As societies move away from what Durkheim calls mechanical solidarity, the claims associated with this kind of spontaneous social morality weaken, creating a need for more abstract and individual strategies of justification. Since on the neo-Durkheimian account the self is viewed as a recognitive achievement, founded on mutual recognition in the light of unquestionable and sometimes ineffable normative constraints, it follows that societies of the premodern kind are characterized by elevated levels of spontaneous social solidarity. In modernity, that solidarity gets weakened.

Existential meaning, an authorized sense of selfhood constituted within traditional symbolic structures of recognition, an understanding of the moral bond as essentially communal, referring the individual to the community, and a vision of society not as a conglomerate of individuals in need of establishing formal relations but, rather, as a unity of mutually recognizing and solidaric agents—these are on a neo-Durkheimian account the most important variables for theorizing the nature of the loss incurred by secularization.

---

30. Georg Lukács, *The Theory of the Novel*, trans. Anna Bostock (London: Merlin, 1978), 41.

To a considerable extent, these are conservative commitments: they articulate, as conservatism always does, a demand for what Marcel Gauchet calls "dispossession," the desire to see oneself not as free and separate but as dependent on, and part of, a larger collective organization whose foundation is inscrutable. For the embedded, "desubjectivated" member of such an organization, the experience of personal contingency is neutralized. Instead, risk is represented as shared among all members of the community, relieving the individual of much of the burden associated with assigning meaning to suffering, loss, separation, and death.[31] On this view, secularization fundamentally involves the loss of contexts in which dispossession becomes possible—in short, the loss of meaningful communal existence in tandem with the emergence of the self committed to full freedom from fixed dogmatic content and heteronomy. Yet this understanding of loss does not necessarily have to be accounted for in merely conservative terms. As I start analyzing the Kantian and post-Kantian thinking about "*Rettung*," it will become evident that the neo-Durkheimian account of secularization allows for a wide variety of more complex and dialectical visions of what it would mean to retrieve an element of dispossession in human experience. Except for Nietzsche's, none of the views I reconstruct call for a response to secularization that would consist simply in restoring an authoritarian and tightly knit social order. Instead, as they articulate their views of the fate of religion in modernity, they express and balance that quest for community in tandem with commitments to personal autonomy and modernization.

Taylor's Paradoxical Faith

Identifying as a neo-Durkheimian thinker of religion, Charles Taylor is a philosopher for whom a linear secularization narrative, or what he calls a subtraction narrative, a simple story of loss, must be rejected. In his *A Secular Age* (2007), he maintains that the "*Enstehungsgeschichte* of exclusive humanism" was a constructive and unruly process whereby secular orientations, rather than flowing exclusively from a commitment to the value of reason and science, often were the outcome of religious initiatives and imageries. Taylor sees in modernity a complex shift toward the adoption of "an immanent frame" combined with various, mostly compensatory, efforts to

---

31. For the analysis of risk as a category of social self-representation, see Ulrich Beck, *Risk Society: Towards a New Modernity*, trans. Mark Ritter (Washington, DC: Sage, 1992).

rescue the existential integrity of faith grounded in appeals to authenticity and unhampered self-expression.

Taylor's vast and sprawling yet also pathbreaking study of the conditions and implications of secularization considers religious faith neither in terms of its potential for obtaining rational support, nor as forming a theory of some kind, but as amounting to a kind of "lived experience," opening the believer to a set of ways of interpreting and viewing the world rather than placing her in some validity-apt relation to God or other religiously charged phenomena. Lived experience, he claims, is always situated, involving numerous ways of exercising one's moral/spiritual calling. Taylor's initial characterization of faith sets the stage for his entire discussion and deserves to be quoted extensively.

> We all see our lives, and/or the space wherein we live our lives, as having a certain moral/spiritual shape. Somewhere, in some activity, or condition, lies a fullness, a richness; that is, in that place (activity or condition), life is fuller, richer, deeper, more worth while, more admirable, more what it should be. This is perhaps a place of power: we often experience this as deeply moving, as inspiring. Perhaps this sense of fullness is something we just catch glimpses of from afar off; we have the powerful intuition of what fullness would be, were we to be in that condition, e.g., of peace or wholeness; or able to act on that level, of integrity or generosity or abandonment or self-forgetfulness.[32]

As I mentioned, secularization is often approached in terms of faith. Sometimes faith is analyzed individually, leading researchers and intellectual historians to question what motivated individuals to adopt humanist or atheist stances of various kinds. As a subset of such investigations, questions may be raised not only about explicit reasons, being transparently available to the reflective agent, but about such less rational sources of persuasion as those of ideology, structural social changes, unconscious forces, and the exercise of pedagogical authority, each calling for its own type of functional or causal explanations. However, as Taylor emphasizes, the question of faith may be looked at collectively as well.

When faith is viewed in terms of lived experience and as a collective achievement, Taylor becomes able to distinguish inquiries into atomistic, belief-centered scenarios from inquiries focusing on the shared *conditions of belief*.

---

32. Charles Taylor, *A Secular Age* (Cambridge, MA: Harvard University Press, 2007), 5.

The shift to secularity in this sense consists, among other things, of a move from a society where belief in God is unchallenged and indeed, unproblematic, to one in which it is understood to be one option among others, and frequently not the easiest to embrace.

[...]

Secularity in this sense is a matter of the whole context of understanding in which our moral, spiritual or religious experience and search takes place. By "context of understanding" here, I mean both matters that will probably have been explicitly formulated by almost everyone, such as the plurality of options, and some which form the implicit, largely unfocussed background of this experience and search, its "pre-ontology," to use a Heideggerian term.[33]

Unlike Habermas, who in *Also a Philosophy of History* predominantly (though not exclusively) understands faith as a rational commitment, calling on the believer to provide reasons, Taylor considers the "fullness" associated with faith as a horizon that structures human sense making, a background that informs activity even when not being explicitly thematized.[34] On this account, agents may count as religious or religiously inclined even in cases where they do not explicitly identify with particular credos and perhaps also in states of religious denial. Since one's identity is so deeply tied up with religious traditions and commitments, there can be no easy or comprehensible path of individual secularization. For secularization to occur, whole traditions need to wither.

Taylor offers a multipronged approach to secularization, analyzing secularity in terms of public spaces, religious belief, and practice as well as cognitive conditions of belief. Restricting his analysis to "Latin Christendom," he moves from a position (predominantly the Middle Ages) in which belief in God is unchallenged (and indeed impossible to challenge, cognitively, psychologically, and socially) to one in which belief either is not on the horizon at all or is simply an option among others, often presented in narrow, expressivist terms as something that enhances one's sense of wellbeing or provides a greater sense of authenticity.

According to Taylor, the most consequential shift in the history of secularization from the Middle Ages until today has been the disenchantment of the world. Providing a Heideggerian account of this fundamentally Weberian claim, Taylor describes disenchantment as the progressive dismantling

33. Taylor, *Secular Age*, 3.
34. Jürgen Habermas, *Auch eine Geschichte der Philosophie*, 2 vols. (Berlin: Suhrkamp, 2019).

of the porous boundary that once existed between personal agency and an environment suffused with meanings and experienced intentions. Five hundred years ago, the mind was viewed as integrated into, and exposed to, a larger order of extrahuman yet intracosmic subjects. The "porous self" could feel objectified by such powers—by the world of spirits, demons, and other moral forces. Or, which was just as common, the self could experience itself as an agent vis-à-vis them, employing magical practices, prayer, and various other means of influencing them and controlling their impact. Melancholy, for example, rather than being experienced as an affliction caused by a mental or physical process within the subject, would be felt as an invasion by evil meanings.[35]

By contrast to the porous self, the modern self is "buffered": it thinks of itself in terms of a sharp contrast between the inner and the outer, between mind and body, and it considers meanings to inhere exclusively in the inner space, in beliefs, intentions, and desires. The world outside the inner has lost its enchantment; it is viewed as material, governed by contingent, unintended, humanly indifferent causal laws. In its Cartesian configuration, the buffered self, while making available a vast domain of causal understanding and prediction (providing, as Heidegger emphasizes, a view of the world as essentially controllable, ready to be transformed technologically), not only rejects the existence of external forces and meanings, but also finds itself disposed to skepticism regarding other minds and even skepticism about the external world. As the Cartesian mind is able to experience the world only indirectly, via its representations, an epistemic gap, seemingly unbridgeable, opens between mind and reality.

In telling the story of how the descendants of Latin Christendom went from the porous to the buffered self and to the secular humanism of late modernity, Taylor vehemently rejects the linear account familiar from classical secularization narratives. Such accounts, he argues, that think of secularization in terms of a "subtraction story" whereby a concern with theological illusions is diminished so as to leave only the purported reality of modern humanism, presuppose a single and stable *explanans*, operating uniformly across a wide swath of human activities, belief systems, and institutions, such as the rise to explanatory prominence of scientific reason. However, even a cursory glance at the history of Christianity since the late medieval period indicates that such a single and unified form of explanation does not exist. Instead, we see a complex zigzag movement in which a number of

---

35. Taylor, *Secular Age*, 37: "Consider melancholy: black bile is not the cause of melancholy, it embodies, it *is* melancholy. The emotional life is porous here again; it doesn't simply exist in an inner, mental space."

factors interconnect to produce a given outcome, and the process of secularization is just as much the result of immanent tendencies within the church itself as of outside factors.

Of particular interest to Taylor are the many unintended consequences of Christian pursuits of purity. The Reformation, for example, responded to the theological-political excesses of the Roman Church by reestablishing respect for the authority of scripture and for personal faith. However, by doing that it had the effect of evacuating a sense of divine presence in the world, of disconnecting the individual from the religious community, and of furthering the disenchantment of the world—all of which increased the level of secularization both individually and institutionally. Indeed, Taylor moves across a vast terrain that includes not only the Reformation but the rise of experimental science, the abstract and deist visions of divinity during the Enlightenment, the emergence of liberalism (with its individualistic view of natural rights), and several other major transformations. As he arrives at the "immanent frame" of modernity, he in particular highlights a shift toward an "ethics of authenticity." The animating concern behind such an ethics hinges on self-expression, the idea that faith must be viewed as a function of untrammeled expression of a supposedly authentic self being hidden behind layers of other commitments structuring the modern self. Given this dispensation, the point of religious activity becomes exclusively subjective. All it does is to give vent to that purportedly real self, allowing it to express itself independent of cultural form and collectively sanctioned meaning. Thus, religion today tends toward being a lifestyle issue and a choice; it becomes privatized and trivialized.

Taylor's historicism has as its central task and function to view agents *within* particular, and institutionally shaped, horizons of significance. As we have seen, the modern horizon, according to Taylor, is fundamentally one of *immanence*: the so-called immanent frame in which there no longer exist any traces of a binding, religious form of the kind that existed before the Enlightenment. Inside the immanent frame, faith becomes one option among many, expressive of a chosen identity. Just as important, whatever quests there may be for transcendence will tend to be in terms of "experience," subjective events defined (perhaps through feeling) as distinct from changes in one's actual being and the object they ultimately refer to. How then, under these conditions, are conversions to Christianity possible that do not only express the inner life of a person? How can the intentional arc, as it were, pick out something transcendent and *mean* it? In short, is faith in God even possible any longer? Taylor's answer seems clear enough. Contemporary moves from an immanent perspective to a spiritual one do exist and must be explained, Taylor avers, by something other than "the internal economy of the immanent theory, say a Freudian one, in which the various forces which count are purely intra-psychic."³⁶ Indeed, experiences of guilt, alienation, and internal division, for example, may be "found at least in part in the aspiration to something transcendent."³⁷

> The convert's insights break beyond the limits of the regnant versions of immanent order, either in terms of accepted theories, or of moral and political practice.... And this may require her to invent a new language or literary style. She breaks from the immanent order to a larger, more encompassing one, which includes it while disrupting it.³⁸

Taylor operates with a less totalizing framework of interpretation than Heidegger. However, if the logic of faith is as interwoven with a form of life (and with what it is that representative agents in an actual, historical life may take as authoritative) as he lays out in the opening chapters of *A Secular Age*, then the worry seems unavoidable that what people in late modernity may think of as faith does not really count: it cannot be more than self-delusion.

In his foreword to Marcel Gauchet's *The Disenchantment of the World: A Political History of Religion*, Taylor addresses this tension head on and seems to struggle with it. He points out how Gauchet, following Durkheim, considers religion "the original socially embedded understanding of the universe as sacred order, in which humans are contained."³⁹ In modernity, as that sacred order is destroyed and agents no longer find any religiously sanctioned subject positions with which to control the effects of personal and social contingency, religion itself becomes at best mere personal faith but more likely just the arbitrary adoption of exotic traditions that no one can any longer vouch for. Gauchet's view seems clear: although self-reported believers still exist, they find themselves in a postreligious society; thus their faith cannot count as fully genuine.⁴⁰ Taylor, however, does not accept this assessment. He argues, first, that "When the culture dies, faith can be left as a residue in certain individuals."⁴¹ Indeed, the modern

---

36. Taylor, *Secular Age*, 731.

37. Taylor, *Secular Age*, 731.

38. Taylor, *Secular Age*, 732.

39. See Taylor's foreword to Marcel Gauchet, *The Disenchantment of the World: A Political History of Religion*, trans. Oscar Burge (Princeton, NJ: Princeton University Press, 1997), xiii.

40. Gauchet, *Disenchantment of the World*, 206.

41. Taylor, foreword, xiii.

structure displays tensions: as one may find to have been the case in several previous periods, though Christianity may institutionally be threatened, that does not necessarily preclude individuals' harboring genuine faith. Taylor, second, holds that tensions in the modern religious structure—the evident existence of scattered individuals holding on to certain traditions and espousing certain beliefs despite the equally evident loss of communally binding religious practice—can "perhaps," he writes, "only be explained by supposing that something like what they relate to—God, Nirvana—really exists."[42] However, the object has no determinate existence outside the language games and horizons of intelligibility that make truth claims possible in the first place. As Taylor has made clear in subsequent writings on language and epistemology, he does not believe that perception is able to make a concept-independent contribution to knowledge: while intuitions rationally constrain our thinking, concepts and intuitions are inseparable.[43] As a result, the existence of God (regardless of our conscious, intentional relation to any such entity) cannot explain our propensity to form determinate beliefs about Him. If, in what is effectively a postreligious age, we are to follow Taylor's historicism and think that the conditions of belief have withered, it can no longer be clear what it is that may even count as a divine being. On the other hand, if we are to take seriously his remarks about the perennial possibility of faith, we must discard the account of what it is that constitutes God as an *intelligible* option. The kind of faith that modern agents could entertain would at best be thin, abstract, without the slightest foundation in the words they actually use, in order to make sense of their experience.

Blumenberg and the Theological Origins of Secular Modernity

Hans Blumenberg shares with Taylor the view that secularization should not be considered a linear process exclusively dependent on pressures external to religion itself. Indeed, Taylor's rejection of a "subtraction" view of secularization remains indebted to Blumenberg. However, unlike Taylor, Blumenberg seems to take the idea of secularization to mean that religious belief is no longer a live option. His highly influential study *The Legitimacy of the Modern Age* presents itself as an attempt to criticize Karl Löwith's

42. Taylor, foreword, xv.

43. This claim is discussed and defended in Charles Taylor and Hubert Dreyfus, *Retrieving Realism* (Cambridge, MA: Harvard University Press, 2015).

so-called secularization thesis, the view that central positions in modernity simply repeat religious commitments, though in a secular register. According to Löwith, the modern concept of progress, for example, simply reiterates or reproduces the religious faith in Providence; liberal conceptions of inviolable human dignity are just secular versions of the idea that man is born in the image of God; the modern work ethic is a secular version of saintliness; and so on. However, it does a lot more than that. In *The Legitimacy of the Modern Age*, Blumenberg provides a vision of modernity as an entirely new order. Considered as the outcome of tensions and dilemmas inherent in Christianity in particular, modernity generates a framework for thought and action that undermines the very possibility of forming a religious attitude and of seriously entertaining religious belief.

The framework constitutive of this new order is highly complex, but its organizing principle, according to Blumenberg, is "self-assertion" (*Selbstbehauptung*). "Self-assertion," he writes, "does not mean the naked biological and economic preservation of the human organism by the means naturally available to it. It means an existential program according to which man posits his existence in a historical situation and indicates to himself how he is going to deal with the reality surrounding him and what use he will make of the possibilities that are open to him."[44] For the agent committed to self-assertion, the bad or negative aspects of the world, rather than being metaphysical markers of a divine principle or punishing distributor of justice, are considered fact-based, as challenges and barriers to be overcome. Opening a horizon of practical futurity, the commitment to self-assertion makes possible visions of incremental human progress brought about by prudential application of scientific and technological achievements. It dignifies the human agent, who, within this program, is viewed as able to take responsibility for his own fate. Although it leads to disenchantment, it calls for secularizing human history, individual destiny, and the world itself, which increasingly is viewed in materialist terms, excluding any reference to divine forces and purposes. All orders, whether of a scientific, moral, aesthetic, or juridical nature, must be interpreted in terms of man's activity and autonomous acts of creation and constitution.

On Blumenberg's account, this principle aims to ground modernity as a separate epoch and, more important, to allow the theoretician to view it as an autonomous human project or undertaking. The modern age, he claims, produces its own form of legitimacy. It is an age in which human

---

44. Blumenberg, *Legitimacy of the Modern Age*, 138. For an excellent account of Blumenberg's fundamental thesis, see Michael Allen Gillespie, *The Theological Origins of Modernity* (Chicago: University of Chicago Press), chap. 1.

agents discover the world as an arena for realizing their own projects, and in which it must be possible to view the creation of a valid order as a reflection of man's own powers. While conceptions of God may continue to inform human projects and ethical self-interpretation, they cannot be granted legitimacy as elements of a fully realized modernity. On the contrary, such elements will have to count as premodern.

Blumenberg's story of how the modern world attains this autonomy is tremendously complicated, involving numerous claims about the early modern rise of science and the transformation of philosophy and theology. He tracks the rise of the antireligious sentiment of "self-assertion" as having its origin in a crisis pertaining to the reigning theological worldview of the Middle Ages. In the cosmos envisioned by high Scholasticism a universal order prevailed in the totality of being, including both creation and creator. With God as its highest guarantee and expression, this *ordo* provided human agents with a sense that the articulation and actualization of God's will in the created universe was essentially benign and rationally predictable, the expression of divine *logos*. However, as a number of medieval nominalist thinkers, including Duns Scotus and William Ockham, came to see, this view harbors a tension between a commitment to God's unrestricted power and freedom and a conception of God's subjection to a universal order, however self-created. If God's will is unrestricted, then it must be that, at any moment in time, God may decide either to abolish or to change that order.

The late medieval rise of nominalism was predicated on the desire to underwrite God's omnipotence by showing that He can do everything, that is, everything except something that would involve entertaining contradictory propositions. (For the early nominalists the idea of God's contradicting Himself would be incoherent: to think a contradiction would make God unintelligible even to Himself.) In the older Aristotelian view, God created not only the finite, material world but all its universals. In a universe in which universals were thought to have a real existence and be *ante rem*, God was restricted. He could not act in ways that would run counter to His own world plan, expressed by the universals. The universe of the nominalists, by contrast, in which God's power is absolute and unrestricted, contains no material limit on what is possible. For the believer, the uneasiness and despair about mundane possibilities arising from nominalism calls for the pursuit of salvation. However, because the created world is devoid of any natural order, any claim of human reason to interpret reality—including the mere construction and imposition of classificatory matrices—must be viewed as an act of self-assertion. In a universe deserted by any sense of divine ordering and governed by a God who not only may call all rational expectations into question but may at any moment decide to transform or destroy, humans are faced with a radical sense of contingency, prevailing from moment to moment, as they face no alternative to passive submission except to find measure and self-worth in nature: "The radical materializing of nature is confirmed as the systematic correlate of theological absolutism. Deprived by God's hiddenness of metaphysical guarantees for the world, man constructs for himself a counterworld of elementary rationality and manipulability."[45]

Although responding to the late medieval and early modern sense of extreme contingency by constructing man-made orders may have been a powerful and effective facilitator of secularization, calling, as in Kant and Fichte, for the self-constitution of the modern subject as an agent self-reflectively responsible for any normative order, it cannot in itself be regarded as a sufficient explanation of the gradual turn away from religion. As Michael Gillespie argues, in some cases, such as the Reformation, it may even have increased spiritual fervor.[46] For Luther, who struggled with the vision of God inherited from nominalism, the response consisted in *sola fides*, *sola gratia*, and *sola scriptura*.[47] Rather than works whereby the believer hoped to justify himself in the eyes of God, the Protestant invested all his hope in the purely inward process of spiritual receivership. As we encounter and are transformed by His word in scripture, God, based solely on grace and in ways that are humanly inscrutable and beyond the grasp of reason, may take possession of us and ensure salvation.

However, while the spiritual fervor of the Reformation was strong and its view of creation not entirely negative, Protestantism did not manage to bridge the gap that nominalism had opened up between an abstract and distant, transcendent God and the material world of human existence. Indeed, the continuum connecting creator and creation was irretrievably lost. Thus Luther's God is a *deus absconditus*.[48] As such, while it informed subsequent attempts—for example in Pietism—to salvage religion by protecting it from rationally grounded skepticism of the kind we find in Hume and the French materialists, the withdrawal of divine presence had a long-term impact on the process of secularization.

---

45. Blumenberg, *Legitimacy of the Modern Age*, 173.

46. Gillespie, *Theological Origins of Modernity*, 101–28.

47. For a particularly succinct expression of these ideas, see Martin Luther, "On the Freedom of a Christian," in *The Essential Luther*, ed. and trans. Tryntje Helfferich (Indianapolis: Hackett, 2018), 74–94.

48. Luther gives an account of the Hidden God in the 1525 text "The Bondage of the Will" (*De servo arbitrio*), *Essential Luther*, 169–77.

Blumenberg's account points to a changing time horizon as agents no longer orient themselves primarily with reference to pregiven orders expressed in traditional symbolic manifestations and practices but, rather, look to the future in which projected orders are to be actualized. Pre-Reformation Christianity was committed to the radical heteronomy of the self—and with that to the heteronomous configuration of meaning. Its source of orientation came out of the past; it was understood to be sacred and unshakable, expressive of an eternal order different from the contingencies of material existence. Secularization weakened religion's hold on political imagery, institutions, and the whole panoply of collectively accepted modes of legitimate self-presentation. It divided state and church; it created an entirely new space for autonomous scientific research and technological development; it made possible a new dynamism both culturally and socially; and it exacerbated the privatizing of faith that had followed in the wake of the Reformation and the Wars of Religion.

The concept of self-assertion carries a number of connotations in *The Legitimacy of the Modern Age*. As the principle behind what Blumenberg thinks of as a "second overcoming of Gnosticism"—the overcoming of a conception of creation as inherently evil or, from the point of view of reason, contingent, and of hopes for salvation in some radically "other" world as its only remedy—"self-assertion" no doubt relates to the Kantian and enlightenment call for rational self-determination. Modernity is the epoch when man has to view himself as responsible for all orders. It is also, however, a principle of liberal individualism, of art and philosophy, and, most important, of science. The dawning of the modern age signaled the liberation of the previously theological category of "*curiositas*," which the medieval mind tended to see as designating something sinful. Excessive interest in the material world was considered suggestive of a mind uninterested in God. In Augustine's *Confessions*, for example, such interest is interpreted as seductive rather than fulfilling, a temptation one should resist.[49]

Modern science takes an interest in the contingent, material world for its own sake. Yet, in tandem with the rise of capitalism, it also makes possible an enormous expansion of technology and mass production. It is important to see that Blumenberg's point is different from the typical secularization paradigm. He is not claiming, at least not primarily, that

---

49. The Franciscan monk William of Baskerville in Umberto Eco's novel *The Name of the Rose* exemplifies this attitude to the full. His empirical investigations, driven no doubt by *curiositas*, not only threaten the Benedictine monks and their way of life but upset them deeply. See Umberto Eco, *The Name of the Rose*, trans. William Weaver (Boston: Mariner Books, 1994).

the spread of what one may call technoscience—and with that, specific forms of reasoning tailored to achieving scientific results and technological ends—creates pressures of various kinds that delegitimize, marginalize and, in the final instance, suppresses and undermine religion. The claim, rather, is that technoscience becomes possible through the liberation of *curiositas* from the grip of religious interpretation. While obviously enforced by capitalist expansion and the rise of an aspiring European bourgeoisie interested in breaking with the old bonds and restrictions of nobility and clergy, technoscience steps in, as it were, to fill the vacuum left by the loss of the Catholic *ordo*. One might think that, for Blumenberg, the category of self-assertion carries very broad connotations, and to some extent that is true. We have already seen how he uses it to refer to a liberation of the subject from a conception of teleologically structured processes, pointing to a divinely sanctioned order, and as such it connotes freedom as both independence and self-determination. However, the effect of such innocuous-sounding forms of self-assertion, when viewed in actual historical contexts of acting within some institutional setting, could hardly have been more transformative. As Blumenberg emphasizes, self-assertion signals the advent of an entirely new attitude toward the world and one's place in it. While ancient and medieval philosophical theory aimed to show how life can be fulfilled (such that some form of *eudaimonia* would be possible), the new, Baconian ideal centered on mere domination over nature, in total disregard for any aspiration for self-understanding, wisdom, and genuine fulfillment. The "old" theoretical motivation sprang out of the "lifeworld": it responded to a need to understand one's place in the great chain of being and act so as to actualize oneself fully. The "new" theoretical motivation simply arose from the perceived indispensability of science as a means of maximizing utility. As a "science industry," a *Wissenschaftsbetrieb*, it has no meaning beyond the mere fact of its social and technological necessity.

In other words, I suggest that Blumenberg, by tying self-assertion so closely to the liberation of *curiositas*, describes what Horkheimer and Adorno would call a dialectic of enlightenment: the shift within the sphere of reason itself from a vision of freedom and independence to one of necessity and dependence. Although self-assertion in Kant, for example, takes on a heroic form, conceiving of the transcendental subject as the self-reflective, self-determining origin of both theoretical and practical orders, as *curiositas* becomes tied to the Baconian project of dominating nature, self-assertion separates from the structure of personality, including its aspirations to freedom, and becomes inherently meaningless, an imperative of domination for its own sake.

Unlike influential critics of modernity such as Nietzsche, Heidegger, and Adorno, Blumenberg never deplores or even questions this dialectic. On the contrary, Blumenberg's central goal is to defend modernity (*Neuzeit*) by demonstrating, against Karl Löwith and Carl Schmitt, that, rather than itself comprising a repetition of possibilities internal to a seemingly bygone tradition of Christian medieval culture, it is *legitimate*: it not only follows but stands responsible for its own principles and commitments. Moreover, insofar as modernity enjoys legitimacy, it deserves to be affirmed.

From Weber to Adorno and Horkheimer's Negativism

Blumenberg's affirmative attitude toward the modern consequences of the project of self-assertion stands squarely opposed to that of Max Weber. In the 1917 essay "Science as Vocation," unpacking the implications of what he calls "intellectualization" and "rationalization" (both associated with the rise of natural science to an exclusive position of epistemic authority in modern society), Weber offers his famous definition of "disenchantment" (*Entzauberung*), which for him is the central characteristic of secularization.

> Thus the growing process of intellectualization and rationalization does *not* imply a growing understanding of the conditions under which we live. It means something quite different. It is the knowledge or the conviction that if *only we wished* to understand them we *could* do so at any time. It means that in principle, then, we are not ruled by mysterious, unpredictable forces, but that, on the contrary, we can in principle *control everything by means of calculation*. That in turn means the disenchantment of the world.[50]

In the fully disenchanted world, the natural sciences enjoy unquestioned authority. Every challenge is now essentially a technical one—a question of calculation and the use of instrumental, end-indifferent reason. The fully disenchanted world contains no inherent value; thus, end-oriented reason can have no object. While scientific (purely descriptive, abstract, fallibilist) thinking may identify the best means to stipulated ends, about ends it must either be silent or, as Weber claims, ready to *decide*, though on an irrational

---

50. Max Weber, *The Vocation Lectures*, trans. Rodney Livingstone (Indianapolis: Hackett, 2004), 12–13.

basis.[51] Disenchantment, since it excludes from reasoning the concept of objective purpose, that actions can have an intersubjectively binding purpose, thus implies a *loss of meaning*: While tailored to a stipulated end, the point of any possible action or action plan can only be tied to its causal effectiveness, the capacity to bring about a further end in an indefinite chain of cause and effect; it cannot be related to any understanding of the objectivity of value. This thought brings Weber to make the following statement:

> Apart from the overgrown children who can still be found in the natural sciences, who imagines nowadays that a knowledge of astronomy or biology or physics or chemistry could teach us anything about the *meaning* of the world? How might we even begin to track down such a "meaning," if indeed it exists? If anything at all, the natural sciences are more likely to ensure that the belief *that* the world has a "meaning" will wither at the root! And in particular, what about the idea of science as the path "to God"? Science, which is specifically alien to God? And today no one can really doubt in his heart of hearts that science is alien to God—whether or not he admits it to himself. Release from the rationalism and intellectualism of science is the fundamental premise of life in communion with the divine.[52]

One may doubt, especially considering the apparent resurgence of religious attitudes during the first two decades of the new millennium, whether in modernity science as an institution holds the undisputed position of authority that Weber attributes to it. Moreover, one may question Weber's abrupt dismissal of noninstrumental end setting. What about the universalisms of Kantian descent? Is silence or decisionism about value really the only alternative? That said, Weber's analysis of the fully disenchanted society, while bleak in its diagnosis of nihilistic technocracy, is grounded in his famous account of Protestantism. Through his account of

---

51. Weber formulates his famous claim about decisionism, of what it means to choose one's own god, in *The Vocation Lectures*, 27: "The assumption that I am offering you here is based on a fundamental fact. This is that as long as life is left to itself and is understood in its own terms, it knows only that the conflict between these gods is never-ending. Or, in nonfigurative language, life is about the incompatibility of ultimate *possible* attitudes and hence the inability ever to resolve the conflicts between them. Hence the necessity of *deciding* between them." Of course, the very notion of being able to decide between such incompatible sources of authority only means that their claim to authority is a sham: from the vantage point of reason, the subjective decision is completely arbitrary.

52. Weber, *Vocation Lectures*, 16.

"inner-worldly ascesis" among agents in early capitalist societies seeking to prove their status as elect in the eyes of God, Weber pioneered the notion of secularization as being intimately tied to the development and implications of Protestantism.[53]

On Weber's view, secularization is an inevitable dimension of Western modernity and its commitments. Secular modernity precludes agents from asking questions about purpose: not only why things are the way they are (calling for causal accounts), but for what purpose they exist. Thus questions regarding the fundamental meaning of human experience, including the meaning of love, happiness, suffering, and death, become moot. In a disenchanted universe, there is a place neither for the divine nor for the effects of God's will.

While modern life renders questions of meaning cognitively moot, thereby undermining the motivation behind religious dispositions, it creates vast new spaces for the exercise of instrumental reason. In tandem with the continual expansion of capitalism that Weber, in *The Protestant Ethic and the Spirit of Capitalism*, sees as connected to the spread of instrumental attitudes, the most fundamental norm of practical rationality becomes efficiency, of most effectively attaining one's goals with ethically indifferent means, where efficiency becomes based on successful planning and calculation. Modernity, therefore, means ethical contingency. It points, as T. J. Clark writes, "to a social order which has turned from the worship of ancestors and past authorities to the pursuit of control over nature, or infinities of information."[54] In the absence of such acceptance of given, socially sanctioned authority, embedded and expressed in stories, myths, images, and ritual, meaning understood as collectively constituted patterns and practices of evaluative self-understanding and interpretation is inevitably going to be, as Clark puts it, "in short supply." "Secularization," to quote Clark again,

---

53. Max Weber, *The Protestant Ethic and the "Spirit" of Capitalism*, trans. Peter Baehr and Gordon C. Wells (New York: Penguin Books, 2002), 82–87. As Kippenberg points out, Weber did not conceive of secularization exclusively in terms of the disenchanting effects of Protestantism in modernity. In fact, "secularization" is a concept Weber uses more extensively in conjunction with his study of the history of law, particularly with regard to the transfer of land, institutions, and persons from ecclesiastical to secular law. See Hans G. Kippenberg, "Dialectics of Disenchantment: The Devaluation of the Objective World and the Revaluation of Subjective Religiosity," in *Narratives of Disenchantment and Secularization: Critiquing Max Weber's Idea of Modernity*, ed. Robert A. Yelle and Lorenz Trein (London: Bloomsbury Academic, 2021), 9.

54. T. J. Clark, *Farewell to an Idea: Episodes from a History of Modernism* (New Haven, CT: Yale University Press, 1999), 7.

is a nice technical word for this blankness. It means specialization and abstraction; social life driven by a calculus of large-scale statistical chances, with everyone accepting (or resenting) a high level of risk; time and space turned into variables in that same calculus, both of them saturated by "information" and played with endlessly, monotonously, on nets and screens; the de-skilling of everyday life (deference to experts and technicians in more and more of the microstructures of the self); available, invasive, haunting experience; the chronic revision of everything in the light of "studies."[55]

In facing up to this condition, Weber takes a stoic position. The loss of meaning associated with modernization, he maintains, must be accepted as the price agents pay for their inclusion in a modern order. Modernity fragments all unifying visions of authoritative wholeness, situating agents before tasks whose operational terms fall squarely within the logic of calculability. The dominance of instrumental reason turns everyone into a specialized agent of abstract risk management able—if at all—to find personal satisfaction exclusively in the private sphere of subjective enjoyment.

Horkheimer and Adorno's *Dialectic of Enlightenment* draws on Weber's claim about the loss of meaning in modernity to provide a more fully articulated philosophy of history that itself may be read as an account of secularization; and on their view the stoicism one finds in Weber yields to a form of deep moral and intellectual despair.[56]

By launching an account of how reason and progress are implicated with forces of regression, the stated goal of the *Dialectic of Enlightenment* is to provide the theoretical background to such manifestly regressive phenomena of twentieth-century life as the rise of fascism, communist totalitarianism, and widespread commodification of minds and cultural items. In a clear nod to Weber it associates "enlightenment thinking," by which Horkheimer and Adorno understand instrumental and subsumptive thinking, and essentially all human strategies that serve to extend human domination over nature and selves, including one's own self, with "the disenchantment of the world."[57] The disenchantment of the world, they continue, "means the extirpation of animism . . . On their way toward modern science human

---

55. Clark, *Farewell to an Idea*, 7.

56. Max Horkheimer and Theodor W. Adorno, *Dialectic of Enlightenment: Philosophical Fragments*, trans. Edmund Jephcott (Stanford, CA: Stanford University Press, 2002).

57. Horkheimer and Adorno, *Dialectic of Enlightenment*, 1.

beings have discarded meaning. The concept is replaced by the formula, the cause by rules and probability."[58]

In the 1966 *Negative Dialectics* Adorno puts forward a complex, dialectical response to the diagnosis of disenchantment provided in the *Dialectic of Enlightenment*. On the one hand, unless some understanding or account of transcendence is available, the world of immanence associated with instrumental and subsumptive reason appears to be both morally and existentially unacceptable and unbearable. Without transcendence, there is ultimately no rejoinder to the most radical and destructive forms of domination (and here Adorno instances Auschwitz). On the other hand, whatever moment of transcendence there may be, it must be able to escape the logic of sameness and repetition characteristic of reason in modernity. Indeed, transcendence, Adorno argues, can coherently be thought only in conjunction with a notion of transience associated with the material world of finite beings. It cannot permit mastery in the form of conceptual representation or instrumental control.

What would the complete achievement of secularization therefore involve? Rather than mere Weberian *Sinnlosigkeit*, it would signify a form of materialism without instrumentalization and subsumptive reasoning, the experience of sensuous immediacy being taken up in such a way as to encourage receptivity, responsiveness, and mutuality.[59] Adorno criticizes identitarian reason and religious claims to transcendence based in reified forms of cognition. At the same time, he searches for ways to retrieve experiences of transcendence beyond, or outside, the perimeters of standard forms of meaning-making in modernity.

Adorno's aim, therefore, is to outline a radicalized process of secularization. There is a step beyond disenchantment, promising not only a more complete overcoming of the traditional opposition of the real and the ideal, the finite and the infinite, but also the recovery, now within a materialist framework, of a claim to meaning associated with transcendence.

Exactly what kind of experience does Adorno have in mind? What, indeed, does he mean by the surprising and provoking term "metaphysical experience," which he alternately associates with beauty, especially natural beauty, and with art and even Proustian moments of spontaneous

---

58. Horkheimer and Adorno, *Dialectic of Enlightenment*, 3.

59. I spell out the implications of such a claim in Espen Hammer, *Adorno's Modernism: Art, Experience, and Catastrophe* (Cambridge: Cambridge University Press, 2015), 59–64. For an attempt to base a critical sociology on this claim, see Hartmut Rosa, *Resonance: A Sociology of Our Relationship to the World*, trans. James C. Wagner (Cambridge, UK: Polity Press, 2021).

recollection? In what sense is such an experience cognitive? Who may hope to undergo such experiences? These are questions that would call for a separate study. My only interest here lies with the structure of Adorno's argument. While accepting the basic outlines of Weber's account of secularization (though with a different and historically more comprehensive *explanans*), he claims that its associated loss of meaning can be countered by *radicalizing the process of secularization itself*. It is because the process of secularization has become centered on rationalization, the increase and intensification of formal and instrumental reason to all spheres of human commitment and existence, that it shows up the kinds of regressive and alienating characteristics that Adorno and Horkheimer analyze in the *Dialectic of Enlightenment*. Indeed, these characteristics, resulting from the hypostatizing and reifying of the subject and of structures of domination tied up with repetition and sameness, and of "ideality" set over against "reality," are themselves remnants of the religious hypostatizations that a successful process of secularization ought to have eliminated. If secularization could take place differently, along a different axis of progression, bringing human agents to the point of becoming fully aware and reflective of their embodied, situated condition in a material world, then the possibility would emerge of a greater sense of meaning and fulfillment.

As I will argue, Kant, Hegel, Feuerbach, Marx, and Nietzsche present views of what a fully secular form of modern life ought to look like that to some degree dovetail with at least some aspects of Adorno's conception. They seek to identify a version of secularization that, by radicalizing and ultimately transforming trends in the actual process of modernization, may be able to retrieve some of religion's erstwhile claims to meaning within a secular setting. However, being able to make such a search intelligible means that secularization must be viewed not just as a loss of faith but as a social process.

[CHAPTER TWO]

The Kantian Compromise

The centrality and foundational role of Kant's thinking for a large number of discourses of modern philosophy has never been in doubt. Since the publication of the *Critique of Pure Reason* in 1781, his critical philosophy has set both theoretical and practical philosophy—including epistemology, moral and political philosophy, aesthetics, and metaphysics—on entirely new and productive paths. To the conception of a comprehensive revolution in philosophy, a tectonic shift in the very space of accepted intellectual possibility, must be added his philosophy of religion, which vehemently opposes any interpretation of Christianity based on appeals to revelation or grace while placing moral purity at the heart of what it means to have faith.

Kant's approach to religion is multipronged. There is, first, the critic of rationalism who, in the *Critique of Pure Reason*, attacks the rationalist proofs of the existence of God, leaving no room for cognitive involvement in religious matters. Second, there is the quintessential Protestant and indeed Pietist thinker who painstakingly defends the integrity of faith by limiting the scope of knowledge and establishing a moral theology in which faith becomes interpreted in terms of pure practical reason. Finally, there is the theorist of cultural modernity (or what Kant calls *die Aufklärung*) who differentiates reason into its cognitive, practical, and purposiveness-attentive uses (in art criticism and biology), sees the capacity for rational self-determination and critique as its liberating telos, and limits the exercise of truth-apt judgment to the scientific domain. In the version of his philosophy of history found in the 1793 *Religion within the Boundaries of Mere Reason*, he unites all these themes in an anticipatory vision of a "kingdom of God" founded exclusively on a commitment to morality (and thus effectively being an "ethical community"). While arguing that this complex theoretical edifice offers the only possible coherent account of how religious faith may be combined with a genuine respect for human dignity, making faith possible even for the most uncompromising *Aufklärer*, his interpretation of divine authority as a mere function of *human* rational authority has led interpreters to suggest that what he ultimately provides is a more or less straightforward secularization narrative.

Kant *critiques* religion, at least in its rationalist version. However, he also attempts to *rescue* it as a component of morality. My aim in this chapter is to reconstruct and critically assess Kant's critique/rescue strategy. I start by situating Kant within a discourse of modernity in which the value of self-determination becomes paramount. Given his philosophically grounded vision of enlightenment as the attainment of rational self-sufficiency, it becomes evident from the outset that Kant will be dismissive of any account of religious experience that is grounded in divine revelation. Known as the *Alles-Zermalmer* (Jacobi), the "universal pulverizer," of rational religion, Kant further dismisses all available proofs of the existence of God as incoherent and as appealing to a conception of objectivity that must be rejected. Having reviewed this part of Kant's treatment of religion, I turn to his positive views of religion. I analyze his arguments in favor of adopting beliefs in the existence of God and in the immortality of the human soul as postulates of pure practical reason. Claiming that none of the strategies for doing so are fully compelling, I propose a diagnostic approach according to which the transcendence Kant insists on as a necessary addendum to moral reasoning should be viewed as offering a dialectical response to his understanding of the existential consequences of viewing our practical identity purely in rational terms. As such, and by holding open the possibility of transcendence in a world of rationalized immanence, Kant sets up a dialectic that deeply influences the subsequent, post-Kantian generation.

Kant and Rationalized Modernity

Kant's philosophy both reflects and anticipates key features and aspirations of Western modernity. He is committed to the fundamental outlook of post-1789 bourgeois society and, within a nineteenth- and twentieth-century context, of a liberal and capitalist industrial society, needing to account both for nature in terms of a system of law (inviting the judicious application of instrumental reason in technology and various commercial activities) and for the human subject as an agent, an active creature of reason, responsive to reasons and constituted to be able to formulate and subject itself to rational principles. On Kant's view the older social formation, based on submission to external authority within an organic, static order grounded in religious authority, can enjoy no legitimacy. Instead nature, the social order, and the subject are viewed as constituted by dynamic principles referring to the capacity for rational self-determination.[1]

Just as expressive, however, of the overall commitment to modernity and an essentially modern form of life (interpreted, of course, in a particular manner) is Kant's differentiation of spheres of cognitive-rational value. While premodern dispensations have tended to be oblivious of these differentiations, Kant, with attention to their constitutive principles, delineates the mode or manner of rational activity within each of these spheres. As students of his three *Critiques* know well, this differentiation is fundamentally a tripartite distinction between three types of judging: determinative judging about nature in the formal and nomothetic sciences; practical and principled reasoning about one's duty in morality and law; and reflective judging about purposiveness in aesthetics and biology. In addition to specifying the type of rational activity that is pertinent to each of these value spheres, the differentiation provides modern agents with ideals regarding the proper use of reason. For agents committed to this differentiation (for Kant, that is all rational agents), nature cannot be rationally approached other than as a system of natural laws. Morality and law, on the other hand, can be rationally approached only as a system of practical laws. Finally, the kind of reference to purposiveness that is pertinent to aesthetics and biology must be made via the regulative exercise of reflective judgment in its "subjective" and "objective" configurations.

Kant's differentiation calls into question a number of commitments that, at least before the Reformation, have been crucial to, and indeed constitutive of, religion and a religious worldview. For example, it implies that, except by acting regressively, intentions or purposes cannot "constitutively" be ascribed to natural events. While, in the *Critique of the Power of Judgment*,

---

1. Kant does not use the term modernity. The closest he gets is with his well-known and frequent use of *Aufklärung*, serving both descriptive and evaluative purposes. It designates a particular age or epoch, the century of the enlightened monarch Frederick, moving Kant to exclaim in the essay "An Answer to the Question: 'What Is Enlightenment?'" that "we do live in an age of *enlightenment*." However, by denying in the same essay that "we at present live in an *enlightened* age," he clearly assigns an evaluative dimension to *Aufklärung*. It is something one may or should be committed to and hence expressive of certain normative requirements in the light of which a particular social order may be considered. Kant seems to admit that ages other than his own may count as enlightened. However, "the Enlightenment" seems mainly to refer to the "century of *Frederick*." It is primarily in this latter sense that we are justified in attributing to Kant a definite awareness of living in modernity. For the passages from Kant's essay on the Enlightenment, see Immanuel Kant, "An Answer to the Question: 'What Is Enlightenment,'" in *Kant: Political Writings*, ed. H. S. Reiss (Cambridge: Cambridge University Press, 2005), 58.

Kant explores the possibility of rationally judging "as if" nature lends itself to purposiveness (that is, "regulatively"), such judging cannot rationally be employed to suggest the actual existence of any goal-directed powers (that is, "constitutively"). Thus any attempt to view nature as "enchanted," comprising, perhaps animistically, powers or agents that somehow direct themselves to achieving ends, would be disqualified as irrational. On Kant's differentiation view, nature is "silent." It cannot address us; and while inviting scientific experimentation and technological advancement, it leaves no room for assertions of objective, subject-transcendent value. Nor can it in other ways be considered an arena in which divine powers may inhere or be present. The differentiation view rules out miracles. As I mentioned, Kant finds extensive uses for reflective judgment understood as a regulative capacity for discerning natural objects and events "as if" there were subjective (in aesthetics) or objective (in biology) purposiveness. These, in particular the judgments made about pure beauty in his sections on aesthetics, do go some way toward remedying the implications of a completely disenchanted nature, especially with regard to the deeply Kantian problem of ascertaining the prospects for agency (and hence moral responsibility).[2] However, they do not change the fact that constitutively, nature is interpreted in terms of a disenchanted system of laws.

Kant's differentiation also precludes any rational recourse to notions of virtue that presuppose conceptions, familiar for example in Catholicism, of a fixed human nature. Since nature is defined in terms of appearances standing under natural law, being sharply contrasted with the space of reasons in which moral imperatives are formed and justified, there can be no way a person can qualify as "self-actualized," if by that one means this human being has attained all the features that together are deemed necessary and sufficient for an individual to count as fully developed and thereby fully human. The demand for self-perfection—which for Kant emerges in conjunction with his account of imperfect duties—can consist only in subjecting oneself rigorously and consistently to the categorical imperative. It is, in other words, as creatures of reason that human beings can seek improvement. However, no such effort can ever count as self-actualization if that means being able and disposed to act virtuously as a function of having accepted God's path for oneself.

Of great centrality to Kant's modernism—and his at least implicit theory of cultural modernity—is also that within each of the separate value spheres, human agents represent themselves as rationally autonomous

---

2. I refer here to the "*Übergangsproblem*," of showing that there can be a transition between freedom and nature.

beings. Thus Kant famously defines enlightenment in terms of the injunction to "think for oneself" ("*Sapere aude!* Have courage to use your *own* understanding!"[3]). To be modern in this precise, normative sense is to accept no pregiven authorities—that is, authorities untested by reason in its self-legislative role. It is to reject dogmatism.

The implications regarding the standing of religion in an enlightened, modern order are rife. Rationally self-reflective, modern agents will inevitably call into question, and simply dismiss, all forms of dependence, especially when referring to pregiven forms of authority, including God, Christ, the church, and even scripture. Although such relations of dependence, in which one's (typically moral) commitments are represented as dogmatically adopted from, or inculcated by, an external source, may successfully be transformed into expressions of self-determination if the recipient of the claims manages to rationally own up to them (which is how Kant typically views the correct Christian response to, for example, the commands of Christ), as such they are regressive and antimodern.

Kant's modernism is at least prima facie at odds with religious commitments. Not only does religious belief typically involve accepting some form of inexorable dependence on supersensible powers, weakening or preventing the decisive commitment to rational self-determination so deeply engrained in Kant's thinking, but religious belief standardly refers to, and is embedded within, horizons of meaning situating the subject in a living tradition exceeding the present and its self-assertive projections of future significance. Christian theology since Augustine, Origen, and Joachim de Fiore has interpreted history soteriologically and eschatologically. Although such notions of history implicate agents in structured projections of future meaning, they do not call for the kind of bracketing and neutralization of conventional meaning that we find in Kant. On the contrary, on such accounts, the religious observer finds herself located within a fixed, collective, and divinely sanctioned trajectory offering promise and hope.

Kant's ontology—with its mechanistic view of nature, its differentiated view of reason and cognitive value, and its emphasis on rational self-determination—may seem to involve not only skepticism of religion but downright hostility. When, in addition to this, one adds that his transcendental idealism restricts claims to objective knowledge to the order of appearance, precluding the possibility of transcendent, metaphysical knowledge (knowledge referring to the noumenal order), then one may seem justified in concluding that he must have been an agnostic or probably even an atheist.

3. Kant, "Answer to the Question: 'What Is Enlightenment?'" 54.

Of course, looking at his main writings as well as his biography, Kant does not seem to have been an agnostic or an atheist. While rationalist forerunners such as Descartes, Leibniz, and Wolff sought to secure religion from the onslaught of mechanistic natural science by demonstrating that human reason is indeed able to provide cognitive assurance to religious belief, Kant's positive account of religion starts by limiting knowledge in order to prevent skepticism about religious claims and by distinguishing rigorously between cognitive and religious claims.

Kant's complex battle with, and ultimate defense of, religion is more precisely taking place on two fronts. On the one hand he faced the kind of skepticism of religion one finds in French materialism or in Hume, according to which an antireligious stance is grounded in a materialist view of the universe and in a certain view of human reason as, in cognitive terms, fundamentally limited to whatever can be presented to the senses and so give rise to impressions. Those kinds of views, Kant believed, undeniably imply agnosticism or atheism. On the other hand, he confronted rationalist views, arguing that their implicit model of cognition must be viewed as incoherent. As a result, the rationalist approach to religion is equally likely to generate skepticism.

The critique of the proofs of the existence of God in the *Critique of Pure Reason* serves to curb the rationalist desire to provide metaphysically relevant conclusions based on reasoning from a priori principles. Kant claims that reason, in its inherent search for the unconditioned, is led to postulate the existence of a primordial being, an *ens realissimum*, capable of conditioning the possibility of all things as their *ground*. However, the ontological, the cosmological, and the physicotheological proofs, while purporting to demonstrate the existence of such a being based on inference from indubitable premises, are all subjected to severe criticism. The ontological argument, for example, which Kant seems to believe is the strongest and most ingenious, infers the necessary existence of God from a premise appealing to the necessary predicates of a perfect being. God must exist because His perfection necessarily entails that He does. The mere concept of the *ens realissimum*, a being that necessarily contains all reality and therefore all predicates, must, since existence is a predicate, carry with it the absolute necessity of that being. However, as Kant famously argues, existence or being is not a predicate.[4] Rather than enlarging or determining the concept to which it is attached, it merely determines the logical form of the judgment.

---

4. Immanuel Kant, *Critique of Pure Reason*, trans. Paul Guyer and Allen W. Wood (Cambridge: Cambridge University Press, 1998), B626.

While the critique of the proofs of the existence of God is central to Kant's approach to religion, it does nothing to establish a positive ground for Kant's own defense of religion. Nor, for that matter, does it pose much of a threat to the Christian believer for whom faith is not viewed exclusively in cognitive terms. Indeed, unless one is drawn to the rationalist view of religion, this critique is itself insufficient to establish whether claims to faith might have a claim to legitimacy outside the rationalist framework.

A more positive yet related dimension of Kant's strategy is the doctrine of transcendental idealism, based on which he believes himself entitled, as he puts it in the second Preface to the *Critique of Pure Reason*, to have "denied knowledge in order to make room for faith."[5] Transcendental idealism distinguishes between two orders of possible knowledge: on the one hand the order of appearances (*Erscheinungen*), which is constituted by the objectivating conditions of space and time as well as by the categories of judgment, and, on the other, the order of things as they are in themselves, which by definition is not constituted by any objectivating conditions (but figures as the object of a possible intellectual intuition, unavailable to human agents who depend on sensuous intuitions to form truth-apt judgments).

By restricting human knowledge to the order of appearances, Kant may be understood as making possible a philosophy of the noumenal and of transcendence, one that, in the transcendental dialectic of the *Critique of Pure Reason*, takes the form of a conditional and hypothetical *metaphysica specialis*: even if God and other transcendent, metaphysical entities exist, we cannot know them. All we can rationally do is to permit assent in the form of *faith*. Although cognitively unassured, faith has the *potential* to refer to something real. Modally, it exists within the space of the thinkable and the possible—the space, as we shall soon see, of hope. However, as we shall also see, the hope in question arises from the structure of practical reason; and in the absence of the moral law, it would not animate and inform the nature of faith. Thus, equally central to Kant's theological enterprise is securing a space for freedom, for uncaused causes, permitting the formation of personal autonomy. Transcendental idealism, by distinguishing between the world of causal necessity at the level of appearance and the world of freedom at the level of the thing in itself, makes such a view possible.

Employing the conceptual divisions of transcendental idealism, Kant immunizes Christian faith against theoretical inquiry and skepticism, thereby compartmentalizing faith and knowledge in a manner respectful

---

5. Kant, *Critique of Pure Reason*, Bxxx. See Kant, *Kritik der reinen Vernunft* (Frankfurt: Suhrkamp, 1988), Bxxx: "Ich mußte also das Wissen aufheben, um zum Glauben Platz zu bekommen."

of both. Science has its domain, which for Kant is coextensive with nature understood as the totality of spatiotemporal objects and events standing under natural law. Theology is assigned a different field, coinciding with the transcendent, postulated reality of the objects of *metaphysical specialis*. By criticizing the aspirations of rational inquiry and (philosophical) rationalism to be able to settle questions of religious faith, and by assigning to knowledge its rightful role in immanent theoretical inquiry, Kant has taken the first step in defending the integrity of faith. He is on his way not only to critique but to rescue.

Summum Bonum and the Postulates of Pure Practical Reason

First published in 1793 and in complex ways building on the achievements of the three preceding Critiques as well as some of the key essays on history, *Religion within the Boundaries of Mere Reason* belongs to Kant's late phase. It starts by offering an account of radical evil understood as man's purportedly natural yet free disposition to adopt maxims that contravene the demands of the moral law. An agent who incorporates in his maxim an inclination stemming from empirically mediated self-love (or desire), according to Kant, is *evil*. By contrast, an agent who determines his will in accordance with the moral law and who does his duty for duty's own sake—for the sake of the unconditional bindingness and value of duty—is *good*. Kant further introduces his doctrine of the *summum bonum*. After applying these notions to various anthropological questions such as whether man was created good or evil, he turns to religion, trying to interpret especially Christianity in light of his own theory of morality. As he spells out in the 1784 "Ideas for a Universal History with Cosmopolitan Intent" and the 1797 *Metaphysics of Morals*, the supporters of such a moral religion need to seek legal protection of the free exercise of their wills in an ethical commonwealth. However, their concept of God must be thought of as exclusively moral: they represent God as an ethical lawgiver, though only in the sense that God serves as the necessary yet cognitively unassured condition under which their rationally motivated hopes for the achievement of the highest good are able to make sense.

All possible (and by implication historically existing) religions, Kant claims, can be divided into two categories. On the one hand are religions of *rogation* (of "mere cult") or of mere worship aiming to win favor, which exclusively appeal to man's quest for *happiness*. Kant's characterization of these religions is nothing less than acerbic. In these religions, he writes, "the human being either flatters himself that God can make him eternally happy (through the remissions of his debts) without any necessity on his part *to become a better human being*; or else, if this does not seem possible to him, that *God* himself *can make him a better human being* without his having to contribute more than to *ask* for it, and, since before an omniscient being asking is no more than *wishing*, this would amount in fact to doing nothing, for, if improvement were a matter of mere wishing, every human being would be good."[6] On the other hand, there is *moral religion*: "According to moral religion, however (and, of all the public religions so far known, the Christian alone is of this type), it is a fundamental principle that, to become a better human being, everyone must do as much it is in his power to do; and only then, if a human being has not buried his innate talent (Luke 19:12–16), if he has made use of the original predisposition to the good in order to become a better human being, can he hope that what does not lie in his power will be made good by cooperation above."[7] If the notion of making use of the original predisposition to the good in order to become a better human being is interpreted externally, as doing deeds that are supposed to "flatter" or in other ways impress or influence God, then the concept of moral religion may suggest an affinity to Pelagianism. However, what Kant has in mind is neither action nor works as such but, rather, the cultivation of moral purity such that the believer can feel justified in hoping for the existence of God and for salvation. In the great sixteenth-century debate between Luther and Erasmus over the existence of freedom and the role of self-improvement (including repentance, baptism, and conversion) in religious life, Kant likely would have sided with Erasmus in emphasizing man's own responsibility for his "eligibility" to be saved.[8] Since human beings are endowed with freedom, the Lutheran doctrine of predestination must be wrong. However, he would have agreed with Luther that human beings are incapable of bringing themselves to God or working out their own salvation. According to Kant, all that human agents can do in these matters is to make themselves *worthy* of salvation. On that basis they can *hope* but never *know*.

Kant's Lutheran rejection of knowledge is based on the doctrine of transcendental idealism. According to this view, faith (*Glaube*), rather than being an intellectual enterprise, a claim to knowledge on a par with (and therefore also in competition with) science, is to be thought of as a "matter of the heart." However, unlike sentimentalist views, such as that of Jacobi,

---

6. Immanuel Kant, *Religion within the Boundaries of Mere Reason*, trans. Allen Wood and George Di Giovanni (Cambridge: Cambridge University Press, 2018), 82.

7. Kant, *Religion within the Boundaries of Mere Reason*, 82–83.

8. Erasmus and Luther, *The Battle over Free Will*, ed. Clarence H. Miller, trans. Clarence H. Miller and Peter Macardle (London: Hackett, 2012).

in which faith is considered in terms of mere feeling—some state of the subject, devoid of a rational structure—Kant claims that faith is articulated propositionally: it is a species of "conviction" (*Überzeugung*) whereby the subject aspires to universal validity.

For a conviction to be successfully formed, it must appeal to some objective ground on which the claim to universality may be based. Claims to knowledge (*Wissen*) do precisely that. They rest on evidence whose bindingness (for or against the putative truth value of a proposition) has been guaranteed by the a priori conditions of objective experience. Yet if faith is supposed to be a "matter of the heart," then why classify it as being based on objective grounds? What grounds might they be?

To be sure, Kant operates with a category or mode of assent that appeals to no such objective ground whatever. In the *Critique of Pure Reason*, he calls such nonobjective judgments "persuasion" (*Überredung*).[9] Persuasions, he argues, have "only private validity." In accounting for why one is of a particular persuasion, a person can do no more than report what it is that predisposes her to be persuaded. Examples of such reports—which, because they refer to one's own subjective constitution, cannot claim universal validity—might include emotional states or sensations of various kinds. There is a parallel to this conception in the analysis of taste in the third Critique. A so-called empirical judgment of taste refers to the speaker's own sensation of pleasure in drinking, say, a particular type of wine. According to Kant, one's approval of the wine would come with no claim on how others should or ought to experience the wine. It would not amount to a statement about the wine as such. Instead, it would simply report to others how the speaker happens to experience the wine. Based as it would be on the particular and contingent facts surrounding how the wine, when touching the palate, causally produces a sensation in the drinker, its validity would be only private.

If *Glaube* indeed had the logical form of "persuasion," it would lend itself to the kinds of analyses one finds in skeptical views of religion. One might then ask questions about *how* someone reached the point of thinking of himself as religious—and perhaps provide a genealogical account that would reveal the history and the mechanisms that together predisposed him to take up the attitude of faith. However, it would effectively prevent Kant from viewing faith as being based on a ground that could legitimate a claim to the "necessary validity for everyone."

Now, even the most cursory look at the history of monotheism, and Christianity in particular, suggests that claims to being in possession of faith

---

9. Kant, *Critique of Pure Reason*, B848.

have frequently been based on some claim to a special, private dispensation. However, someone who claimed to have become a believer, and to have received grace, based on some kind of revelation necessarily unavailable to others, would on Kant's view qualify as no more than irrational or idiosyncratic. Thus, in *The Book of Adler*, Kierkegaard raises the question whether a revelation could authoritatively be presented as an objective ground of faith.[10] His answer is that it can, but only if the individual experiencing the revelation finds a way to present his experience, and hence himself, as *authoritative*. In Kierkegaard's existentialist view, authority depends on the quality of the subjective stance itself, its "intensity" or "inwardness." The believer must identify some way of presenting his own experience as valid for everyone. Unfortunately, since pastor Adolph P. Adler, Kierkegaard's main character in the *Book of Adler*, finds himself in an age of "objectivity" in which every claim is met with the demand for some sort of proof, this attempt is doomed to fail. While Kierkegaard considers revelation an impossible source of authoritative faith owing to the pressures that in modernity make people disinclined to trust anything but the objectively demonstrable, Kant dismisses revelation *because it necessarily remains private*: since its grounds are subjective (idiosyncratic or irrational), it *cannot* command universal assent.

What, then, might the grounds of Kantian *Glaube* be? The answer, very generally stated, is that faith obtains its legitimacy through the structure and needs of practical reason, which as such are considered to be necessary and universal. Interpreted as a mental state, faith may arise in response to all sort of experiences, including revelation. Kant does not deny that over the course of human history, many people will have experienced their faith in ways that do not accord with the strictures of practical faith. Indeed, in *Religion within the Boundaries of Mere Reason* he frequently acknowledges the existence of other types of faith. However, insofar as it may claim intersubjective validity and thereby transcend the merely irrational, it must have the structure that Kant outlines in conjunction with his account of practical reason. That structure, more specifically, is tied to the doctrine of the Highest Good and the two postulates of pure practical reason that supposedly follow from this doctrine: God's existence and the immortality of the soul.[11]

---

10. Sören Kierkegaard, *The Book of Adler*, trans. Howard V. Hong and Edna H. Hong (Princeton, NJ: Princeton University Press, 1998).

11. There is, of course, a third postulate of pure practical reason, namely that of freedom. However, while freedom is of paramount importance to Kant's account of moral responsibility, it only indirectly relates to religion. Without freedom, there would be no morality, and without morality there would be no faith and no religion. In this sense

In the *Critique of Practical Reason*, Kant deduces as a fact of reason the moral law, which based on pure reason alone is supposed to constrain any rational agent unconditionally and immediately (by the practical rule itself). As the mere form of law itself, the moral law commands by requiring that one act "so that the maxim of [one's] will could always hold at the same time as a principle in a giving of universal law."[12] The good will, understood as unconditional, a standing disposition to act for the sake of duty alone, constitutes, according to Kant, "the Supreme Good." It is a condition for being worthy of happiness. However, *supremum* must be distinguished from *consummatum*. While both can mean "the highest," the whole and complete good is understood by Kant as the *summum bonum*, the Highest Good.

The Highest Good (when interpreted, as I will do from now on, in terms of the criterion of *consummatum*) adds happiness to virtue. Kant defines it as *an ideal state of affairs in which all agents have achieved virtue and happiness is distributed in accordance with virtue*. As opposed to the supreme goodness of virtue considered as such, it makes up a totality (hence its theoretical location in the dialectic of pure practical reason) that cannot figure as part of any larger whole or order of the same kind.

It is not hard to see why Kant considers the Highest Good to consist of these elements. Virtue is the Supreme Good. However, it cannot be the Highest Good. A virtuous person may be devoid of whatever it is that would make her happy, and she may indeed be deeply unhappy, which cannot be unconditionally good. Virtue without happiness is supremely yet not consummately good. Happiness, on the other hand, without virtue, while desirable for people of a questionable character, cannot be the Highest Good for the simple reason that, lacking the supreme good of virtue, it is consistent with a life of depravity and evil. For the Highest Good to be an object of practical thought, the two elements must be united: since the connection cannot be cognized analytically, by the mere analysis of discrepant concepts, there must be a synthesis between them such that the totality of the object may emerge. Both elements must coexist in this synthesis. The one cannot be reduced to the other.

In order to bolster the idea that, for the Highest Good to be an object of pure practical reason, there must be a synthesis of virtue and happiness in proportion to desert, Kant, in the *Critique of Practical Reason*, considers two ancient views, both of which he finds reductive. The Stoics, he argues,

---

freedom is important for Kant's understanding of religion, yet freedom does not point directly toward religion.

12. Immanuel Kant, *Critique of Practical Reason*, trans. Mary Gregor (Cambridge: Cambridge University Press, 2015), 28.

viewed happiness as consciousness of one's virtue. Happiness is therefore a function of virtue. The Epicureans, by contrast, interpreted virtue as being conscious of one's maxim leading to happiness. For them, considerations regarding how to achieve happiness disclose the nature of virtue. On closer inspection the Stoic fails to account for how virtue can make one happy. While the use of freedom involved in acting on unconditional principles may be able to provide a sense of pleasure, the moral feeling of the *Groundwork of the Metaphysics of Morals*, it "cannot be called happiness because it does not depend upon the positive concurrence of a feeling; nor is it, strictly speaking, *beatitude*, since it does not include complete independence from inclinations and needs."[13] Of course, had Kant's view of happiness been closer to the eudaimonistic conception he finds in Stoicism, he might have thought twice about ruling out the possibility that virtue might embody happiness. However, with his sensualist view of happiness as involving an uninterrupted feeling of "agreeableness of life" made possible by the consumption of a desired object, such a view will necessarily be ruled out from the outset. The Epicureans, on the other hand, simply presuppose the existence of a virtuous disposition in those they deem to have attained happiness. Yet while, according to Kant, it is true that no morally upright human being will enjoy life unless she is conscious of, and responsive to, duty (which allows to her to have moral worth), such a disposition does not automatically prevail in the subject pursuing happiness. It must come from somewhere else.

There is thus an irreducible difference between virtue and happiness. They differ semantically, allowing for no reduction of the one to the other. Considered as an object of pure practical reason, however, the Highest Good represents their unity qua synthetic achievement.

The doctrine of the Highest Good can be interpreted as containing two layers, sometimes referred to as its ectypical versus archetypical dimensions, forming a demand and a promise. As Lawrence R. Pasternack points out, the two layers or dimensions correspond to the bifurcation of the Highest Good as *demand* and as *promise*.[14] Considered as a demand, the Highest Good presents a duty to which all rational beings are bound. In the critical literature on Kant, the nature of this duty has generated a lot of debate. On one interpretation, there is a particular duty to promote the Highest Good. Pasternack, for one, views it as an imperfect duty, "one that

---

13. Kant, *Critique of Practical Reason*, 96.

14. Lawrence R. Pasternack, *The Routledge Philosophy Guidebook to Kant on "Religion within the Boundaries of Mere Reason": An Interpretation and Defense* (London: Routledge, 2014), 31.

we are obligated to positively promote, rather than a perfect and negative sort of duty, such as the prohibitions against lying, stealing or killing."[15] A problem with this interpretation, however, is that it leaves unresolved how such a duty might be grounded or justified. Kant does not explain how it can be derived from the moral law, nor does any of the formulas of the moral law have the Highest Good as its content. Rather than identifying some unaccountable duty *in addition* to all the particular duties we have that are derived from the moral law, a more promising interpretation would hold that human reason unavoidably represents all particular duties as leading toward the promotion of the Highest Good.[16] On this latter account, the duty to promote the Highest Good, Kant claims, "does not increase the number of morality's virtues but rather provides these with a special point of reference for the unification of all ends."[17] In other words, each time a rational agent determines her will in accordance with the categorical imperative, it may justifiably be represented as contributing to actualizing the Highest Good. As Kant argues in the *Religion within the Boundaries of Mere Reason*, this striving can make full sense, and be fully justified to individuals, only insofar as each acting agent finds herself within an indefinite community, comprising all rational (and hence morally obligated) beings.

However, the *summum bonum* is also serving as a promise and thus as an ideal. As such it takes a distributive form, calling for the distribution of happiness in proportion to our moral worth. In critical writings from the 1780s and the 1790s, Kant provides dozens of formulations of this ideal. The *Critique of Practical Reason*, for example, quite paradigmatically defines the archetypical layer of the Highest Good as follows: "happiness distributed in exact proportion to morality (as the worth of a person and his worthiness to be happy) constitutes the *highest good* of a possible world."[18] Likewise, in the *Critique of Pure Reason*, he asserts that "everyone has cause to hope for happiness in the same measure as he has made himself worthy of it in his conduct, and that the system of morality is therefore inseparably

---

15. Pasternack, *Routledge Philosophy Guidebook to Kant on "Religion within the Boundaries of Mere Reason."*

16. For the (in my view unpromising) notion that we have a duty to promote the Highest Good that is separate, and logically different, from our regular moral duties, see Lewis White Beck, *A Commentary on Kant's Critique of Practical Reason* (Chicago: University of Chicago Press, 1960), 244–45, and Allen Wood, *Kant's Religion* (Ithaca, NY: Cornell University Press, 1970), 95–96.

17. Kant, *Religion within the Boundaries of Mere Reason*, 41.

18. Kant, *Critique of Practical Reason*, 90.

combined with the system of happiness, though only in the idea of pure reason."[19] While the Highest Good as duty expresses how agents who honor the moral law necessarily conceive of themselves as obligated to contribute to actualizing this ideal, the Highest Good as ideal expresses what those same agents would create were it in their power. They would create what they could hope for *as* those kinds of agents. The actualizing of the Highest Good would make life for those who deserve it happy and even blissful, but only in proportion as they indeed deserve it.

We have seen how Kant's doctrine of transcendental idealism situates us as empirical beings within a domain of immanence—in short, the domain of the rationally masterable: what permits empirical experience in light of its unavoidable transcendental conditions and rational responsiveness in light of self-chosen principles or maxims. However, especially while conceiving of us as being constrained by the moral law, which calls on us to regulate our actions so that the maxims they are based on can be universalized, Kant admits to a great deal of contingency. Actions may have unintended consequences. Other agents may act on impermissible maxims. The body is fundamentally weak and exposed, constituting the agent as a being of needs that, depending on luck and on the decisions both of oneself and of others, may or may not be satisfied. According to the First Part of *Religion within the Boundaries of Mere Reason*, Kant implies that, while ultimately "inexplicable," a "propensity to evil" lurks inextricably and universally in the human heart, causing our moral striving to forever take the form of a struggle.

In this Kantian world of rationalized immanence, the promises of happiness seem few and far between. Sociality, being together with others and enjoying their presence as rational beings able to listen and intervene, is one of them. The experience of beauty and sublimity is another. Beauty in particular, the enjoyment of "purposiveness without purpose," on which Kant expounds in the first half of the *Critique of the Power of Judgment*, presents an occasion when the human subject experiences an object as it pleases the senses devoid of both conceptual determination and empirical interest. All that, in addition to the senses, mediates this experience is the imagination as it freely relates to the rules (and conceptual determinations) provided by the understanding. Like other experiences of pleasure,

---

19. Kant, *Critique of Pure Reason*, A809/B837. Kant, *Kritik der reinen Vernunft*, A809/B837: "daß jedermann die Glückseligkeit in demselben Maße zu hoffen Ursache habe, als er sich derselben in seinem Verhalten würdig gemacht hat, und daß also das System der Sittlichkeit mit dem der Glückseligkeit unzertrennlich, aber nur in der Idee der reinen Vernunft verbunden sei."

it nevertheless remains exceptional and contingent on the existence of certain objects to which, in lucky circumstances, one may relate. Then, finally, there is happiness as undiluted satisfaction of sensuous need.

The account of the *summum bonum* stands out as the location where Kant's philosophy introduces a conception of *transcendence*, a state of being, though conditional on the satisfaction of the distribution requirement, in which agents may find genuine (and, of course, also deserved) fulfillment. As opposed to epistemic transcendence, which the restriction thesis of the *Critique of Pure Reason*—the claim that objective experience, based as it is on an interplay between intuitions and concepts, extends to the order of appearance yet not to the order of the thing in itself—has declared impossible, the transcendence associated with the quest for happiness makes sense as an *aspiration*. It is something that all humans necessarily long for and, to the extent they deserve it, are justified in longing for. As such, it is not surprising that it figures as the touchstone of Kant's interpretation of religion's promise. The happiness involved in the vision of the Highest Good is thus the subject of *hope*. In addition to "What can I know?" (the epistemic and metaphysical question) and "What should I do?" (the moral question), it functions as a separate yet crucial question in the critical project as a whole: "What may I hope?" (the religious question).[20]

It is the connection to morality that, in the *Critique of Pure Reason*, provides hope with a normative element (an a priori principle). The hope of happiness, rather than a mere fact about individuals (there the question would have been "What do I hope?"), finds its principled mode of motivation when attached to morality. In "Was darf ich hoffen?" the German verb *dürfen* makes it abundantly clear that the hope at stake necessarily is subject to a normative requirement. According to the principle of proportionate distribution that we have already come by when analyzing the concept of the Highest Good, an agent is rationally justified in holding to the hope of happiness insofar as she has become worthy of receiving it.

The hope, in other words, that Kant has in mind is not just a psychological occurrence, and it should not be equated with wishful thinking. It flows, and is derived from a commitment to morality. In the *Critique of Pure Reason*, which provides the first treatment that Kant gives of the Highest Good

---

20. In *Jaesche Logic*, in *Kants Werke*, ed. Hartenstein, 8:25, Kant adds as a fourth fundamental question of his critical philosophy "What is man?" While understanding this as an anthropological question, a likely interpretation might be that Kant, who takes the fourth question to encompass the first three, has in mind his whole critical project insofar as it evolves from an ongoing attention to the human subject in its transcendental capacities.

in the critical phase, it unites morality and happiness by making the hope for happiness an intrinsic element of moral motivation. It is true that later writings on morality, such as the *Groundwork of the Metaphysics of Morals* and the *Critique of Practical Reason*, hold duty as such to be a sufficient incentive for action. Awareness of their duty provides agents not only with an understanding of the constraining norm as such but with sufficient reason to act. However, before his critical phase and well into the early critical phase, Kant's moral thinking displayed both rationalist and sentimentalist theses. He subscribed to a lawlike, principled view of morality. At the same time, however, he believed that, shorn of the requisite feeling, an individual would not have a motivation to perform an action that, on rational grounds, she realizes it is her duty to perform. As he puts it in the so-called Mrongovius notes, "When a man has learned to appraise all actions, he still lacks the motive to perform them. . . . The understanding has no *elateres animi* . . . man has no such secret organization, that he can be moved by objective grounds."[21] The notion of such a motivational deficit enters with great consequence in the Canon of Pure Reason of the first *Critique*, where Kant writes that "the majestic ideas of morality are, to be sure, objects of approbation and admiration but not incentives for resolve and realization."[22] What then, given that Kant at this point has left his sentimentalist impulses behind, could function as such incentives?

The answer, in short, is the idea of the Highest Good considered as an ideal. What it takes for morality's injunctions to be accepted as motivating commands is the promise of deserved happiness, standing in exact relation to morality: for fear of punishment (the absence of happiness or even negative sanction) it prevents us from trespassing against the moral commands; by the hope of reward, it steers us toward accepting duty as decisive for how we conduct ourselves practically.

Yet the *summum bonum* cannot be hoped for in the sensible world of causal laws. Perhaps the most important reason for this relates to the problem of moral contingency, that the outcome of human action, even when performed by a good will, is never fully controllable. Also, since moral actions are sanctioned from within, through conscience, no individual can control other people's moral activity. At best, individuals may find themselves able to educate other people's moral dispositions or influence them in other ways. However, scenarios have of course been historically abundant

---

21. Pasternack, *Routledge Guidebook to Kant on Religion within the Boundaries of Mere Reason*, 44.

22. Kant, *Critique of Pure Reason*, A813/B841.

in which, despite their best efforts, the morally committed become overwhelmed not only by the contingency of natural events but by intentionally evil action perpetrated by other agents. Indeed, as Kant in his pessimistic moments seems to intimate, they are typical. Why, in short, should an agent be bothered to act morally when evil so often seems to triumph? What reason is there for acting morally when good intentions are so easily defeated? It is only, Kant argues, by postulating the existence of a perfectly just lawgiver and an infinite duration in which to set things right that morality may connect with our wills to promote action.

Kant's God serves as a bridge between morality and happiness, making the thought of the *summum bonum* both possible and coherent. For Kant, to believe in God is to place one's trust in a supreme, intelligent will (and a cause of nature) capable of securing an inviolable and necessary connection between morality and the happiness deserved by those who are worthy of it. Endowed with that trust, which figures as the entry point of religion, an agent finds that her motivational needs can be satisfied: when this "postulate" is accepted, the world ultimately appears just and, as such, a meaningful arena of moral action. An agent may act morally and sacrifice immediate interest while entertaining a practical belief in the ultimate possibility of deserved happiness.

Kant also puts forward as a postulate of practical reason the immortality of the soul. Like the postulate of God's existence, this postulate springs from, and supplements, the logic of the moral law. The thought of the *summum bonum* not only requires the postulate of God as an ultimate provider of happiness to those worthy of it, it also involves an extension of life beyond this one in which rewards and punishments can be meted out and the moral subject can perfect itself. To the purely motivational argument of the first Critique, the *Critique of Practical Reason* adds that the idea of the *summum bonum* can be formulated coherently only if we assume that complete conformity to the moral law is a viable human goal. Without such an aspiration, the Highest Good would be unthinkable as a human ideal. Indeed, since this conformity is possible only if we assume moral perfection, the *holiness* of a will devoid of impure motives, it requires *infinite* striving. Thus the soul must be viewed as, or believed to be, immortal, capable of forever improving and purifying itself.

Many critics have felt considerable unease about the deduction of *Glaube* in the first Critique's Canon of Pure Reason. Indeed, in the form it attains in this early account, Kant manifestly ignores a distinction that, especially in the *Groundwork*, is crucial, namely that between motivation for the sake of the moral law alone (in which respect for the moral law is taken to be the sole determining ground of the will) and motivation based on an aspiration to happiness. Either the "majestic ideas of morality" are sufficient incentives for resolve and realization, in which case the motivational argument is superfluous and should be dismissed, or morality needs such a supplement, in which case the idea of the purity of moral motivation, so central to Kant's vision and account of human reason, must be rejected, leaving huge questions surrounding his moral philosophy unanswered.

Material practical principles (assertoric imperatives) can in Kant's view never be more than contingent; whether they should apply depends not on the universal structure of human reason but on the empirical constitution and conditions of each individual subject. Whether a person can expect happiness from adopting a principle of this kind depends on who this person is and can never be settled in advance with any certainty. Needs and desires exist empirically; what satisfies one person, giving pleasure and happiness, may be a source of dissatisfaction for another. While certain rules of skill, or what Kant calls hypothetical imperatives, may inform one's principles of self-love—rules, in short, dictating to a rational agent what the best means of obtaining one's ends may be—they can never function as more than pragmatic principles grounded in observation of causal relations. Practical precepts formed with reference to such principles, if directed toward attaining happiness, are thus in a double sense contingent: they rely on knowledge of how the world works ("flour is needed to bake bread") and on what it is that, given one's empirical constitution, satisfies desire ("I would like to eat bread"). In contrast to such principles, the moral law is supposed to command the will unconditionally: where hypothetical and assertoric imperatives constrain the will conditionally, the moral law determines the will purely by virtue of its own form, independent of sensible conditions.

The motivational argument in the Canon of Pure Reason in the first Critique is at best unstable. If the Highest Good is construed as necessary for moral motivation to be possible, then the idea of duty as itself sufficient to motivate us to act, central to Kant's whole vision of autonomous morality, becomes unsustainable. Thus, in the *Critique of the Power of Judgment*, Kant modifies this argument. On the one hand, he insists on the unconditional and formal nature of moral laws; they obligate rational agents without regard to ends. Even if one were to become convinced that there is no *summum bonum* and hence no God prepared to mete out a just distribution of rewards and punishments to indefinitely self-perfecting agents, it would be a mistake "on that account ... to hold the laws of duty to be merely imaginary, invalid, and nonobligatory."[23] They do motivate in an action-guiding sense.

---

23. Kant, *Critique of the Power of Judgment*, trans. Paul Guyer and Eric Matthews (Cambridge: Cambridge University Press, 2002), 451.

On the other hand, however, the hope of happiness is introduced as a supplement to a successfully executed moral life, a set of dispositions and convictions that, while they do not undermine the autonomy of the moral law, help us psychologically to stay on the right course morally. If the argument in the Canon of Pure Reason purports to be pointing to a rational structure, appealing to what it is for a reason to motivate sufficiently, the argument in the *Critique of the Power of Judgment* centers on all the disappointments we may face as moral agents, "the purposeless chaos of matter," and "all the evils of poverty, illness, and untimely death."[24] Much of the gist of Kant's exposition hinges on the notion of resilience. In the Parable of the Righteous Atheist, offered in the third Critique, Kant imagines a person whose respect for the moral law has been unrestricted and impeccable. However, devoid of hope that his efforts will ever be rewarded, and overwhelmed by the futility of human action in a world of evil and contingency, his resolve will gradually be weakened.[25] Ultimately, the righteous atheist may succumb to despair and give up altogether on his commitment to morality. When resilience fails, in other words, the result, Kant seems to intimate, is cynicism. Overcoming cynicism, the theist may rest his commitment to morality on the belief that all the suffering and injustice in this life will be met with justice—and with happiness in proportion to desert—in the next life.

Kant at this point gets close to offering religion as a solution to the perennial question—the Job question, as it were—regarding the meaningfulness of human existence. According to his doctrine of practical reason, human beings lead lives of meaning and purpose insofar as they can recognize themselves as free agents capable of unconditionally observing moral precepts. They are then able to see themselves as originators of actions that reflect their highest aspirations and that, if consistently undertaken, affirm their sense of self-worth and dignity. When, as with the righteous atheist, that project becomes unsustainable, the very rationale of existence—the reason to exist—may seem to be threatened, if not entirely undermined. While Kant refers to cynicism, he clearly also references despair; and *Glaube* is presented as their only real and abiding remedy.

While the strategy in the first Critique's Canon of Pure Reason runs into difficulties owing to its failure to differentiate sufficiently between duty and the hope of happiness, the strategy in the third Critique may seem to make the hope of the *summum bonum* as an ideal circumstantial and indeed wholly dependent on one's actual situation together with one's psychological, evaluative, and interpretive dispositions. To the extent that adopting

---

24. Kant, *Critique of the Power of Judgment*, 452.
25. Kant, *Critique of the Power of Judgment*, 452.

faith was supposed to be more than a matter of mere contingency, something that happens to occur in certain individuals, and instead a reflection of fundamental and a priori principles of practical reason, it needs a firmer and more principled grounding. The way Kant accounts for it in the *Critique of the Power of Judgment* makes it not only contingent but also peripheral to our moral striving. If the postulates of pure practical reason are merely serving as psychological support systems, then the door seems open to an indefinite variety of alternative systems of moral self-help, reducing religion to just an unnecessary instrument of personal edification.

In the *Critique of Practical Reason* Kant backs away from both the motivational and the psychological arguments, arguing instead that the Highest Good, in accordance with practical reason's quest for the unconditioned condition of itself, functions as an unconditioned totality on which practical reason depends. Since this stipulation is based exclusively on a rational need for completion, closure, and totality, familiar from the transcendental dialectic of the *Critique of Pure Reason*, it remains unclear how a subject, considered as a moral agent, is supposed to experience the force of this argument. It seems to remain a mere logical requirement flowing from the structure and dialectic of pure practical reason. Also, as Pasternack argues, it makes it a condition of duty (and its *ought*) that the ideal expressed in the *summum bonum* can be realized. However, Kant elsewhere argues that the moral law binds rational agents independent of whether the Highest Good can be realized.[26]

A more compelling strategy appears in the preface to the first edition of *Religion within the Boundaries of Mere Reason*, where Kant returns to the idea of motivation, though in a manner that deviates significantly from the earlier efforts. The guiding idea in *Religion* is that while determining oneself based on the moral law does not, and should not, take place with reference to the possible or actual ends of one's action, a truly conscientious agent cannot be indifferent to the *actual outcome* of her actions. For example, while morally obligatory (though only as imperfect duties), acts of benevolence that never produced any good outcomes and never improved anyone's life would seem pointless, calling for some sort of account of why they should have been undertaken in the first place. Kant's expression of this important idea is worth quoting in full.

> But although on its own behalf morality does not need the representation of an end which would have to precede the determination of the will, it may well be that it has a necessary reference to such an end, not as the

---

26. Pasternack, *Kant on Religion within the Boundaries of Mere Reason*, 50.

ground of its maxims but as a necessary reference to such an end, not as the ground of its maxims but as a necessary consequence accepted in conformity to them.—For in the absence of all reference to an end no determination of the will can take place in human beings at all, since no such determination can occur without an effect, and its representation, though not as the determining ground of the power of choice nor as an end that comes first in intention, must nonetheless be admissible as the consequence of that power's determination to an end through the law (*finis in consequentiam veniens*); without this end, a power of choice which does not [thus] add to a contemplated action the thought of either an objectively or subjectively determined object (which it has or should have), instructed indeed as to *how* to operate but not as to the *whither*, can itself obtain no satisfaction. So, morality really has no need of an end for right conduct; on the contrary, the law that contains the formal conditions of the use of freedom in general suffices to it. Yet an end proceeds from morality just the same; for it cannot possibly be a matter of indifference to reason how to answer the question, *What is then the result of this right conduct of ours?* Nor to what we are to direct our doings or non-doings, even granted this is not fully in our control, at least as something with which they are to harmonize.[27]

Some qualifications are called for at this point. Kant cannot mean that considerations regarding the outcome of actions should ever serve as relevant reasons in assessing their moral worth. If he did, then he would immediately come into conflict with his own deontological commitments. The sole basis for assessing the moral worth of an action must, if Kant is to be consistent, remain the maxim on which that particular course of action was based—whether it permits universalization along the lines of what the moral law requires. However, when assessed more widely, the actions of a rational agent must also allow for considerations of their efficacy. In the passage just quoted, Kant explicitly states that what the result of our conduct might be cannot be "a matter of indifference to reason." In other words, while morally a rational agent restricts her assessment to the maxim on which an action purports to be grounded, *qua* rational the agent must consider the effects of the action.

In *Religion*, Kant takes an extremely strong view of what this might entail. The view is not just that rational agents cannot help caring about outcomes (which would be a psychological claim), or that they ought to care (which would be a claim conditional upon other interests), but that the very

27. Kant, *Religion within the Boundaries of Mere Reason*, 4–5.

determination of the will, understood as a condition of all action, including moral action, presupposes a rational consideration of possible ends. How, exactly, does this claim square with his deontology? If a morally obligatory action is one in which the will is exclusively determined by a universalizable maxim, then how can the same will necessarily be determined by considerations of possible ends as well? It seems that the only interpretation capable of providing a consistent view of agential self-determination would have to involve seeing (and assessing) actions under distinct aspects. Considered in terms of its candidacy for moral acceptance, an action must have been undertaken exclusively for the sake of duty. However, considered in terms of its rationality qua action as such, reflecting upon the projected ends becomes unavoidable. As Kant admits, actions undertaken for morally acceptable and relevant reasons may be *irrational*: they are irrational if the agent does not care to make sure they are likely to produce the desired outcome. In addition to the relevant unconditional imperative determining the will, it follows that the agent must be able to form, and act on, a hypothetical imperative, staking out how ends, related to the action, are to be achieved. For example, if one is to refrain from lying (which is one of Kant's most famous impermissible maxims, constituting a perfect duty), then to be rational one must be committed to a hypothetical imperative informing oneself of how a particular action actually produces the effect of not deceiving someone. In a specific situation, such a hypothetical imperative may, for example, direct oneself to speak truthfully when asked a question.

Of course, an agent may have luck. Yet luck itself does not make an agent who is indifferent to the outcome of his actions any more rational. The hypocrite, in other words, who has worried so many students of Kant's moral philosophy, may, on this view, be criticized. The problem with this figure is not that he is falling short of the demands of morality but, rather, that he is oblivious to the outcome of his actions. Indeed, the hypocrite does not even consider the possible outcome of his actions. The hypocrite just acts, interpreting his actions as morally laudable—but without subscribing to a fundamental norm of rationality.

To be rational, we thus need to take a rational interest in the possible "whither" or "what-for" of our actions. Not only must we believe that they promote an end, that they are undertaken with a certain purpose in mind, but we must also conceive of our actions as in fact conducive to bringing about the rationally chosen end, which involves knowledge about causal efficacy. Finally, we need to order our ends so as to unify them with reference to some higher end that incorporates or makes manifest such ordering. The concept of the Highest Good provides the requisite principle of such ordering, calling for the realization of happiness in proportion to the observance of morality. The idea here is that without such a rational desire to order and unify ends, our wills would always be frustrated. We would experience a perpetual division between the demands of morality and the desire for happiness. Armed with the concept of the *summum bonum*, and thus with the postulates of a just God and immortality, we become able to project a unified ordering of our ends that can satisfy us rationally.

The Highest Good, in other words, gives one confidence in oneself as a moral agent. It suggests that as one goes about setting ends for oneself, they will be not only realizable but conducive to happiness. Thus, as Kant puts it, "morality . . . inevitably leads to religion, and through religion it extends itself to the idea of a mighty moral lawgiver outside the human being, in whose will the ultimate end (or the creation of the world) is what can and at the same time ought to be the ultimate human end."[28]

The argument in the first preface of *Religion* seems closer in spirit to the formal derivation of the Highest Good in the *Critique of Practical Reason* than to the motivation arguments of the first and third Critiques. Although it does not completely dismiss the notion that moral agents need the Highest Good in order to overcome feelings of despair that could compromise their commitment to the moral law (this is reflected in the anxiety regarding one's own possible impotence as a moral agent), the emphasis is not on despair but rather on the centrality of the concept of the Highest Good to our practical identities and lives. The agent modeled in *Religion* simply finds that the general structure of his rational agency is such that he will want to justify his actions in terms of a realizable *whither* (all actions are teleological), and he will want that whither to issue in a harmony between morality and deserved happiness. He ipso facto will want there to be conditions such that he can reasonably hope to achieve such a harmony: hence the postulates of pure practical reason; hence religion.

Perhaps in *Religion* the biggest question mark pertaining to the strategy relates to the claim that the structure of rational agency demands that the whither of any possible rational action must anticipate a union of morality and happiness in proportion to desert. The notion of ordering ends according to some standard seems to flow quite naturally from an understanding of what a reasonable agent would consider to be binding. However, it is not evident that such a commitment necessarily calls on a rational agent to adopt the postulates of pure practical reason and anticipate (or hope for) the realization of the *summum bonum*. Indeed, when considering the most ordinary situations in a typical human life, there seem to be many ways ends can be ordered rationally that would not issue in some vision of a transcendent order creating harmony between morality and deserved happiness.

28. Kant, *Religion within the Boundaries of Mere Reason*, 6.

It would not be easy to adjudicate conclusively between the four strategies Kant presents for deriving the concept of *Glaube*. They all seem to have both strengths and weaknesses. A skeptic will have plenty of reasons to reject each of them. On the other hand, a more welcoming interpreter might focus on the strongest and most compelling strategy, perhaps building an even stronger case by developing, and elaborating on, the arguments presented.

It is important to note that while rational agents do tend to hope for the realization of the Highest Good as an ideal, in all the strategies we have looked at, including the one in *Religion*, the only way such agents can come to rationally have such a hope, and thus faith, is through their own predispositions to do good—that is, through attaining a good moral character. Kant's whole view of Christianity centers on the idea of making ourselves worthy of salvation. It is not enough to just "flatter" or pray (an attitude Kant claims to find in both Islam and Judaism); rather, we must prove ourselves electable in the eyes of God, and that can be done only through what Kant calls a "change of heart."[29] Against the evil that Kant, in *Religion* and elsewhere, argues lurks within man's heart—the frailty of human nature, the impurity of motives, depravity and corruption of the human heart, and most seriously, though perhaps not a genuine human opportunity, diabolical evil, when active resistance to the moral law becomes an organizing incentive—for faith and salvation to be possible, there must be a change of heart whereby the supreme incentive of our actions, our consistent principle of rational commitment, becomes identical to the moral law. Such a change, Kant argues, is purely a matter of radical self-transformation. While the only teacher worth following in this regard is Jesus Christ, the change of heart is Kant's version of conversion.

Kant's God

Soon after the publication of *Religion* in 1793 (with a second edition appearing in early 1794), Kant received a royal rescript from the Prussian Censorship Commission (serving under the relatively conservative Frederick William II), prohibiting him from publishing further on matters of religion. Although Kant, as we have seen, does not repudiate religion or flatly deny the existence of God, the Censorship Commission must undoubtedly have felt unease regarding his radical restructuring of the concept of *Glaube*. Indeed, since its publication, *Religion* and all the other texts in which Kant

---

29. Kant, *Religion within the Boundaries of Mere Reason*, 78–79.

addresses the question of religion have generated a great deal of controversy, ranging from those who see in Kant's project a support for Christianity to those who see him questioning religion, including Christianity.

Pasternak belongs to the former camp. According to him, although Kant sets himself the task of reinterpreting theistic language in accordance with the doctrine of the Highest Good, he never rejects it. While he instrumentalizes a number of symbols and liturgical practices, making them means for attaining moral purity, he "neither denies the possibility of revelation and miracles, nor does he deny their utility."[30] As long as they speak to us as practical agents, they can satisfy needs that Kant views as thoroughly religious. He admits, though, that Kant decisively rejects more traditional interpretations of faith, including those grounded in feeling (such as the feeling of divine presence or influence) or in what Kant derogatively refers to as "fanaticism" (*Schwärmerei*): "Pure Rational Faith [*Reiner Vernunftglaube*] = Saving Faith [*seligmachender Glaube*]" is Kant's formula.[31] In a similar vein, Allen W. Wood claims that "Kant's real aim is not to destroy theology, but to replace a dogmatic theology with a critical one."[32] "Kant," he writes, "is fundamentally unable to conceive of the human situation except theistically, and unable to conceive of God in any terms except those of the scholastic-rationalistic tradition."[33]

Gordon E. Michalson belongs to the opposite camp.[34] According to Michalson, Kant replaces the vision of God as an autonomous, self-authorizing lawgiver with a vision of moral duties flowing from the structure of reason, construed as unconditional commands. Kant, in other words, turns the age-old relation between morality and religion upside down: no longer is religious dogmatism supposed to dictate the content of our moral duties. Rather, it is moral duties that dictate whatever it is we can take to be God (and Christ). Moreover, in several of the strategies for deducing *Glaube*, Kant seems to instrumentalize the representation of God: the concept of His will, being generated by the dictates of the Highest Good, has been rationally rather than divinely ordained, serving no other purpose than to properly proportion happiness and virtue such as to satisfy the requirements of an autonomous human and moral rationality. As Michalson puts it, "running powerfully through Kant's philosophy is what might be called a 'principle of

---

30. Pasternack, *Kant on Religion within the Boundaries of Mere Reason*, 246.

31. Pasternack, *Kant on Religion within the Boundaries of Mere Reason*, 190.

32. Allen W. Wood, *Kant's Rational Theology* (Ithaca, NY: Cornell University Press, 1978), 17.

33. Wood, *Kant's Rational Theology*, 17.

34. Gordon E. Michalson, *Kant and the Problem of God* (Oxford: Blackwell, 1999).

immanence' that is finally incompatible with theistic belief and which implicitly leaves Kant's effort at theological mediation in a shamble. The principle of immanence is embedded in Kant's theory of rationality itself, especially in the powerful element of autonomy associated with the Kantian account of rationality. Bluntly stated, autonomous rationality is imperialistic in relation to all that comes before it, including the very idea of God."[35] Ultimately, Kant's effort to make faith intelligible in the light of reason's needs, Michalson argues, threatens to make faith redundant: "Making faith intelligible might also make it redundant, since the mediating maneuver may simply recast what can also be said in purely secular terms. In that event, appeals to divine transcendence are more neatly eliminated than resuscitated, since they merely repeat in unwieldy terms what also comes to expression in neater and more immediately available form."[36] Obviously, what this comes down to is whether Kant, as Wood argues, believed an *ens realissimum* to be rationally inevitable or, since our only way of appealing to God as a *lawgiver* is by addressing our own rational nature, whether talk of God is really just a veiled way of talking about ourselves. To the extent that the Kantian God is a function of how we must understand ourselves if we are going to count as moral creatures, it is hard not to think that the religious element has become dispensable.

In a late text on the philosophical implications of secularization (especially with regard to the Enlightenment, which he considers to have been an important context of secularization), Jacques Derrida supports the latter approach (providing the fundamentals of what might be called a secularization narrative).

> In *Religion within the Limits of Reason Alone* Kant makes a gesture which, in my view, strikes a decisive note with respect to secularization: from the rational point of view, from the point of view of practical reason, he defines the Christian religion as the only moral religion. All other religions promise salvation, allow hope for this or that, but no religion other than the Christian religion requires believers, the faithful, to act well regardless of the hope of salvation or reward. In other words, obedience to a purely moral categorical imperative is an injunction of the Christian religion which therefore emancipates (or gestures at emancipating) the believer from religion itself, so to speak. Even if God did not exist, it would be necessary to conduct oneself well.
>
> Consequently, Kant's analysis privileges Christian religion (since it is the only moral religion), and at the same time it emancipates the moral

---

35. Michalson, *Kant and the Problem of God*, 5.
36. Michalson, *Kant and the Problem of God*, 138.

subject from religion (or from belief in God)—at the limit, even accepting a certain death of God. In other words, the death of God (which is already a Christian theme, the Passion) is a theme which leads us out of Christianity—the death of God is inscribed within the very structure of the moral imperative. There is here a properly secularizing gesture insofar as it dispenses with religion within religion itself.[37]

Derrida seems correct regarding the "secularizing gesture" of Kant's treatment of religion. However, he is hardly right to argue that Kant, as he puts it, "dispenses with religion within religion itself." Although Kant does indeed dispense with any religion of revelation, he is firmly committed to a God of the morally predisposed. His criticism of rational theology notwithstanding, Kant's God, as Wood maintains, has much in common with the God of Descartes, Leibniz, and Wolff. It is a supremely perfect and necessary supersensible being, unconditionally capable of initiating causal series of events; and it is a morally concerned being, the ultimate guarantee of what Fichte later called the "living and operative moral order."[38]

However, while Wood and Pasternack are right in claiming that Kant retains theistic language, its strangeness can hardly be denied. It is the language of a thinker for whom the world is wholly disenchanted (regardless of the intimation of purposiveness in Kant's notion of aesthetic experience of the beauty of nature, which hardly amounts to an encounter with the sacred, let alone with any contentful understanding of a divine entity), being unable to grant neither validity nor value to what Charles Taylor calls "a sense of fullness" and Paul Tillich "the total surrender" associated with "the mystical a priori" of God, "the awareness of something that transcends the cleavage between subject and object" and yet is of "ultimate concern."[39] It is, moreover, the language of a thinker for whom the role of God is primarily judgmental and morally evaluative. While Kant's God is imagined to play a providential role in pursuing final ends, those ends can only be coherently imagined as moral: they are, as Kant makes evident in "The End of All Things," ideas of ends chosen by God as a moral lawgiver.[40] The author of

37. Jacques Derrida, "Christianity and Secularization," *Critical Inquiry* 47 (Autumn 2020): 140.

38. J. G. Fichte, *Werke*, vol. 5, ed. Fritz Medicus (Leipzig: Eckardt, 1910), 130. Quoted from Wood, *Kant's Rational Theology*, 26.

39. Taylor, *Secular Age*, 5. Paul Tillich, *Systematic Theology* (Chicago: University of Chicago Press, 1967), 9.

40. Kant, "The End of All Things," in *Religion within the Boundaries of Mere Reason*, 233–46.

such ends must be conceived of not only as a lawgiver but also as a judge. As we have seen, Kant's God metes out sanctions in the form of rewards and punishments; thus "the end of all things," the Day of Judgment, must be interpreted morally, as the ultimate and unconditional reality of God's supersensible (and hence not temporal) moral judgment.

In psychoanalytic terms, Kant's God would be the agency of the unforgiving, guilt-inducing, and ego-dominating superego, familiar from Freud's metapsychological writings, forever surveilling the ego, prohibiting its transgression, while meting out sanction in the form of bad conscience. As such, the superego plays a crucial role in disciplining individuals. According to Freud, the tyrannical version of the superego becomes especially prevalent in modernity when the civilizational constraints on behavior have reached their historically most pervasive and intense level.[41] Kant's disciplined believer is remarkably similar to the purportedly autonomous bourgeois subject of Freud's Victorian age.

At this point in the dialectic it becomes impossible not to note the antinomy in Kant's account between theistic and secular (or even a-theistic) language. The arguments (related to the concept of the *summum bonum*) in favor of adopting the postulates of pure practical reason speak in favor of theism. The arguments in favor of (a) moral autonomy, (b) the unconditional authority of reason, (c) the ontology of a world standing exclusively under natural laws, and (d) the exclusively penal vision of divine judgment, suggestive of Freud's conception of the superego, all speak in favor of secularism. It might be tempting to just register and accept this tension. As Hegel and others would later argue, Kant's system is quite evidently full of dualisms and oppositions that seem to call for a reconciliation that just never emerges.

In the closing chapter on metaphysics in *Negative Dialectics* titled "Meditations on Metaphysics," Adorno makes a suggestion that is relevant both to the assessment of Kant's tension and to an understanding of the intellectual ambivalence with which this Enlightenment thinker witnesses the process of secularization. Having outlined how Kant employs a double strategy of both *criticizing* and *rescuing* a concept of the intelligible sphere (the strategy, in short, that I have already mentioned, forming the lens through which I

---

41. I have in mind especially the late Freud's reflections on the superego in *Civilization and Its Discontents*, trans. James Strachey (New York: W. W. Norton, 1989), in which, on page 97, he reveals his "intention to represent the sense of guilt as the most important problem in the development of civilization and to show that the price we pay for our advance in civilization is a loss of happiness through the heightening of the sense of guilt."

recommend viewing the accounts of religion in the thinkers being analyzed in this volume), Adorno considers the hope expressed by the postulates an admission that the Kantian conception of rational self-determination is insufficient to generate the kind of motivation and meaning that human orientation ultimately requires. In particular, this conception suggests a kind of confinement imagery whereby reason is only able to confront the results of its making. In the theoretical philosophy, it is expressed through the restriction thesis: the epistemic restriction of objective knowledge to whatever can be presented in accordance with the a priori rules for creating synthetic unity in experience. In the practical philosophy, the imagery is brought to a dramatic conclusion with Kant's exclusion of all morally acceptable aspirations to earthly happiness. While enigmatic and without the kind of rational grounding that rational theology purported to be offering, the intelligible sphere (and God) enters the equation as Kant's attempt to make up for this lack.

> Kant's rescue of the intelligible sphere is not merely the Protestant apologetics known to all; it is also an attempted intervention in the dialectic of enlightenment, at the point where this dialectics terminates in the abolition of reason. That the ground of the Kantian rescuing urge lies far deeper than just in the pious wish to have, amidst nominalism and against it, some of the traditional ideas in hand—this is attested by the construction of immortality as a postulate of practical reason. The postulate condemns the intolerability of extant things [*die Unerträglichkeit des Bestehenden*] and confirms the spirit of its recognition. That no reforms within the world suffice to do justice to the dead, that none of them touch upon the wrong [*Unrecht*] of death—this is what moves Kantian reason to hope against reason. The secret of his philosophy is the unthinkability of despair.[42]

Adorno's minor point in this passage is that Kant's argument for the Highest Good and for the postulates can be read as a plea for some form of absolute justice, one that will be conferred on humankind if indeed God exists and is able to grant immortality. By the power of grace, such a justice would make up for the sufferings and deaths of morally good men. His major point, however, comes out in his reference to the dialectic of enlightenment and to

---

42. Theodor W. Adorno, *Negative Dialectics*, trans. E. B. Ashton (New York: Continuum, 1973), 385. For the German original, see *Negative Dialektik* (Frankfurt: Suhrkamp, 1982), 377–78.

the notions of "hoping against reason" and "the unthinkability of despair."[43] In other sections of "Meditations on Metaphysics," Adorno explains this dialectic in terms of an ongoing process of secularization and disenchantment whereby human experience increasingly, and with great success, becomes subject to self-imposed norms of "identitarian thinking"—in short, thinking that, in the service of self-preservation, prioritizes the capacity for abstraction, for creating identity and consistency by employing higher-order concepts and categories, and for viewing one's responsibility to oneself, to others, and to objects in one's surroundings in terms of one's coordinating and instrumentalizing capacities. Although Adorno does not ignore the fact that Kant does allow for end-oriented (and not just formal or instrumental) reasoning, he considers the transcendental project to be an expression, though in an elevated conceptual form, of precisely such a tendency. Kant's rationalistic immanentism—his conception of the constitutive role of the transcendental subject, in both its theoretical and its practical roles, and his restriction thesis—becomes strikingly similar to what one may think of as the project of secular modernity: formalism, immanentism, disenchantment, a wholesale rejection of any aspiration toward transcendence. What Adorno sees as crucial in Kant's deduction of *Glaube* is the recognition that, considered in this light, the dialectic of enlightenment (whereby reason, in its capacity to disenchant and control nature, itself becomes naturelike and compulsive) generates a further dialectical twist. In the attempt to escape despair (*Verzweifelung*)—and in Kant, especially when he worries about the ability of pure practical reason to motivate action and calls for a commitment to the possibility of the *summum bonum* in order to support and even make possible a vigorous commitment to morality—the feeling or intimation of despair creates an urge to seek out and articulate some form of transcendence. To be sure, both Kant and Adorno understand that vision of transcendence to be epistemically indefensible. As Kant argues, it cannot be made into an object of regular human knowing. And as Adorno maintains, the appeal to transcendence relates to a possibility that as such exceeds the parameters of everyday, objective judgment.

Adorno frames his reading of Kant not only within the so-called dialectic of enlightenment on which he and Horkheimer elaborate in the *Dialectic of Enlightenment*, but also with reference to the radical evil of Auschwitz. He does this in part in order to make concrete and historical Kant's concerns about the prevalence of radical evil in human nature (although the kinds

---

43. For a lucid account of Adorno's rejoinder to Kant's theory of autonomy, see Martin Shuster, *Autonomy After Auschwitz: Adorno, German Idealism, and Modernity* (Chicago: University of Chicago Press, 2014).

of evil Kant had in mind, exemplified by tribal warfare and ritual slaughter, may in hindsight seem innocent compared with the industrialized horrors of Auschwitz), but, more philosophically, also in order to intimate a world of literal immanence, one from which there is no escape except death, which for Adorno figures as the extreme conclusion to the dialectic of enlightenment in which reason progressively refuses to grant existence to anything transcending its own range of domination and control. As theologians of the Holocaust such as Emil Fackenheim have argued, a world of such diabolical immanence calls for some kind of claim to transcendence.[44] For Adorno, alluding to Kant, the alternative would be some form of unmitigated despair over the way of the world.

I have made this brief detour through Adorno's reading of Kant's account of the *summum bonum* in order to suggest an interpretation that escapes the seemingly irresolvable opposition between theistic and nontheistic readings. Moving beyond this opposition, I hope it may be granted that what Kant provides is not only an unstable and, for reasons I have been rehearsing in this chapter, inherently problematic account of a form of supposedly necessary supplement to the morality of reason, making up the foundation for an extensive reinterpretation of the Gospels, but also a conceptual transition from morality to religion that can form the outline of an attractive philosophical response to the process of secularization.

But Kant's strategy is not without precedent. In Rousseau's "Profession of Faith of the Savoyard Vicar" in the fourth book of *Émile, or On Education* (which Kant studied repeatedly), the idea of God also arises—and is justified as a hypothesis worth adopting—via the belief that, even if the world is wicked, the just person will ultimately have to be rewarded.[45] Yet the strategy he appropriates from Rousseau and does so much to develop

---

44. Emil Fackenheim, *To Mend the World: Foundations of Post-Holocaust Jewish Thought* (Bloomington: Indiana University Press, 1994).

45. Jean-Jacques Rousseau, *Émile, or On Education*, trans. Allan Bloom (New York: Basic Books, 1979), 292: "If I do a good deed without a witness, I know that it is seen, and I make a record for the other life of my conduct in this one. In suffering an injustice, I say to myself, 'The just Being who rules everything will certainly know how to compensate me for it.'" What mediates one's relationship with God, according to Rousseau's Savoyard Vicar, is neither blind faith, nor some metaphysical proof, but the experience of being constrained by one's sense of duty and the belief that this constraint must reflect some larger moral order of which God is the ultimate provider and guarantee. In such an order, morality is inevitably going to be rewarded. While Kant interprets this line of thought squarely within the framework of his own moral theory, including the transcendental idealism on which it is predicated, there can be no doubt that he supports and indeed adopts Rousseau's general strategy.

and refine within the context of his transcendental idealism should ultimately be regarded as expressive of a doubt regarding the full completion of the process of enlightenment, at least to the extent that enlightenment entails an unflinching commitment to the principle of rational autonomy and secularization.

Kant critiques and morally rescues religion. However, in rescuing religion he at least implicitly makes it clear that the proud project of critique confronts limits of its own making. Also, in Kant's moral religion one may detect an existentially felt exposure to contingency. Calling for its overcoming, he displays an awareness of existing in a world forever mired in suffering, evil, and ill intentions, a world in which meaning is in short supply. This is the immanence that generates a desire for transcendence.

Kant neither sought to reverse secularization nor, as some of the German Romantics such as Novalis would call for, return to a world in which the church plays the unifying role it once did. However, he detected reasons to be disappointed with the enlightenment project. As such, he set the stage for the rich and complex discourse that started with Hegel's idealism, and in many ways culminated with Nietzsche.

[CHAPTER THREE]

Hegel's Rescue Mission

Among the many thinkers concerned with the fate of religion in modernity, Hegel holds a special place. He is a distinctly Christian philosopher, according Christianity a privileged status in all his philosophical writings. At the same time, however, his commitment to Christianity appears as the result of a sustained effort to interpret this religion philosophically while assessing its ultimate conceptual significance within specific historical configurations ranging from the late Roman period and the European Middle Ages via the Reformation and the Enlightenment to the post-1789 modernity of his own day. In the reading I offer, while Hegel cannot be said to have escaped the onto-theological tradition entirely, he criticizes the familiar hypostatizing of God as the supersensible other of finite, human reality, arguing that, as spirit (*Geist*), God must be viewed as the animating, "logical," and "dialectical" element of all human understanding and self-understanding as they develop historically. On Hegel's view, God's ways are those of *kenosis*: He exhausts himself in His own creation, becoming one with it as its logical, rational dimension. In modernity, he claims, the development of spirit (and our comprehension of it, which amounts to a form of self-understanding) has reached a level such that God must be theorized as the rational "Idea" (*Idee*), the sum of all the conceptual mediations of subject and object that make rational comprehension possible. As such, the God of supersensible reality "dies." All that is left of religion has been translated into the language of philosophy. On the one hand there is God as an all-embracing conceptual and rational reality. On the other hand there is no longer a God in relation to whom one may entertain various propositional attitudes. Hegel's modern world is prosaic; its rationality is immanent in, though not reducible to, the possible configurations of conceptual activity and their operations within social and institutional existence.

A full account of how Hegel negotiates the various pressures involved in this complex enterprise would exceed the space of this book. My aim is far more modest. I will first be discussing his early *Tübingen Essay*, written approximately ten years before the articulation of his first philosophical system. The *Tübingen Essay* is relevant not only because it introduces Hegel's approach to the critique/rescue dialectic, but also because it is framed as an attempt to challenge central features of Kant's philosophy of religion, including its rigorous separation between reason (and law) and empirical inclination. Anticipating the concept of spirit, Hegel understands religion (especially Christianity) as a set of meaning-providing and normatively binding social practices capable of offering spiritual and moral renewal.

After the turn of the century, and especially with the publication of *The Phenomenology of Spirit* in 1807, Hegel expands elements of his religiously inspired critical social philosophy to become the full-fledged philosophy of spirit with which he is generally associated. He also starts to think about religion in terms of his account of spirit. While in Hegel's view, Christianity is the only religion that proclaims "the death of God" and, owing to the figure of Christ, the complete unification of divine being with finite, created existence, it also, in his interpretation, provides the figurative basis for the development of the mature system. Christianity teaches Hegel how social and philosophical division can be overcome; it outlines a vision of free subjectivity that inspires his account of modernity and, thanks to its conception of reconciliation, inspires the ultimate layout not only of his philosophical account of identity, truth, and reason, but also of the fundamental ideals of modern existence. However, as spirit for Hegel exhausts itself in the institutional life of modernity, securing its immanent claim to rationality, the kind of room for authoritative religious practice that once existed is shrinking to the point of nonexistence.

Exploring these claims, I ultimately see Hegel as a theorist of secularization *malgré lui*. Unlike Kant, who harbors a conception of transcendence, Hegel transforms religion to the brink of atheism. The social world of *Elements of the Philosophy of Right* is decisively disenchanted: there are no remnants of the sacred, no promises of transfiguration, no understanding of God as wholly other. Yet, as I seek to demonstrate, it is precisely this prosaic world of modernity that for Hegel most conclusively actualizes the promises of Christianity.

The Early Hegel's *Volksreligion*

The so-called *Tübingen Essay*, composed in 1793 when he was only twenty-three years old, stands as one of the earliest expressions of Hegel views of religion.[1] While stylistically modeled on critical yet publicly accessible

---

1. Note that Hegel never finished the essay. He began it in Tübingen, and also did some work on it while at home with his family in Stuttgart. For a brief account of the

essays written by Enlightenment figures such as Lessing and Voltaire, its central philosophical concern, which would preoccupy Hegel throughout his career, revolves around the question of how religion can survive and remain compelling under modern conditions. In that it sets an agenda that keeps recurring, few essays are more instructive for understanding what the challenges to such an undertaking are taken to be, and for setting up some of the theses that later will guide Hegel in formulating his philosophy of religion.

Like so much in the early Hegel, the Kantian background to this essay is all important, forming both a platform for argument as well as a view against which its author feels compelled to polemicize. At the same time, the piece emerges as having been profoundly shaped by a sense of religious malaise—a sense, more specifically, that religion, in the wake of its enlightenment and rationalist onslaught, finds itself in a crisis, being unable to command allegiance based on rational persuasion alone. Its appeals to "the heart" and to "love" resonate with Romantic themes that for some time had attracted his seminary friends Hölderlin and Schelling as well. However, its enthusiastic tone scarcely manages to cover up the underlying sense, familiar from the late Hölderlin's hymns, that the spontaneity and proximity to the gods that they all claim had characterized the ancient Greeks' religious activities have vanished. The people who felt close to the gods have "fled from the earth."[2] Not only does Hegel display a strong historical awareness of being situated within a post-Enlightenment dispensation in which the world has come to be fundamentally disenchanted, he also considers the God of ontotheology, claimed to be accessible to human reason, as having—most powerfully with Kant's *Critique of Pure Reason*—become subject to devastating forms of skepticism. Whatever religion is supposed to be conceived as, it can no longer rest on an appeal to rational cognition of the supersensible.

According to much Enlightenment culture, religion has become incapable of commanding any authority or allegiance. For the early Hegel, however, a complete loss of religion would have incalculable consequences for our self-understanding as moral beings, including what it is to flourish and live well and to find meaning and purpose in life. A fully rationalized world

---

composition, see H. S. Harris, *Hegel's Development: Toward the Sunlight, 1770–1801* (Oxford: Clarendon Press, 1972), 119.

2. G. W. F. Hegel, "The Tübingen Essay," in *Three Essays, 1793–1795*, ed. and trans. Peter Fuss and John Dobbins (Notre Dame, IN: University of Notre Dame University Press, 1984), 58. The *Berne Fragments* of 1793–94 (contained in the same volume) are written in much the same vein as the *Tübingen Essay* and complement it.

(to use Weber's formulation) would be one in which no authority other than reason, which for the young Hegel is both motivationally weak and liable to skeptical attack, would offer practical guidance and direction. While Hegel is by no means dismissive of the value of reason, in what continues to be a Kantian spirit he seeks to limit the role of reason, assign it to its proper domains of legitimate use, *and* interpret faith as an authoritative and collectively embedded constraint and enabler of practical engagement.

The account on offer here considers religion primarily in its social role, as a unifying and authoritative set of symbolic practices capable of restoring cohesion in a social order that would otherwise threaten to fragment. As Thomas A. Lewis puts it, "Hegel writes not as a theologian but as a social theorist exploring how a civil religion might function as the social glue to hold together a fragmenting social order."[3] We do, in other words, see the rough contours of an *avant la lettre* Durkheimian view of religion, in which its authority is considered a function of the unreflective ethical relations sustaining a sense of selfhood and practical identity among mutually recognizing agents. As I have already suggested, on such a view, the process of secularization largely follows the course of what Durkheim calls anomie and Hegel soon will think of as objectivism, intellectualism, and positivity: in both thinkers' accounts, a religion loses its grip as agents in a rationalizing social order come to substitute shared social meaning for individually held principles and reasoning. Following Lessing and Herder, the young Hegel's response to this process consists in fashioning himself as a *Volkserzieher*, a public educator, bringing religion's role in motivating action to the attention of the community. If sufficiently powerful sources of inspiration can be presented, he hopes that people—and indeed readers of the *Tübingen Essay*—will be attracted by this critical yet enthusiastic vision of how a community might be reconstituted. Thus the concerns with *zōon politikon* and with *homo religiosus* would merge and become indistinguishable. Of course, as Hegel later comes to realize with some bitterness, the notion of *Volksreligion* in particular, because it does not do sufficient justice to the role of reason and the claims of individual autonomy, simply cannot satisfy modern agents: given its idealized vision of ancient Greece, it remains an anachronism.

In the *Tübingen Essay*, Hegel fundamentally distinguishes between "objective" and "subjective" religion.[4] Objective religion comprises the *fides*

---

3. Thomas A. Lewis, *Religion, Modernity, and Politics in Hegel* (Oxford: Oxford University Press, 2011), 25.

4. Although Hegel was not a Pietist, it is far from unlikely that the distinction stems from—or at least is inspired by—the Pietism he had been exposed to in Württemberg,

quae creditur, the body of faith that is actually believed—in other words, the sum of everything related to one's faith that can be rendered as discursively structured knowledge-claims. With regard to objective religion,

> understanding and memory are the powers that do the work, investigating facts, thinking them through, retaining and even believing them. Objective religion can also possess practical knowledge, but only as a sort of frozen capital. It is susceptible to organizational schemes; it can be systematized, set forth in books, and expounded discursively.[5]

Subjective religion, by contrast, "expresses itself only in feelings and actions,"[6] and, while objective religion has its place as an archive of accepted propositions, useful as reminders of the various abstractions that unite believers at a very general level, it is only subjective religion that has, as Hegel puts it, "inherent and true worth."[7]

Being a matter of the "heart" rather than understanding and memory, subjective religion is lived and therefore indexed to particular individuals and communities. While knowledge secured and expressed through the understanding and memory tracks facts and, in its ability to discern causal relations, can make agents calculative and prudent by helping them to find the most efficient means to their ends, considered as such it carries no motivational power. Hegel's argument, at this point, takes a pronounced Humean course: "No printed code or manner of enlightening the understanding could ever prevent evil impulses from taking root or even flourishing."[8] Feelings and, in particular, the will may be confronted with all sorts of principles and still be left unmoved. Only the heart, Hegel submits, and the way subjective religion interacts and is united with the sensuously embodied dispositions of the believer, can move and ultimately determine the will. For the sake of establishing and maintaining a well-functioning moral life, a good heart (and the subjective religion animating it) is crucial.

---

where he received his elementary education. It is also worth noticing that his friend Hölderlin grew up in an environment steeped in Pietism. Politically, Pietism had tended to be opposed to the more conservative Catholic church, advocating the value and importance of democratic powers of self-transformative faith over Catholicism's dogmatic allegiance to the authority of the clergy.

5. Hegel, "Tübingen Essay," 33.
6. Hegel, "Tübingen Essay," 33.
7. Hegel, "Tübingen Essay," 35.
8. Hegel, "Tübingen Essay," 40.

The understanding, in other words, always remains "cold." The heart, by contrast, is "warm" and, as Hegel frequently puts it, capable of *love*: "A heart that does not speak louder than the understanding . . . , or that just keeps silent, allowing the understanding all the time it needs to rationalize some course of action—a heart like that isn't worth much to begin with: there is no love in it."[9]

The ambivalent relationship to Kant may start to become apparent. Hegel at this early stage accepts the broad contours of Kant's moral religion. For Hegel, the Kantian project of limiting reason to make room for faith becomes a call to determine and restrict the role of reason both in religion and in moral life, while viewing religion essentially in moral terms. Viewed from the vantage point of religion, reason cannot aspire to the motivational power of the heart. Although Kant never claimed it would make sense for human, sensual beings to aspire to a "holy will" (a will determined purely, exclusively, by reason), he did believe that when determining themselves morally, moral agents must be able to set aside inclinations based on sensuous desire. Against this view, Hegel holds that "man needs motives other than pure respect for the moral law, motives more closely bound up with his sensuality."[10] A more realistic account is called for, in tune with the natural and social facts of human life. While not ruling out the enterprise of systematic theology, he sees true religion as primarily a social phenomenon, involving affects rather than reason. Reason's only genuinely religious role, he maintains with Kant, centers on the formulation of moral postulates, to be accepted in order to make the demands of practical reason as motivationally effective as possible: "And I classify as religious only such knowledge of God and immortality as is responsive to the demands of practical reason and connected with it in a readily discernible way."[11]

However, Hegel qualifies the teaching regarding the postulates, claiming that even they should be embedded in practices shared by all members of the community: "When we go on to speak of religion as public we still of course take it to include the concepts of God and immortality as well as everything connected with them, but specifically insofar as these constitute the conviction of a whole people, influencing their actions and ways of thinking."[12] To be sure, since Hegel follows Kant in interpreting religion morally, the emphasis is always on desert: To be a believer is not to

9. Hegel, "Tübingen Essay," 38–39.
10. Hegel, "Tübingen Essay," 46.
11. Hegel, "Tübingen Essay," 35.
12. Hegel, "Tübingen Essay," 32.

expect particular favors from God in return, say, for fidelity, sacrifice, and so on. Nor is it to derive from one's vision of God's will specific grounds for actions where mere prudence would be sufficient. Rather, the extent to which one is a believer hinges on one's willingness to become *worthy* of salvation; and the only way to display such a willingness is through commitment to moral purity.

Although he invokes the Kantian postulates, for the young Hegel the more important source of moral motivation relates to his conception of how a *Volksreligion* actually operates. As I have indicated, its central task is to move members of the religious community to act virtuously. While reason only stakes out the morally right course of action, the feelings inculcated in believers through participation in religious practice are supposed to "imbue the soul with power and enthusiasm, with a spirit indispensable for the noble exercise of virtue."[13] Hegel brings up several points that are central to his account of this kind of moral cultivation.

For one thing, a *Volksreligion* should not be imposed from the outside, through some act of force or as the result of mere irrational processes such as fantasy; rather, the adoption of a *Volksreligion* must be consistent with what members of the community can recognize as reasonable and in this sense be an expression of *freedom*. The reference to reason may seem to be in tension with the emphasis placed on participation in already constituted practices. A *Volksreligion*, he maintains, must contain a significant amount of historically constituted meaning in the form of traditions that members identify with via their active participation in customs and ceremonies. While the tension between freedom and participation in socially endorsed practices with a conventional meaning may seem stark, it can be lessened if we grant that Hegel at this point anticipates his later conception of spirit. The form of life in question, while appearing conventional and arbitrary from the outside, is not simply given. For its members and participants, it is historically occurring as a collectively self-determining entity, providing free self-actualization. If, as is likely, given the numerous affirmative references to ancient Greece in the *Tübingen Essay*, Hegel is already anticipating his conception of Greek ethical life, then what he characterizes is a social order in which individuals do not yet stand out as independent

---

13. Hegel, "Tübingen Essay," 47. In *Hegel: A Biography* (New York: Cambridge University Press, 2000), 41, Terry Pinkard points here to the influence of Rousseau and, indirectly, the Earl of Shaftesbury: "For the young Hegel . . . , the idea of Enlightenment reason *alone* motivating us was simply unbelievable. In the essay, he offers no real arguments against Kant's idea that reason provides us with its own incentives for action; instead, he simply voices his conviction that Kant's view is incredible."

and autonomous (or at least are not expected to do so). As members of a collective, they recognize the pregiven authority of its laws and gods. Thus the normativity involved is based less on individual reason-giving than on charismatic (to use Weber's term) modes of expression such as myth and ritual, both of which are said to engage the emotions and the imagination more than reason. These are contexts and arenas that inspire the individual to acquire, maintain, and act upon a sense of virtue. It is the members who institute meaning, though not in a self-reflective, fully rational manner.

Myth, a central concept in Hegel's essay, engages the imagination directly, thereby cultivating particular feelings claimed to predispose the individual to morally praiseworthy behavior. By "myth" Hegel has in mind the historically situated narratives of Christianity. However, he also refers—as either Hegel, Hölderlin, or Schelling (the authorship continues to be unknown) would do in the so-called *Oldest Systematic Program of German Idealism* (*Das älteste Systemprogramm des deutschen Idealismus*), written in 1796/97—to ancient Greek myths, emphasizing the way they seem able to unify spiritual meaning and sensuous embodiment in poetic images of beauty and spontaneity.[14]

Finally, Hegel pays attention to the role of *ceremonies*, claiming they support religion's ability to function morally by providing practically relevant contexts for the expression of faith. Such contexts involve the community at large, thereby invoking the authority embedded in socially endorsed practice, and make believers perform actions, thereby externalizing their faith and making it publicly manifest. Hegel walks a fine line in his discussion of the ceremonial aspects of religion. On the one hand, he distances himself from crude, irrational forms of religious ceremonies, in particular those involving sacrifices, the quid pro quo transactions that he refers to as "mechanical operations."[15] Rather than trying for one's own sake to influence God's will, sacrifice should be used only to cultivate feelings, dispositions, and attitudes that are internal to the moral end of religion. It should express humility. On the other hand, in a gesture opposed to the Pietism that inspired the distinction between subjective and objective religion, the appeal to ceremony is a manifestation of his dismissal of the radical interiorizing

---

14. In comparison with the *Tübingen Essay*, *The Oldest Systematic Program of German Idealism* is much more of an explicitly aesthetic manifesto. Following Kant's *Critique of the Power of Judgment* and Schiller's *Letters on Aesthetic Education*, it proposes to see in beauty the joyful and inspiring synthesis of freedom and nature, capable of (and here the essay is explicitly proleptic) overcoming the fragmentation and reification supposedly existing in modern culture.

15. Hegel, "Tübingen Essay," 55.

of faith that had followed in the wake of the Enlightenment critique of religion. As Lewis puts it, for Hegel "Religion should be intertwined with the general practices of the society, its way of life.... Religion's autonomy from other spheres of life is a danger, not an ideal."[16]

While suggestive, the *Tübingen Essay* leaves questions unanswered. The most pressing relates to the exact status of the appeal to *Volksreligion*. Is he, in part because of his early enthusiasm for the French Revolution, advocating a transformation of modern society in accordance with its actual political demands? Or does the *Tübingen Essay* regurgitate the cultural nostalgia that, since Winckelmann and Goethe and continuing with many of the Romantics, including Hölderlin and Schelling, had been fashionable in Germany of venerating an idealized vision of ancient Greece? Although Hegel never clarifies this issue, a likely interpretation would have to include both commitments. While inspired by contemporary ideals such as Kantianism, Pietism, and the French Revolution (especially via Rousseau's account of civil religion), and also by the worries about social fragmentation displayed in the writings of figures such as Christian Garve and Johann Gottfried Herder, it seems implausible that Hegel would be calling for an acceptance of status quo. At the very least he seems to have been interested in, as Pinkard puts it, "the issue of what conditions would be necessary to bring about a spiritual and moral renewal of 'the people.'"[17] That said, his blueprint for social change appears to have been deeply retrograde. While mediated by Rousseauian ideas of civil religion, the true ideal of freedom is to be found in ancient Greece, in which religion purportedly overcame social opposition, uniting citizens patriotically with their fellow men and preparing them for duty and service. The retrograde character of Hegel's ideals in this essay hardly explains how their implementation might serve to reform contemporary Germany. On the contrary, since the ideals on display in it are so evidently tied to Hegel's account of the religion of ancient Greece, they appear anachronistic, unable to be applied in Hegel's own circumstances. Indeed, just the fact that German society was predominantly Christian and far from pagan suggests that, at the very least, Christianity itself would need to be reformed. The yearning for a more socially unifying and sensuously articulated form of Christian faith was already present in Hölderlin, who, like the young Hegel, was infatuated with the ancient Greeks. Yet exactly what this would require is never spelled out.

This problem—the "modernity" problem—connects with the equally general problem of how commitment to the value of reason, which is of

16. Lewis, *Religion, Modernity, and Politics in Hegel*, 31.
17. Pinkard, *Hegel: A Biography*, 42.

great centrality to the author of the *Tübingen Essay*, is supposed to be balanced against the commitment to less reflective forms of participation in religious practice. In the moral domain in particular, the early Hegel accepts the basic framework of Kant's view of reason as self-legislative, capable of rationally ascribing to itself categorically binding laws. He also refers to reason's role in formulating principles and, with the help of what Kant calls the understanding, identifying hypothetical imperatives, the kinds of imperatives that stake out what it is that obtaining a particular goal requires ("if you want x, you must do y"). However, as we have seen, without any genuine argument he dismisses reason as a sufficient source of moral motivation. In short, it seems the appropriation of Kant, and with that of a modern notion of conscience, is done only halfway, leaving the reader with serious misgivings about Hegel's view of individual freedom under modern conditions. Again, he seems deeply conflicted between a commitment to modern freedom, including individual autonomy, and a support for an antimodern notion of heteronomy in which members of communities leave the morally and politically relevant capacity for decision-making to religiously sanctioned authorities.

That said, while subscribing to Kant's doctrine of the primacy of practical reason and situating faith within an essentially moral framework, the *Tübingen Essay* frames the question of religion within a larger social context of modernization and secularization. Hegel realizes that religious belief stands no chance of being accepted as rationally endorsable and thus that the enlightenment critique of religion, exemplified by Kant's dialectic of pure reason, is irreversible. Moreover, the early Hegel senses that religion in its traditional form is in crisis, being in thrall to long-term trends of secularization, including what Weber would call rationalization and disenchantment. If religion is interpreted socially, along lines that can be recognized as Durkheimian *avant la lettre*, he believes it can be rescued as a meaningful dimension of modernity, although in a form that centers neither on cognitive activity (as in rationalist schools of philosophy from Aquinas to Descartes and Leibniz) nor on inner conviction alone (as in Pietism) but, rather, on what it means to participate successfully in an ethical form of life based on the mutual recognition of one another as free and equal agents. On Hegel's view that mutual recognition finds both expression and authorization in individuals' feeling of trust in the practices sustaining the institutional life of their community. In the absence of that experience of participating in socially endorsed practices, the individual will be without a sense of purpose and orientation; and actions, restricted to coordination and instrumental intervention, will be left without any deeper meaning. This is for the early Hegel where the real threat of secularization lies: an atomized society of narrowly rational agents with no sense of moral unity and no ability to detect in moral reasons any deeper sense of authority or meaning. The *Tübingen Essay* critiques the one-sided rationalizing of Enlightenment universalism and calls for a return of something like the spirit of Greek ethical life.

Faith, System, and Secularization

The early Hegel of the *Tübingen Essay* and, closer to the turn of the century, *The Life of Jesus*, and especially *The Positivity of the Christian Religion* and *The Spirit of Christianity and Its Fate*, formulates a number of ideas that become central in his mature philosophical theology of spirit. We have already seen how, in the *Tübingen Essay*, he invokes conceptions of mindedness, meaning-making, and self-interpretation, each referring to dispositions and capacities made possible by participation in social practices. In *The Spirit of Christianity and Its Fate*, written in 1798–99, he increasingly displays an interest in forms of self-constituted social practice able to overcome division and creating unity without sacrificing the constituent parts or members of any given relation. Love, in particular, the key interpretive device in the early Hegel's interpretation of scripture, supersedes both division and alienation. In a relationship based on love, in which the parties are able to recognize each other as necessary for their own self-actualization, Hegel finds the structure of reconciliation that he soon will ascribe to the more general concept of spirit. For Hegel, Christianity is, more than anything else, *the* religion of self-division and subsequent reconciliation. Not only does Jesus preach the gospel of love, but the very edifice Christianity is based on takes as its starting point the idea that the opposition between God and creation is overcome in the figure of Christ, whose love, while strict, is "infinite." In Christ, God overcomes His otherness and, in an act of infinite mercy, unites Himself with humanity. On Hegel's account, philosophy should be focused on overcoming division, creating unity, and achieving reconciliation. While Christianity presents this process in theological, biblical terms, as revealed truth, the task of philosophy is to understand and conceptualize the underlying thought.

To be sure, Hegel comes to realize that, in order to achieve such a conceptualization, the notion of spirit will have to be formulated in a manner that is consistent with genuinely philosophical demands for generality and universality, familiar to Hegel from his extensive studies of Plato and Aristotle. In 1802, inspired by Schelling, who for a number of years had been calling for a systematic exposition of philosophy, he thus starts constructing his first system; and until he completes the *The Science of Logic* in 1812, he is continuously preoccupied with the question of how a philosophy of spirit can be provided with a strict philosophical form. It is also from this system that he derives the dialectical framework of his *Realphilosophie*, including the philosophy of religion.

I announced at the outset of this chapter that I intend to read Hegel's mature philosophy of religion as articulating a gradual rationalizing of religion that, at least in modernity, coincides with secularization. Yet for readers of this material, any attempt to associate Hegel with such a commitment may seem awkward, if not hopelessly misguided or even patently false. Thus, in the opening paragraph of the 1827 *Lectures on the Philosophy of Religion*, for example, we find Hegel proclaiming that religion "is the loftiest object that can occupy human beings; it is the absolute object. It is the region of eternal truth and eternal virtue, the region where all the riddles of thought, all contradictions, and all the sorrows of the heart should show themselves to be resolved, and the region of the eternal peace through which the human being is truly human."[18] For Hegel, it seems, religion should be imbued with an aura of authority, seriousness, and inherent truth: it is a "region" in which man's highest interests and aspirations, those that define a person as a spiritual and not just a material being, a being with a destiny determined by the will and intention of a divine power, are being negotiated and resolved. So how can this have anything to do with secularization?

While passages such as the one just quoted from the late philosophical lectures on religion seem to reveal Hegel as the Christian thinker he traditionally has been made out to be, earlier texts (and other interpretive frameworks based on those texts) leave readers with a different impression. In the 1801 *Faith and Knowledge*, for example, we find Hegel stating that "the feeling upon which the *religion* of more recent times rests" is that "*God is dead.*"[19] In its stead, modern agents will have to relinquish their religious assumptions in favor of accepting what he calls the "speculative Good Friday," a metaphor of sorts for the replacement of (Christian) faith by philosophy and for the philosophical comprehension of the mystery of incarnation. Moreover, in the *Addition* to §270 of the 1824 *Elements of the Philosophy of Right*, with a view to the social and political arrangements suitable to modern conditions (and to the "needs" of spirit), we find Hegel claiming that

---

18. G. W. F. Hegel, *Lectures on the Philosophy of Religion: One Volume Edition, The Lectures of 1827*, trans. R. F. Brown, P. C. Hodgson, J. M. Stewart, and H. S. Harris (Berkeley: University of California Press, 1988), 75.

19. G. W. F. Hegel, *Faith and Knowledge*, trans. W. Cerf and H. S. Harris (Albany: State University of New York Press, 1977), 190; my emphasis.

"The state is indeed essentially secular and finite, and has particular ends and particular powers."[20] Any attempt, he reasons, to externally ground the state on religion—and thereby to delegitimize its claim to being an autonomously structured power—would, owing to the purported arbitrariness of religious feeling or mere "representational" (*vorstellende*) thought, be repressive and have destabilizing consequences. The state itself, however, "consists in the march of God in the world;"[21] it is, Hegel writes in the *Lectures on the Philosophy of World History*, nothing less than "divine" and divinely sanctioned.

This quick summary of the central tensions in Hegel's philosophy of religion can only serve a stage-setting purpose. Indeed, the challenges facing an interpreter of Hegel's account of the fate of religion in modernity are no doubt vast. Starting with his early call, in 1803–4, as he begins to distance himself from Schelling's theory of the absolute subject-object for a system focused on the notion of spirit, he gradually, from *The Phenomenology of Spirit* to the *The Science of Logic*, the *Encyclopedia of the Philosophical Sciences*, the *Elements of the Philosophy of Right*, and the various versions of his *Lectures on the Philosophy of Religion*, develops a complex, dialectical account of *Geist* in its logical articulation, its historical development, its objectification in nature, its manifestation in the individual mind, and its sociopolitical reality, as well as its self-understanding in the evolving domains of art, religion, and philosophy. While he most explicitly, and at considerable length, deals with religion in *The Phenomenology of Spirit*, *Encyclopedia of the Philosophical Sciences*, and the lecture courses on religion, whatever claims he ultimately makes about this topic hinge not only on these writings, difficult though they are, but on the complete system of the philosophy of spirit that, from 1807 onward, he increasingly comes to oversee and seek to articulate. The theory of spirit *is* his theory of religion. However, the ramifications of his account of *Geist* extend to all corners of Hegel's systemic enterprise, including those that emerge in the seemingly contingent terrain of historical development. There is no "place," whether in philosophy itself or in human reality, where spirit "does not go."

20. G. W. F. Hegel, *Elements of the Philosophy of Right*, trans. H. B. Nisbet (Cambridge: Cambridge University Press, 1991), 302. However, Hegel immediately adds that "its secularity is only one of its aspects, and only a spiritless perception can regard it as merely finite." Note that the German term for Nisbet's "secular" is *weltlich*. See G. W. F. Hegel, *Grundlinien der Philosophie des Rechts* (Frankfurt: Ullstein, 1972), "Der Staat ist allerdings wesentlich weltlich und endlich, hat besonders Zwecke und besondere Gewalten, aber daß der Staat weltlich ist, ist nur die eine Seite, und nur der geistlosen Wahrnehmung ist der Staat bloß endlich."

21. Hegel, *Elements of the Philosophy of Right*, 279.

Does this mean that a responsible reconstruction of Hegel's account of religion is forced to deal with every aspect of his system? Strictly speaking, the answer is yes. Any attempt to isolate religion from the rest of the system is bound to be misleading. The lectures on religion, for example, which were given in different versions in 1821, 1824, 1827, and 1831, deliver systematic accounts of (a) religion's object (the kinds of metaphysical claims implicitly or explicitly being made in prayer, ritual, or liturgy, referred to as "the concept of God"); (b) religion's dialectical history and development ("determinate religion"); and (c) religion grasping itself as spirit in Christianity ("consummate religion"). However, the ultimate meaning of the lectures becomes apparent only when placed within the larger systematic framework of spirit's self-understanding as absolute spirit, which itself serves as the completion of a much larger enterprise.

At the risk of doing violence to Hegel's overall purpose in constructing a system of philosophy—a violence, by the way, that no interpreter of Hegel can fully avoid—I will be assuming that, while keeping in mind the larger architectonic of the system, and realizing that the question of religion is one approach among several to the larger question of spirit and its purported process of self-actualization, it is possible to explore religion, and religion's exhaustion in modernity, as a separate (though not independent) issue. As will soon become apparent, for Hegel the specificity of the religious experience can become manifest only if handled dialectically, as *both* separate and determinately individuated in (and by) its relations to spirit's other configurations, whether in the shape of art and philosophy (which, in addition to religion, are modes of spirit's own self-comprehension), or in the shapes of the respective levels of logic, nature, and spirit. Like many commentators before me, including Peter C. Hodgson, Walter Jaeschke, and Thomas A. Lewis, I thus take seriously Hegel's claim to have a separate philosophy of religion, even though its claim to separateness depends on its place in, and determination by, other dimensions of the system.[22]

A more obvious challenge to "orthodoxy" centers on my claim to detect in Hegel's reflections on religion an account of secularization. As I have already intimated, the standard view is that Hegel, remaining true

22. Lewis, *Religion, Modernity, and Politics in Hegel*; Peter C. Hodgson, *Hegel and Christian Theology: A Reading of the Lectures on the Philosophy of Religion* (Oxford: Oxford University Press, 2005); Walter Jaeschke, *Reason in Religion: The Foundations of Hegel's Philosophy of Religion*, trans. J. M. Stewart and Peter C. Hodgson (Berkeley: University of California Press, 1990). The literature on Hegel's philosophy of religion is extensive. These three names, in my view, are representative of the most accomplished recent scholarship.

to his early Christian faith, reinterprets, rearticulates, and even tries to *transform*, religion along rationalist lines: his Christianity, then, as an element of a modern society, is that of the believer motivated by philosophical insight. This would make his view coherent with those of medieval rationalist theologians such as Anselm and Aquinas, for whom the notion of philosophy as being a "handmaiden" to revealed truth meant that philosophy would be saddled with the task of providing a rational articulation of faith's content or commitments, albeit with no implications for the nature and integrity of faith itself, which was supposed to remain formally independent of reason.[23] To my knowledge, the only one among the commentators I just mentioned who in fact applies the terms "secularization" and "secularization theory" to Hegel is Jaeschke. At one point Jaeschke, considering the connection Hegel draws between the rise of Protestantism and disenchantment, whether causal or not, situates the theory as being "close to the theory of secularization."[24] However, he quickly modifies this statement, adding:

> The radical desacralization of the world is, to be sure, the hallmark of the present epoch; it is, however, characterized in a derogatory fashion, and as a passing phenomenon. It is regarded as precondition, to be fulfilled before "the spirit can venture to sanctify itself as spirit in its own shape

---

23. In *The Philosophy of St. Thomas Aquinas* (New York: Dorset Press, 1948), 52, Étienne Gilson puts this point very well: "Such appear to us the points of contact and the distinctions between Reason and Faith in the system of St. Thomas of Aquino. Faith and Reason can neither contradict each other, nor ignore each other, nor be confused. Reason may well try to justify Faith: it will never transform Faith into Reason, for as soon as Faith were to abandon authority for proof, it would cease to believe; it would know. And Faith may well move Reason externally or guide it internally; Reason will never cease to be itself, for once it renounced the proof of its assertions, it would deny itself and would vanish to make room for Faith. It is, therefore, the inalienability of their proper essences which permits them to act upon each other without contaminating each other."

24. Jaeschke, *Reason in Religion*, 164. See also Hermann Lübbe's more direct statement in *Säkularisierung: Geschichte eines ideenpolitischen Begriffs* (Freiburg: Karl Alber, 1965), 37: "Diese Theorie Hegels vom Zusammenhang der modernen politischen und geistigen Welt mit ihrer christlich-reformatischen Herkunft ist sicherlich Theorie eines Zusammenhangs, den wir heute durch die Kategorie der Säkularisierung aussagen könnten. Zugleich läßt sich behaupten, daß Hegel mit solchen Theorien aktiv in den Säkularisierungs-Prozeß eingreift." Jean-Claude Monod, *La querelle de la sécularisation de Hegel à Blumenberg* (Paris: Libraire philosophique J. Vrin, 2016), 62, sees Hegel as "le *premier philosophe de la sécularisation*, justifiant, dans le cadre d'une théodicée philosophique, la *Verweltlichung* du christianisme."

and reestablish the original reconciliation with itself in a new religion," consecrating the world no longer in alien fashion but its own.[25]

Yet what is this "new religion" that Hegel, according to Jaeschke, speaks of? This is what needs to be explored. Insofar as he claims to defend religion philosophically, Hegel commits himself to a view of religion as being a credible expression of spirit's claim to truth and authority. However, he retains a conception of faith and refuses to believe that it has been completely superseded by the rational culture of modernity. How does he justify this apparent settlement? What does it mean?

His distinction between content and mode of expression throws some light on the settlement. In the *Encyclopedia of the Philosophical Sciences*, religion is theorized as a "representation" (*Vorstellung*) of spirit, dependent on symbolically charged expression in the form of sensible imagery.[26] As such it is placed in the second tier of the tripartite manifestation of absolute spirit comprising art, religion, and philosophy. In the *Encyclopedia*, religion is characterized as having the same content as art and philosophy, namely the absolute. It expresses absolute truth. However, it is inferior to philosophy insofar as it formally relies on representation in the form of imagery. It is not conceptual in the strict, dialectical sense.

The distinction between content and mode of expression carries a number of implications. To be relying on *Vorstellung* means that the subject, in order to arrive at a fully transparent form of self-understanding as absolute (which, after all, is the goal of spirit), must utilize a mediating medium to direct itself to the object. As Hegel notes in the introduction to *The Phenomenology of Spirit*, the notion of such a medium standing between the subject and the object, mediating their relation and purportedly ensuring a cognitive grip, tends to generate skepticism. It suggests that since direct epistemic access is restricted to the medium (the idea, the *Vorstellung*), there can be no straightforward way of ascertaining that the medium in fact effectively secures objective knowledge.[27] Regardless of the medium being

---

25. Jaeschke, *Reason in Religion*, 165.

26. Hegel, *Philosophy of Mind (Hegel's Encyclopedia of the Philosophical Sciences)*, trans. A. V. Miller (Oxford: Clarendon Press, 1971), 176.

27. See Hegel, *The Phenomenology of Spirit*, trans. Terry Pinkard (Cambridge: Cambridge University Press, 2018), 51: "Or, if the testing of cognition which we supposed to be a *medium* made us acquainted with the law of its refraction, it would be just as useless to subtract this refraction from the result, for it is not the refraction of the ray but rather the ray itself through which the truth touches us that is cognition, and if this is subtracted, then all that would be indicated to us would be just pure direction or empty place." This is not an easy sentence to translate. See Hegel, *Phänomenologie*

deployed, from a cognitive point of view it will appear arbitrary, offering at best an indirect view of the object, which thus in the way it is presented will have to count as a mere appearance. By contrast to such a picture, a conceptually mediated self-understanding, while not dependent on any medium, is supposed to be able to know the object universally and in a mode of full freedom and rational transparency. This is the key reason philosophy is a higher mode or form of knowledge than both art (being directly restricted to sensuous presentation) and religion (being dependent on *Vorstellung*, whether sensuous or not) can ever be. Unlike his early commitment to religious practice in the form of mythically informed celebration and poetic image-making, the mature view calls for an apprehension of the absolute in the form of conceptual self-transparency in its unrestricted and rational form. Hegel is not rehearsing the standard atheist view of religious symbolizing as somehow being a manifestation of superstition. Religion has cognitive content: it makes a meaningful claim to truth (and, as we will see, its object, God, exists). It is just that it restricts the believer to an understanding of God that lacks rational (*vernünftige*) grounding. As such it can neither be "fully true" (or "true to its concept" in Hegel's sense) nor be compatible with humanity's aspiration to full freedom.

Yet what conception of God does Hegel have? And how does it differ from that of the religious believer who is dependent on the form or medium of representation?

No student of Hegel can ignore the fact that, rather than viewing religion negatively, as a possession unworthy of humanity in its mature state, familiar from certain strands of the Enlightenment and from thinkers such as Marx, Nietzsche, and Freud, he imbues religion with a tremendous aura of authority, seriousness, and inner truth. Hegel never thinks that the *content* of religion, which he identifies with spirit or God, is somehow illusory.[28] On the contrary, although God (or spirit) can be grasped only inadequately, God exists and is the most real "entity" or power there can be. "God is the beginning and end of all things. God is the sacred center, which animates and inspires all things."[29]

---

des Geistes (Frankfurt: Suhrkamp, 1986), 69: "Oder wenn die Prüfung des Erkennens, das wir als ein *Medium* uns vorstellen, uns das Gesetz seiner Strahlenbrechung kennen lehrt, so nützt es ebenso nichts, sie im Resultate abzuziehen; denn nich das Brechen des Strahls, sondern der Strahl selbst, wodurch die Wahrheit uns berührt, ist das Erkennen, und dieses abgezogen, wäre uns nur die reine Richtung oder der leere Ort bezeichnet worden."

28. Hegel, *Elements of the Philosophy of Right*, 292: "The content of religion is absolute truth, and it is therefore associated with a disposition of the most exalted kind."

29. Hegel, *Lectures on the Philosophy of Religion*, 76.

The most direct expression of Hegel's devotion to such a metaphysical conception of God appears at the very end of the *Encyclopedia*. Here he quotes Aristotle, who in *Metaphysics*, book Lambda 7, articulates the nature of the "prime mover." Aristotle reasons that, in order to avoid an infinite regress, all process and change in the universe will ultimately have to presuppose the existence of an unmoved mover, capable of causing process and change without itself being subject to them. The unmoved mover, Aristotle argues, must be an immutable substance acting eternally and, by being necessarily in accord with the demands of reason (*logos*), in ways that cannot but be good. In so doing it apprehends itself and becomes an object for itself: "And thought thinks itself because it shares the nature of the object of thought; for it becomes an object of thought in coming into contact with and thinking its objects, so that thought and object of thought are the same."[30]

In these passages it is possible to recognize a precursor to Hegel's commitment to the divine as a wholly self-sufficient "substance"—the, as it were, universal and logical structure of the world, necessarily actualizing itself by externalizing itself and then reappropriating itself while identifying with its particular other. Hegel's God is a self-thinking, self-reflective form of logos that, while actualized in humanly comprehensible ways (and as humans participate in spirit and carry it forward), permeates the world, attaining unity in ever widening circles of self-alienation and subsequent overcoming.

The late Hegel's approach to religion is ambiguous. On one hand, he attempts to rescue religion from both enlightenment criticism and Pietist subjectivation and emotionalism. Spirit—Hegel's fundamental reality (and "the absolute")—not only is objective but is supposed to unite "the infinite" and "the finite," God and the natural and historical reality of man. By claiming that human self-consciousness, human history, and even the state (insofar as it objectifies and expresses spirit) are *geistige* achievements, Hegel effectively renders human existence divine and considers reconciliation, symbolically represented in scripture, to be available in human institutions and their self-representation. On the other hand, as spirit exhausts itself in history—and, in modernity, as it finally obtains adequate and exclusive expression in the universal medium of conceptual thinking, thereby liberating itself from all forms of givenness, dependence, and limitation—its specifically *religious* interpretation can no longer be accepted as authoritative. Philosophy must take over. While religious practices may continue,

30. Aristotle, *The Complete Works of Aristotle*, vol. 2 (Princeton, NJ: Princeton University Press, 1984), 1695.

the modern, post-Reformation, post-Revolutionary Europe of Hegel's own time must be considered to be essentially rational yet also prosaic: if considered a transcendent being, opposed to the finitude of human reality, God is essentially "dead."

Hegel's theological rescue mission thus comes at a remarkably high price. While the content—the absolute, or "truth"—remains unchanged as, in modernity, philosophy takes over the baton from religion, its authoritative form changes completely. Rather than being an object of religious veneration, spirit comes to know itself conceptually, as the dialectical movement of a priori concepts and their relations. Thus, like art, religion will find itself "to be a thing of the past."

To interpret this coherently depends on introducing Hegel's historical narrative. Ultimately it is religion that undergoes a transformation. Hegel's God is always a function of what human agents as *geistige* beings can interpret as authoritative. Humans are self-interpreting agents. Thus the overall claim is going to be that while the religious interpretation of God loses authority, the content of the religious interpretation will survive and yet be formally sublated as, in modernity, philosophy becomes the most authoritative interpretation of spirit.

Hegel's story of Western secularization is complex and lends itself to various interpretations. However, a key idea that, for him, must be associated, and indeed identified, with secularity is the complete loss in modernity of any authoritative vision of divine *transcendence* (entailing, importantly, the conception of some object of representation). The essential teaching of Christianity—and, obviously, the scriptures—is that God is *fully revealed* (*geoffenbart*): any otherness or externality pertaining to God has been overcome. Given that God, understood as a transcendent being, is conceived of not only as *capable* of dying but, in the figure of Christ, as *actually* dying, Christianity differs crucially from all other religions. In Christ's resurrection and ascension, which the religious community receives in the form of the Holy Spirit, Hegel detects the possibility of a reconciliation of transcendence and immanence, universality and particularity, in the mediated unity of spirit.

Hegel's interpretation of God's ineluctable death follows from his understanding of spirit as essential self-revelation, the attainment of self-knowledge and transparency in and through the other. The making of the world, he writes in the 1827 *Lectures on the Philosophy of Religion*, "is God's self-manifesting, self-revealing."[31] Drawing its inspiration from, among others, Jacob Böhme, Hegel's idea is that spirit can actualize itself only insofar as it makes itself

---

31. Hegel, *Lectures on the Philosophy of Religion*, 129.

manifest to itself.³² It must make itself known to itself. Inert unity accounts such as Spinoza's, in which the substance is unitary, containing no moment of self-differentiation—involve no self-manifestation and hence no moment of creation, of coming into being or actuality. For that to be possible, there must be some form of objectification followed by an appropriation of the objectification such that the subject can reflexively know itself as identical with its objectified other. Actualization is thus self-differentiation followed by reunification or reconciliation with the differentiated other. As spirit actualizes itself, it rationally comes to know itself in the successive determinations arising from the process of self-differentiation and reunification. The death of God is simply the highest expression, in any religion, of precisely this essential process of spirit's own self-manifestation. In the suffering of Christ, God—considered as an abstract, transcendent, and universal entity—is conceived of as dying away from Himself, being transformed into the self-reflective practices of the community of believers who commemorate this death in acts of worship. For Hegel, with its discovery and articulation of the dialectic of self-differentiation and reunification, Christianity is the only true or, as he puts it, *consummate* religion. It is the religion of the fully revealed God, in which the divine, when adequately understood, is no longer presented in an alienated, projected, or transcendent form. Hegel's God is identical with spirit, and while divine, spirit achieves full reconciliation with itself through human efforts at self-interpretation and self-articulation. Since this is a rational process, spirit's highest and most adequate articulation takes place philosophically. In this respect, Hegel's God is *nous*, thinking being.³³

Hegel on Political Secularization

We have seen that Hegel most certainly is a believer, if this means he holds the view that a divine substance exists. However, we have also been able to ascertain that God's divinity (conceived in Hegel's *The Science of Logic* as *die*

---

32. Hegel, *Lectures on the Philosophy of Religion*, 431: "Jacob Boehme was the first to recognize the Trinity in another manner, as universal. His way of representing and thinking is rather wild and fanciful; he has not yet risen to the pure forms of thinking. But the ruling foundation of the ferment in his mind, and of his struggles to reach the truth, was the recognition of the presence of the Trinity in everything and everywhere."

33. Hegel, *Lectures on the Philosophy of World History: Introduction, Reason in History*, trans. H. B. Nisbet (Cambridge: Cambridge University Press), 35: "For divine providence is wisdom, coupled with infinite power, which realises its ends, i.e. the absolute and rational design of the world; and reason is freely self-determining thought, or what the Greeks called 'nous.'"

Idee, comprising the full overcoming of all dualisms, the organic unity of all dialectical movements conceived as a whole) actualizes itself via externalization (*Entäusserung*) or *kenosis*, arriving at full self-revelation. Thus, while this view grants that Hegel did subscribe to the existence of a divine being, it also forms the basis for thinking not only about *how* the externalization and self-appropriation takes place, which, I take it, is the object of Hegel's philosophy of spirit as a whole, but also about whether externalization and self-appropriation—and with that the full overcoming of all appeals to transcendence—can justifiably be characterized in terms of secularization.

The apparent ambiguity of Hegel's position—the endorsement of Christianity coupled with the belief that the modern world is largely secular—comes out clearly in his assessment of the role of religion in the modern, rational state. In the Addition to § 270 of the *Elements of the Philosophy of Right*, Hegel claims, as I mentioned earlier, that "The state is indeed essentially secular and finite, and has particular ends and particular powers."[34] The reasoning at this point is complex. However, the thrust of his argument is that any attempt to externally ground the state in religion (as in Islamic sharia or forms of Judaism), by making it dependent on the arbitrariness of emotionally charged piety or the internal structure of representational thought (religious dogma, etc.), is bound to destabilize the state. In the interest of protecting individual freedom, the state should be tolerant of various religious practices as long as they do not interfere with the business of governing and do not prevent its members from performing their most basic duties toward it (such as military service); and religion can functionally unite communities around goals that coincide with the interests of the state and even serve to "integrate the state at the deepest level of the disposition of its citizens."[35] Designers of a rational state should, however, not let religion enter into politics and political deliberation more generally, and fundamental laws and principles of the state should be founded not on religious creeds and commitments but on reason alone. If not, the danger arises that its claim to be a rationally structured entity is undermined, opening the door to fanaticism.

> Thus, if religiosity sought to assert itself in the state in the manner which it usually adopts on its ground, it would subvert the organization of the state; for the differences within the state are far apart, whereas everything in religion invariably has reference to the totality. And if this totality sought to take over all the relations [*Beziehungen*] of the state, it would

---

34. Hegel, *Elements of the Philosophy of Right*, 302.
35. Hegel, *Elements of the Philosophy of Right*, 295.

become fanaticism; it would wish to find the whole in every particular, and could accomplish this only by destroying the particular, for fanaticism is simply the refusal to admit particular differences.[36]

Hegel's commitment to the essential secularity of the modern state is mediated by his even more significant commitment to the rational nature of the state, and thus to its essential actuality as spirit, requiring self-knowing in the form of principled cognition. The state, he famously claims, is divine. Rather than the kind of excessive political mysticism Hegel has sometimes been associated with, this means that its rational structure is supposed to be based on an adequate articulation of spirit in its unfolding as the actual shape and organization of a political entity.[37] In other words, unlike Kant, Mill, or Rawls, Hegel is not a straightforward theorist of the modern, secular state. Rather, the secularity of the state follows from his theory of spirit, which in the state objectifies itself to achieve full expression and manifestation.

The account of the state in *Elements of the Philosophy of Right* should not be confused with a historical account of the nature of actually existing modern states (say of Hegel's own post-Napoleonic state of Prussia, ruled by King Friedrich Wilhelm III in accordance with the written constitution of the reform administration of Chancellor Hardenberg).[38] In terms of the issue of secularization, all that can be conclusively gathered from this writing is that to the extent that it is rational, the state will have to be secular, founded not on religion in the traditional sense but on spirit as expressed in Hegel's philosophy of objective spirit. Since Hegel's political theory is oriented around a conception of self-actualization, in *Elements of the Philosophy of Right* there is no claim that the modern state actually (or "empirically") is secular. However, Hegel's theory of the fully rational state is related to his view of history. If history itself, as he argues, can be viewed as a rational process, then locating the fully self-actualized state formation at the end of history does make sense.

---

36. Hegel, *Elements of the Philosophy of Right*, 303–4.

37. Hegel, *Lectures on the Philosophy of World History*, 95: "The divine principle in the state is the Idea made manifest on earth."

38. The debates at this point have been complex and long-standing, going all the way back to the immediate post-Hegelian response. In the one camp were people like Erdmann and Rosenkranz representing the right-Hegelian view that Hegel was referring to the actually existing state, and, in the other, left-Hegelians like Strauss, Bauer, and Feuerbach, representing Hegel's theory in ideal terms, as an instrument, however ideological, of social critique.

The passages in which his direct assessment of contemporary secularity is to be found are elsewhere. Most striking in this regard may be his comparisons of contemporary Europe with the Roman Empire. Thus, in the 1821 version of the *Lectures on the Philosophy of Religion*, referring to the Roman Empire, Hegel indirectly describes a modern society—familiar from Weber's account of *Entzauberung*, the desacralization and demystification of the world—in which instrumental reason is rampant, rationality mainly a privately exercised capacity to secure rights and goods, and a common life based on religion, Taylor's "horizon" or "background," has been irretrievably lost.[39] Rather than genuine faith and understanding of God, there is an abundance of historical and technical information (mere "facts" carrying neither intrinsic meaning nor significant connection with rationally organized systems of propositions) as well as moralistic views and purely subjective feelings and sentiments. What is left is only "finitude [turned] in upon itself, arrogant barrenness and lack of content, the extremity of self-satisfied disenlightenment (*Ausklärung*, a derogatory play on *Aufklärung*)."[40] Hegel's modernity is indeed barren, offering limited resources for anyone in search of existential meaning.

Hegel's Secularization Narrative

To obtain an adequate sense of why Hegel may count as a theorist of secularization, we must look beyond the philosophy of right to Hegel's views of history as they appear in his recounting of the history of spirit.

In both the 1824 and the 1827 lectures on the philosophy of religion, Hegel's account of the development of religion from "nature religion" and magic via Asian, Greek, Jewish, and Roman religion to, finally, "the consummate religion" of Western Christianity covers a large terrain. In very general terms, it suggests that no culture ever existed without religion and that religion in this sense is universal. However, the lectures also describe transitions in the history of religious development that can be interpreted as instances of secularization.

One such—relevant for the history of Western religiousness—is the transition from Greek to Jewish and Roman religion. As is familiar from many

---

39. G. W. F. Hegel, *Vorlesungen über die Philosophie der Religion*, lecture manuscript and various transcriptions, part 1 (Hamburg: Felix Meiner, 1983), 158–62.

40. Hegel, *Vorlesungen über die Philosophie der Religion*, 159–60. I borrow the translation from Stewart and Hodgson in Peter C. Hodgson, ed., *G. W. F. Hegel: Theologian of the Spirit* (Minneapolis: Fortress Press), 203.

of Hegel's writings—including *The Phenomenology of Spirit*, the various *Lectures on the Philosophy of Religion*, and the *Aesthetics: Lectures on Fine Art*—in Greek religion, or what Hegel often calls the "Religion of Beauty," the divine is represented as being present in the world. In myths that provide shape and meaning to the ethical and political life of the community, the gods and their ways become intelligible. Religion thus essentially serves to integrate the community. Given the lack of self-reflection and interiority, as well as the spontaneous participation in socially endorsed roles and structures, that Hegel ascribes to the ancient Greeks, there is no room for a sense of alienation from the divine. As in Hegel's account of the *Volksreligion*, the divine is universally present in the rituals and symbols of social life. While sacred and "shining," the divine is not incommensurable with the lives of humans; and while different from humans in their power, dispositions, and abilities, the gods can even take a human shape or appearance.

In the 1827 lectures and elsewhere, the Greek religion, while presenting a "beautiful" and deeply satisfying unity of the human and the divine, is viewed as dialectically inadequate. First, it fails to liberate the divine from the finite, making representations of the divine dependent on representations of human embodiment, which is transient and mortal. Second, Greek religion lacks a moment of active endorsement—the apperceptive element of taking oneself to believe based on considerations and reasons that mark oneself as a rational being. Mere existence in an enchanted universe, while on some theorists' view the prototype of all religion, is for Hegel a form of immediacy, deficient in its self-knowledge, calling for an overcoming in the form of some sort of rupture or transcendence.[41] In *The Phenomenology of Spirit*, that overcoming is brought about by the irresolvable conflict between the human and the divine law epitomized by the tragic standoff between Creon and Antigone in Sophocles' tragedy *Antigone*.[42]

Jewish religion, or what Hegel calls "The Religion of Sublimity," interprets the absolute in terms of pure transcendence, devoid of mediation with the world of finite existence. While God acts out of internal necessity, from the vantage point of human existence His actions will inevitably seem inscrutable and incomprehensible, and the world of finite existence appears arid and without meaning or purpose. The community is rule-based.

---

41. The theorist of secularization Marcel Gauchet (*The Disenchantment of the World*, 27) argues that religion in its "original pure state" requires the complete dispossession of human freedom and self-reflection, a desire to merge with an enchanted nature, a socially endorsed conception of the social order as immutable, collective social organization, and the "absolute predominance of a founding past."

42. See Hegel, *Phenomenology of Spirit*, 279–89.

However, the authority of the rules remains completely mystical. In *The Phenomenology of Spirit* this is the world of the unhappy consciousness experiencing alienation from the absolute.[43] By contrast, Roman religion, or the "Religion of Expediency," involves the at least partial withdrawal of the divine from communal life and the essential privatizing of belief, which now (as in Stoicism) takes on a compensatory quality. In Roman religion, what matters is political dominion, and the gods' primary function is simply to realize this "universal purpose." Thus the Romans instrumentalize their pantheon. Jewish religion is alienating as the result of the sublimity and purely abstract quality of the absolute. However, Roman religion is alienating due to its cold, utilitarian vision of the divine and the transformation of the public realm from an arena of spontaneity (as Hegel saw in the Greek polis) into a system of rights and entitlements, leading to social atomizing and a loss of cohesion.

Hegel is hardly claiming that Jewish and Roman communities are more secular than the Greek ones. In fact, as a configuration of religious life, the ongoing Jewish liberation of the absolute from finite modes of representation and mediation may seem more "pure" than Greek religion, in which the gods, while habitating above the human abode, nevertheless exist in a cosmic continuity with human beings. Also, within Roman religion, for example in Stoicism, there are plenty of attempts to "idealize" the gods and disentangle them from the human realm. From the viewpoint of an account of secularization, however, what matters is the loss in both Jewish and Roman religion of the immediate identity of the subject with the social substance and the consequent alienation of the subject from the absolute. As Taylor points out, secularization does not necessarily follow a path of subtraction, a critique and demystification of the divine, leading along more or less rational routes toward a weakening of religious

---

43. There is a puzzling discrepancy between the treatment of Judaism in *The Phenomenology of Spirit* and the 1827 *Lectures on the Philosophy of Religion*. In the former writing, the Jewish religion makes a cameo appearance in the early section of the self-consciousness chapter on unhappy consciousness, next to Hegel's discussions of stoicism and skepticism. It is, however, not present in Hegel's long chapter on spirit, in which he accounts for the transformation from Greek to Roman and then to Christian society and religion, culminating with the European Enlightenment. In the *Lectures*, however, he inserts a brief discussion of Jewish religion between the characterizations of the Greek and Roman worlds. As Hodgson argues in *Hegel and Christian Theology*, 228–37, Hegel's treatment of Judaism changes significantly from the perspective of the *Early Theological Writings*, in which alienation is the key, to *The Phenomenology of Spirit*, in which the emphasis is on God's transcendence. The theme of transcendence remains central in all the lectures on the history of religion, including those of 1821, 1824, 1827, and 1831.

fervor. Rather, secularization can and often does come about as the result of collective steps that serve to *alienate* the subject from the absolute and thus weaken the horizon in which faith attains genuine significance and motivational power. As I mentioned, Taylor also suggests that secularization tends to be accompanied by an increased sense of division between subject and object, combined with a turn from the "porous" to the "buffered" self. Both the Jewish and the Roman religions involve such transformations of subjectivity. Judaism views the absolute as transcendent, thereby eliminating the vibrant connection between the subject and the living manifestation of spirit that the Greeks were able to enjoy in their art and religious practices. As a result, when God is viewed as subsisting entirely without sensible shape, the subject starts seeking the law, or the absolute, in thought and thought only.[44] Yet when thought finds no support or evidence in the existing world, it risks becoming empty or dependent on ceremonial service, which itself is abstract and external. By constructing a formal and strictly utilitarian institution of public worship with which the individual subject finds itself incapable of identifying, the Roman religion, on the other hand, equally leads to the constitution of a buffered self. According to Hegel, the subject position publicly available to the Romans can be characterized as being an abstract bearer of rights (property rights but also certain political rights). The result is withdrawal from the community and the setting up of a strict division between the inner and the outer.

> Thus on one hand the individual perishes in the universal, in the sovereign authority, in the Fortuna Publica; but on the other hand human purposes hold sway and the human subject has an independent, essential value. These extremes and their contradiction are the whirlpool in which Roman life tosses and turns.[45]

In the chapter on spirit in *The Phenomenology of Spirit*, Hegel understands the development of spirit from the ancient Greeks via the Romans to medieval Europe, absolutist Europe, and the Europe of the Enlightenment in

---

44. Hegel, *Lectures on the Philosophy of Religion*, 359: "Thus the unity of God contains one power within it, which is accordingly the absolute power. Every externality, every sensible configuration and sensible image, is sublated in it. For this reason God here subsists without shape—he subsists not for sensible representation but only for thought. The inwardly infinite, pure subjectivity is the subjectivity that is essentially thinking. As thinking it subsists only for thinking, and therefore subsists in its [activity of] judgment. Thinking is the essential soil for this object."

45. Hegel, *Lectures on the Philosophy of Religion*, 385.

terms of alienation.[46] If spirit in the ancient Greek world was too natural, failing to display a capacity for self-reflection, then the subsequent dialectic of spirit takes the form of purifying the subject of everything natural, every nonreflective attachment and commitment, such that spirit (or, in the language of the *Phenomenology*, "the Substance," the "in itself") can finally become subjective (or "Subject," the "for itself"). In *The Phenomenology of Spirit*, the beginning of alienation is to be located in the transition from Greek to Roman antiquity. However, the process of alienation and purification continues beyond that juncture, going all the way to the European Enlightenment, where post-Reformist faith retreats into the inner or "the heart."

After the downfall of the Roman Empire, medieval Europe powerfully and lastingly reasserted the existence of a transcendent and almighty God. However, in Hegel's account, medieval Europe is itself showing tendencies that point toward the sixteenth-century reform movements and the seventeenth and eighteenth centuries of enlightenment. In *The Phenomenology of Spirit*, for example, he describes the development of the nobility and its honor code.[47] Gradually, as the European state becomes more centralized and the court system is established, the nobility adopts an increasingly intense ethics of self-purification, articulating the culture of the empty "flattery" characteristic of the French absolutist court. Indeed, medieval Europe abounds with projects of self-purification—some, as in the example of the nobleman, mostly secular, others, as in Christocentric forms of spirituality, turning inward, focusing on individual actions like fasting, going on pilgrimage, and private prayer, and abandoning the standard forms of devotion, in particular the Mass, in which the individual would find itself more deeply integrated into the community.[48]

Equally important, however, for a dialectical account of the process of secularization is Hegel's observation, particularly in the early Jena period, that Christianity shares with the Roman world an intense desacralization of nature.[49] Whereas the Greek gods animated the world, Christianity

---

46. For a similar emphasis on the concept of alienation, see Terry Pinkard, *Hegel's Phenomenology: The Sociality of Reason* (New York: Cambridge University Press, 1996), chap. 5.

47. Hegel, *Phenomenology of Spirit*, 284–306.

48. Taylor, *Secular Age*, 70–71.

49. See G. W. F. Hegel, *A System of Ethical Life* and *First Philosophy of Spirit*, trans. H. S. Harris and T. M. Knox (Albany: State University of New York Press, 1979), 182. For an account of Hegel's assessment of early Christianity versus the Roman world, see Jaeschke, *Reason in Religion*, 162.

enforces conceptions of transcendence, leaving nature "mute." Responding to this process, Hegel sees medieval Catholicism as attempting to revoke the desacralization. However, this strategy had to fail because the diremption between the ideal and the real, between the divine and man's earthly existence, had already been experienced as historically real, provoking a return of spirit not to nature but to itself in its progressively purer and "denatured" state. According to Hegel, the Reformation can be viewed as a concerted effort to destroy the sanctification of the world imparted by Catholicism. While Catholicism, or what Hegel in *A System of Ethical Life* calls the first form of Christianity or even a "beautiful religion," aspires, with its saints, relics, and magic, to return to mythology, Protestantism accepts the broken unity of subject and object, introducing a feeling of infinite longing and anguish. As Weber would later argue, the return to empirical existence takes the form of reconciling oneself not to an enchanted universe but to a world of commonplace, everyday work and necessity.

Although Hegel is by no means adequately described as an anti-Enlightenment thinker, his analysis of the Enlightenment is in large part negative. Both in *The Phenomenology of Spirit* and in the 1827 *Lectures on the Philosophy of Religion*, the Enlightenment is characterized as a negative movement, devoid of a positive stance and geared toward critique or what Hegel calls "the destruction of externality," though basically in an abstract and sterile fashion. On his analysis, the Enlightenment aims at intellectual self-purification, ridding the subject of any pregiven and nonreflective attachments while overcoming immediacy. The requirement, after all, of successful enlightenment reflection is that no content should be accepted at face value and that everything should be subject to doubt and rational scrutiny. The Enlightenment thus brings about the establishment of a radical ideal of rational agency. Whatever is to be accepted as valid or true must undergo a critical investigation. For religious experience, not surprisingly, the Enlightenment is destructive. By treating faith on a par with scientific belief, it asks for justification where none can be given; and since God's existence "cannot be proven," religion must be rejected.[50]

In Jacobi, by contrast, who builds on Kant and accepts his restriction of knowledge to the order of appearance, the theoretical impossibility of justifying the existence of God is endorsed as an epistemological fact but

---

50. Of course, attempts at proving God's existence were given in Scholasticism and continued in rationalist thinkers like Leibniz and Descartes. However, in the 1827 lectures on religion, Hegel argues that none of the proofs seem to work and, more fundamentally, that they misunderstand the nature of religious faith by construing it as on a par with scientific understanding.

not as a reason to reject faith. Faith, Jacobi argues, is noncognitive, residing in the heart. On Hegel's reading, while Jacobi's strategy is understandable and capable of retaining some sense of the object, it fails to achieve any determinacy and regresses to mere formless emotion, locked inside the self.

> This is what is called the pious life of feeling, to which *Pietism* also restricts itself. Pietism acknowledges no objective truth and opposes itself to dogmas and the content of religion, while still preserving an element of mediation, a connection with Christ, but this is a connection that is supposed to remain one of mere feeling and inner sensibility. Such piety, together with the vanity of subjectivity and feeling, is then turned polemically against the philosophy that wants cognition. The result of this subjectivity is that everything fades away in the subject, without objectivity, without firm determinacy, without any development on the part of God, who in the end no longer has any content at all.[51]

Hegel's 1824 and 1827 lectures on religion are both responding not only to Jacobi's Pietism but also to his concern over Schleiermacher's forthcoming *Glaubenslehre*, of which Hegel had some knowledge, in which the way to save religion from the onslaughts of science and enlightenment criticism was also to locate the origin and meaning of faith in the realm of the noncognitive—feeling, intuition, piety.[52]

For Hegel, Pietism of this kind is expressive of modernity, and in particular of the withdrawal of spirit to the interior typical of enlightened modernity. A central task of the lectures on religion is to demonstrate the partiality of such views. Far from being a satisfying response to the condition of modernity, they serve to intensify disenchantment, the loss of God as a concrete truth shared by members of the religious community. At the end of the day, Pietism is bound to regress into indifferentism and nihilism. As Hegel sarcastically writes, if Schleiermacher's version of Pietism, emphasizing a feeling of dependence and viewing that as key to the nature of faith, were right as an interpretation of Christianity, then "a dog would . . . be the best Christian."[53] Feeling is as such indeterminate and sense-based, and therefore devoid of content (that is, of claims that can express objective truth). By depriving faith of any intentional relation to an object, it risks reducing

---

51. Hegel, *Lectures on the Philosophy of Religion*, 486.

52. For an account of Schleiermacher's role in particular, see Hodgson's "Editorial Introduction to Hegel," in Hegel's *Lectures on the Philosophy of Religion*, 15–24.

53. The passage (from the Berlin years) is quoted from the translation by J. Michael Stewart for Stewart and Hodgson, *G. W. F. Hegel: Theologian of the Spirit*, 166.

religious life to a mere self-relation, in short something psychological and "finite." On Hegel's account, Pietism also rejects the authority of the church and most public displays of religious affiliation. In that regard it sides with secularism.

At the end of the 1827 *Lectures on the Philosophy of Religion*, Hegel distinguishes between the culture of the Enlightenment and what he calls a "third moment" beyond both criticism and emotionalism. The third moment lets theology "take refuge" in the concept (*der Begriff*) and in philosophy: for only philosophy can freely and rationally preserve the content of religion.

> This reconciliation is philosophy. Philosophy is to this extent theology. It presents the reconciliation of God with himself and with nature, showing that nature, otherness, is implicitly divine, and that the raising of itself to reconciliation is on the one hand what finite spirit implicitly is, while on the other hand it arrives at this reconciliation, or brings it forth, in world history. This reconciliation is the peace of God, which does not "surpass all reason," but is rather the peace that *through* reason is first known and thought and is recognized as what is true.[54]

For Hegel, the modern relation to the absolute requires philosophical articulation, the determination of its own conceptual commitments as they play themselves out in our relation to nature, society, the human mind, and culture. However, the world of modernity in which this articulation takes place is going to be devoid of the spiritual fervor with which, say, Hölderlin (and Hegel in his younger days) dreamed of a beautiful Christian community of love or, later, the young Nietzsche would advocate the joyful return to Greek, tragic culture. God considered as a transcendent entity of representation to which consciousness is supposed to relate in faith is no longer a viable, fully authoritative conception. To the extent that God can be said to exist, it must be as a dynamic self-relationship of spirit, the consciousness of absolute spirit, and hence as the basic structure of the absolute in the way it is interpreted by philosophy. Religion, then, since it has failed to elevate the objects of representation to the level of the true self-consciousness of spirit, is necessarily a "thing of the past," the recounting of which must take place via the historically minded dialectic of the lectures on religion.

---

54. Hegel, *Lectures on the Philosophy of Religion*, 489. The reference to the "surpassing of all reason" is an allusion to the German translation of Phil. 4:7: "And the peace of God, which surpasses all reason [*Vernunft*], will keep your hearts and minds in Christ Jesus." Clearly, Hegel wants to intimate that God, in his view, is not beyond reason. On the contrary, reason is able to fully exhaust the meaning of God.

It is important not to confuse this claim to rational comprehension with the descriptive accounts of modernity that can be found in standard secularization theory. They typically point to a de facto loss or transformation of spirituality to be ascertained, say in contemporary Europe, by the actual waning of religious (and especially Christian) practice. However, Hegel never claims that the end of religion means the end of de facto religious practice. He makes no pronouncement to the effect that churches will close, people will stop praying, and the like. His claim is predominantly normative: that such practice (and the commitments that go with and sustain it) is no longer able to carry any claim to authority and that it is dialectically and rationally superseded. According to Jaeschke, the parallel with Hegel's more famous, yet often misunderstood, thesis about the end of art is striking.[55] Hegel's claim in the *Aesthetics* that "art, considered in its highest vocation, is and remains for us a thing of the past"[56] is not implying that artworks will no longer be made or enjoyed. Rather, the claim is that art *in its highest vocation* is no longer available. In modernity, as conceptual thinking becomes the only acceptable candidate for achieving the requisite of universality and freedom, art of this kind comes irretrievably to an end *in its capacity to be taken as presenting the absolute*. This does not, however, deter Hegel from identifying alternative roles for art to play. Among these are the attentiveness to bourgeois existence displayed in Dutch genre painting, the "subjective humor" of Sterne's *Tristram Shandy*, and the lyricism of Goethe's *Divan* poetry.[57] Thus, Hegel's narrative of art's development confirms the general tendency toward secularization that we have already had ample opportunity to detect elsewhere. Art is no longer capable of offering

---

55. Walter Jaeschke, "Philosophical Theology and Philosophy of Religion," in *New Perspectives on Hegel's Philosophy of Religion*, ed. David Kolb (Albany: State University of New York Press, 1992), 15.

56. G. W. Hegel, *Aesthetics: Lectures on Fine Arts*, trans. T. M. Knox (Oxford: Oxford University Press, 1999), 11.

57. For an account of the extent to which Hegel provides conceptual space for "art after the end of art," see Benjamin Rutter, *Hegel on the Modern Arts* (Cambridge: Cambridge University Press, 2010). See also Robert Pippin, *The Persistence of Subjectivity: On the Kantian Aftermath* (Cambridge: Cambridge University Press, 2005), 295: "The modern social world itself may be rational, in other words, but it is, to say it all at once, just thereby not very beautiful, and its 'meaning' is not very mysterious. It has its own kind of domestic and rather small-screen beauty, we can say—hence all that Hegelian praise for Dutch celebrations of the bourgeoisie—but the 'sacredness' of orderly city streets, piano playing, milk pouring, needlework, and fine clothing, does not, given that Hegel's aesthetics is so content-driven, satisfy very lofty aesthetic ambitions."

an *authoritative* presentation of the divine. However, it also reveals ways for art to continue existing in the absence of such authority.

It was Hegel's belief that only the incorporation of Christianity and the Christian God into his system could rescue the Christian religion. Whether or not that move was successful therefore depends at least in major part on the acceptability of the system as a whole. While an assessment of that aspiration would go beyond the framework of this book, it is evident that the critique/rescue dialectic structures Hegel's philosophy of religion down to its most minute details. He relentlessly critiques the Judeo-Christian vision of the transcendent God, and in the name of his philosophy of spirit he questions the historically constituted authority both of the church and of faith and prayer. At the same time, in his system he finds a place for the divine and the absolute and, by implication, in his interpretation of the modern state and modern ethical life. The "religion" he thinks is justified for modern agents is thin, rationalized, and, as Nietzsche will later deplore and mock, without any of the fervor and respect for the sacred that once dominated Christian societies (and, of course, the ancient Greek world). However, the understanding of the modern state as offering a form of life that is authorized by its claim to articulate and objectify "the absolute" and "the Idea" can be read as yet another attempt to find in religion an anticipation of an ethical life able to satisfy the most considered expectations with regard to freedom and self-actualization. The early Hegel tried to transpose religious ideals directly to a social level. Realizing that this would be a philosophically dubious procedure that would tailor modern aspirations to a reactionary framework, he rejected this model and adopted a version of modernity based on achievements tied to freedom and rationality. Kant viewed Christianity in exclusively moral terms, arguing that its promise of happiness and salvation could be retained and interpreted as postulates of pure practical reason. Dismissing Kant's continuing appeal to transcendence, Hegel viewed it more widely as the rational framework upon which modern ethical life at large should be erected. However, they both found the successor to revealed religion to be ethically oriented, though in a manner that aspires to be fully rational.

[CHAPTER FOUR]

A Social Critique of Religion

Feuerbach and Marx

Successful philosophical accounts of secularization should not be confused with the critique of religion, which is a far older genre. David Hume and Voltaire criticized religion. They showed, as in *Dialogues concerning Natural Religion*, that the traditional arguments in favor of the existence of God are incoherent or, as in *Candide*, that claims concerning creation and its purported "perfection" make a mockery of actual human suffering. The critique of religion quite possibly originated with Epicurus, who proclaimed that whatever gods there may be, they are far from us and indifferent to human lives. This critique, Epicurus contended in what became a deeply influential strand of social criticism, aims to relieve humans of fear—fear of the unknown, for example, or fear of inscrutable forms of punishment.[1] Calling for human self-reliance, rational self-determination, and mastery based on rational insight, it belongs to the standard repertoire of enlightenment thinking.

As we saw in the case of Comte, philosophical accounts of secularization may incorporate critique of this kind. However, they also perform tasks that are equally important, if not more so. As a first approximation, it can be stipulated that such theories provide an account of religious motivation. They try to explain, or at least interpret, the hold that religion can have on people's minds. What explains its authority? How is it maintained? What mechanisms and social structures may account for its motivational power? However, philosophical accounts of secularization also explore the conditions under which religious belief and practice, as well as concomitant visions of the sacred, may *weaken* their motivational hold on agents. While historians and sociologists of religion tend to focus on, and causally account for, the empirical expansion of humanist attitudes, more philosophically inclined theorists of religion are interested in broad questions involving value,

---

1. See Epicurus's "Letter to Herodotus," in *The Art of Happiness*, trans. George K. Strodach (New York: Penguin Books, 2012), 111.

meaning, and human self-assertion. Finally, philosophical secularization theorists want to know whether the religious attitude might have a natural or meaningful successor—either a substitute of some sort for religion or a different order altogether.

By claiming that its content—in particular the belief in the existence of a supersensible realm of divine existence—is illusory, Feuerbach and Marx are, in the spirit of the Enlightenment, critiquing religion. Yet in addition to their objections to religion, they both attempt to illuminate its attraction and understand the conditions under which that attraction, including the ideals generative of it, may weaken or, so they hope, be transformed and thereby pave the way for a renewed and rejuvenated ethical life. It is in this latter sense, the moment of rescue, that they interpret the ultimate purpose of a philosophical discourse of secularization.

This chapter analyzes Feuerbach's and Marx's critiques of religion and thinking about secularization. I start by discussing the early Feuerbach's objections to Hegel's idealism. I then examine Feuerbach's projection theory, in which religion is understood to be a projection of humanity's own essence onto a fictitious, quasi-metaphysical level of existence. While in crucial ways indebted to Hegel, Feuerbach's materialism both criticizes and rescues elements of religious faith and practice. Feuerbach criticizes the projection of human essence and the self-alienation it causes. However, by calling for an appropriation of the projected content, he anticipates a state in which humanity is able to actualize the essence that hitherto was associated with transcendence. Marx, on the other hand, locates religious consciousness in a significantly more complex theoretical context. For Marx, religion is a paradigmatic species of ideology, a key component of the societal superstructure, which, by promising happiness and salvation, obscures both the real conditions of human existence and the potential for genuine social transformation. I claim that Marx's strategy hinges on the possibility of a form of secularization centered on what I will call the achievement of finitude. Whereas Marx theorizes finitude both materialistically and historically, thereby anticipating how religion (and the need for it) can be overcome, he retains, like Feuerbach, elements of Judeo-Christian thought, in particular the idea of a communal existence capable of overcoming all forms of alienation.

Feuerbach's Humanism

Both Feuerbach and Marx formulate projection theories of religion. Religious belief and practice incorporate visions of human essence that, while based on human self-interpretation, are projected into a purportedly supersensible realm, thereby leading to, or being expressive of, self-estrangement or alienation. Since they are illusory and ideological, they serve at best to uphold and consolidate the social conditions that ultimately explain the creation of, and need for, such illusions in the first place. As society overcomes the conditions leading to self-estrangement, the illusions are liable, they argue, to be overcome. The natural outcome of the process of secularization, then, is the achievement—as agents become who they essentially are as opposed to projecting that essence onto a sphere of divine otherness—of a particular conception of human self-actualization.

A major part of the appeal of projection theories is that, in a simple manner, they aim to explain the attraction, the vulnerability, and the fate of religion. They hypothesize about how religion creates allegiance, and they typically do so by invoking a conception of social function: religions function to uphold a certain social order. However, they also purport to demonstrate that it is within the social order itself that the conceptual resources for its overcoming are to be found. Projection theories, while not inherently or necessarily critical, thus invite *immanent criticism*, a form of critique whose aim it is to disclose tensions or even downright contradictions in the object of criticism itself. As is well known, the very notion of immanent critique, at least in its respectable philosophical shape, can be traced to Hegel, who in *The Phenomenology of Spirit* launched his account of successive formations of consciousness whose "essence" or "truth," when considered as criteria or standards of knowledge, tends to generate contradiction. The task of the phenomenologist, Hegel claims, is to observe consciousness as it comes to experience the failure besetting its own attempts to attain an adequate definition of its own essence. Like Hegel's formations of consciousness, suffering from inadequate forms of self-understanding, religious consciousness, in Feuerbach's and Marx's senses, rather than receiving the critical impetus from an external point of view—one with no recognized authority in the eyes of religious consciousness itself—is to be viewed as working out its self-contradictions (or "self-estrangement) on its own terms. Secularization, on this account, is thus a "dialectical" process, a kind of "working through" (Freud).

Feuerbach's and Marx's views about religion are difficult, if not impossible, to appreciate fully unless their extremely ambivalent attitudes toward Hegel's philosophy are adequately taken into account. Often referred to as Left-Hegelians (or, in Germany, *Junghegelianer*), while being deeply influenced by Hegel's system, they quickly became dissatisfied by its idealist commitments, which they argued could be corrected and overcome by invoking various dimensions of human finitude, including "sensuousness" (Feuerbach) and "concrete human existence" (Marx). In their attacks on

Hegel, neither Feuerbach nor Marx concentrates on his actual secularization narrative. Instead, their opposition to Hegel focuses almost exclusively on what they see as his hypostatizing of spirit. Partially in line with the interpretation I attempted to provide in the previous chapter, Hegel, they contend, translates into philosophy religion's traditional claim to possess awareness or knowledge of the absolute. This, however, far from signaling that religious consciousness has been brought to a de jure end in rationalized modernity means that philosophy *has become what religion in their eyes has always been*: a system of purportedly ideal insights into the ultimate nature of things, shorn of any mediation by either sensuous-material or sociohistorical existence. As Marx claims in his 1843 *Critique of Hegel's Philosophy of Right*, rather than marginalizing and decentering religion, Hegel totalizes its sublated philosophical substitute to the point of deriving all historical and social determinations from it. Hegel thereby mystifies social life, viewing it solely from the vantage point of essentialist, hypostatized categories.

In raising this objection, Feuerbach and Marx assume that Hegel, along neo-Platonist and Spinozist lines, views spirit as a metaphysical substance, capable of uniting the ideal and the real, or eternal determinations of thought, on the one hand, and nature and human history on the other. Indeed, on this metaphysical reading, which in current scholarship tends to be backed by evidence showing Hegel's sustained interest in the speculative thought of late medieval figures such as Meister Eckhart and especially Jacob Boehme, spirit is interpreted as a structure that is both self-dividing and self-reconciling. From inert immediacy, in which no determination exists, spirit becomes foreign to itself as it splits. However, as spirit, in a temporal, historical, and teleological movement, seeks to become united with its alienated other, it articulates and attains consciousness of itself. Spirit, Hegel often writes, "finds" itself in its otherness, by which—and from which—it overcomes its own self-alienation.

In much recent scholarship, this neo-Platonist approach has met with considerable criticism. In the writings of Robert Pippin, Terry Pinkard, and others, Hegel's *Geist*, rather than being viewed as a metaphysical structure, is understood as the totality of self-reflective social practices, incorporated in historically existing symbolic structures while also being constitutive, in the sense of providing normative constraints, of that which, for members of the life form in which such self-reflective social practices and self-determinations are viewed as authoritative, may count as real.

While Pippin's and Pinkard's unmistakably Kantian interpretation is often referred to as "deflationary," the inspiration for Feuerbach's critique of high idealism can be traced to Schelling, for whom Hegel's philosophy appears as limited rather than idealist in some absolute manner. Distinguishing in his late writings between negative and positive philosophy, associating Hegel only with the former, Schelling invokes a positive, conceptually "nonmediated" otherness—a pure Being (*Sein*, or, in some passages, *unvordenkliches Sein*) that, according to him, has to be assumed for any conceptual and dialectical thinking to even get started. Dialectics, or negative philosophy, deals with *whatness*—conceptual generality in all its forms. The philosophy of Being, or the *Ungrund* (positive philosophy), on the other hand, deals with *thatness* or, as Duns Scotus's followers called it, *haecceitas*.[2]

In his 1839 essay "Towards a Critique of Hegel's Philosophy," Feuerbach focuses directly on the late Schelling, arguing that his philosophy poses a powerful challenge to Hegel's idealism.[3] While acknowledging the evident strands of idealism in Schelling—in particular the early Schelling, whose work sought both to continue and to revise Fichte's subjective idealism—Feuerbach highlights his late philosophy of nature as being especially important for his own work. In the *Weltalter* and elsewhere, Schelling, Feuerbach claims, offers a perspective from which the so-called identical subject-object, the synthesis of spirit and nature, can legitimately be viewed from the vantage point of nature itself. (Indeed, Schelling himself keeps claiming that the "coming into being" of subject/object identity can be viewed from the vantage point both of the subject and of the object: both points of view are equally legitimate and mutually coherent.) In what Feuerbach sees as a rejoinder to Hegel, spirit is said to develop out of nature, the pure immediacy of unstructured matter, available to human agents in their existence as embodied creatures, capable of sensuous experience and consciousness.

In "Towards a Critique of Hegel's Philosophy" there are no direct arguments in favor of such a view. However, Feuerbach highlights some moments in Hegel when that natural immediacy is simply ignored or even actively suppressed. One is the opening, sense certainty section of *The Phenomenology of Spirit*.[4] In that section Feuerbach argues that one may detect a crucial, and indeed irresolvable, tension between idealist commitments

---

2. F. W. J. Schelling discusses this distinction in *The Grounding of Positive Philosophy: The Berlin Lectures*, trans. B. Matthews (Albany: SUNY Press, 2007).

3. Ludwig Feuerbach, "Towards a Critique of Hegel's Philosophy," in *The Fiery Brook: Selected Writings*, trans. Zawar Hanfi (London: Verso, 2012), 53–96.

4. There are no claims in Feuerbach that Hegel's idealism entails immaterialism. The question is not whether Hegel is able to accept the existence of matter. Rather, Feuerbach's challenge is whether Hegel may be able to acknowledge that nature can be said to exist independent of "the truth" or conceptual determination that the mind ascribes to it.

and the purportedly material world of "pure being" (Hegel). As students of this section know, the epistemic norm of this particular formation of consciousness is *immediacy*. To know the world, the proponent of sense certainty proclaims, must be to know it in its immediacy as what it "simply is."[5] This kind of knowledge, it adds, must be both the *richest* (in terms of content it is limitless, knowing no limitation, whether of fineness of grain or of topography) and the most *veritable*, "for it has not omitted anything from its object, but rather, has its object in its complete entirety before itself."[6] Moreover, in its prohibition on any type of projection, constitution, or conceptualization, it must be *receptive*. Incidentally, while considering this conception of cognition, it is worth noticing how well it seems to lend itself to a Feuerbachian view of the subject/object relation. For Feuerbach, as I will soon explore in more detail, while the ideal cognitive state is "sensuous," the real is material immediacy insofar as it is given to the senses and able to affect them. However, contrary to what Feuerbach recommends, Hegel disposes of this picture, instead focusing his investigation on the conditions for such knowledge of the immediately given. In Hegel's dialectic, consciousness has no other way of expressing an intentional awareness of the given than by using demonstratives and indexicals. Thus the indeterminate "this" of the initial indexical attempt to establish a referential relation quickly transforms into a "now" and a "here," themselves yielding to a multiplicity of "nows" and "heres." The lesson, of course, is that sense certainty cannot do without universals. It needs, in Hegel's language, to be able to negate and mediate; in short, consciousness, in order to relate to being, must do so in terms of particulars, where particulars call for concepts that express the continuity of the particular object in its various adumbrations and spatiotemporal locations. Far from being immediate, the real, *Sein*, is a particular, X, known through, and mediated by, the predicates that can be ascribed to it.

Feuerbach's interpretation of this famous dialectical argument (an argument that has also been construed as a straightforward transcendental argument, asking for the a priori conditions of knowledge[7]) is directed at what he finds is Hegel's attempt to sublate and overcome the very existence of the immediately given.

---

5. Hegel, *Phenomenology of Spirit*, 60.

6. Hegel, *Phenomenology of Spirit*, 60.

7. For what is possibly the most influential account of Hegel's argument as being of a transcendental nature, see Charles Taylor, "The Opening Arguments of the *Phenomenology*," in *Hegel: A Collection of Critical Essays*, ed. Alasdair MacIntyre (New York: Doubleday, 1972), 151–87.

My brother is called John, or, if you like, Adolph, but there are innumerable people besides him who are called by the same name. Does it follow from this that my brother John is not real? Or that Johnness is the truth?[8]

The answers to these questions must obviously be negative. According to Feuerbach, pure being is in Hegel's thought experiment never shown to be "unreal." Rather, it is conceptuality and language in general—the necessity, for reference to be established, that universals are in play—that must be dismissed as "unreal." While Hegel may successfully have shown that agents do depend on universals to establish reference, and that descriptions necessarily enter into the picture as they seek to express their experience of particulars, allowing the sensuously given to be viewed as a determinate particular, he does not overcome the distance or division between concept and reality. The house being referred to as "house" transcends the determinations one is able to associate, contingently or essentially, with one's definition of "house." It is possible to think the concept of the house. Yet it is not possible to conceptualize—and hence think—the material object itself. That object is available only in its sensuous immediacy; and while one may or may not be able to express it, it is nevertheless completely real. Indeed, according to Feuerbach, while thoughts and concepts are human creations, permitting tasks to be done and acts of communication to occur, they can never fully represent the object itself. There will always remain an irresolvable gap between concept and intuition.

In Feuerbach's interpretation, Hegel ends up viewing the immediately given as *unreal*. However, for Hegel it is unreal only in the sense that it cannot play a role in a successful account of what it is that may count as establishing an adequate referential relation—and, as the dialectic progresses, a relationship of genuine knowledge—to an object. Hegel's dialectical method of sublation (*Aufhebung*) never purports to question the *existence* of a suggested object of knowledge; on the contrary, what it does is to reflect on the terms and conditions according to which consciousness may lay claim to being cognitively in touch with the object in the first place. Although, in *The Phenomenology of Spirit*, consciousness proceeds to ever more complex levels of self-determination when it comes to its criteria of objective knowledge, it does not invalidate the object's existence. The sensuously given entity is presented to the senses. However, it can be known only through conceptuality (and universals). What it does leave behind in its dialectical experience is its initial *account* of how the object can be known. "This *dialectical* movement which consciousness practices in its own self (as well as in its knowing

---

8. Feuerbach, "Towards a Critique of Hegel's Philosophy," 77.

and in its object), *insofar as, for consciousness, the new, true object arises* out of this movement, is properly what is called *experience*."[9]

While attributing to Hegel a kind of idealist immaterialism that refuses to grant existence to material objects would be false, the real force of Feuerbach's critique lies elsewhere. With Adorno one might think of it as highlighting the nonidentity of subject and object, or rather concept and object. Hegel's idealism is predicated on the absolute idealist notion that the object-determining concept (*Begriff*), constituted by the self-reflective subject in acts of epistemic self-legislation, reaches "all the way" to the object and determines it without remainder. However, as Feuerbach contends, it must be granted that there is an "otherness" pertaining to this operation. Indeed, even if Hegel rejects (as he does) the idea that any claims to "givenness" or "objecthood" external to the conceptual framework projected by consciousness are able to play an epistemic role, he provides no reason to think that this givenness or objecthood has no genuine existence. This is precisely the point at which Feuerbach's insistence on existence makes sense. On Feuerbach's view, Hegel forces the object into a framework that, while coherent on its own terms, fails to do justice to the otherness of the object. Although Hegel never dismisses the idea of mind-independent, material objects, the conceptual apparatus invoked in order to know them may potentially screen the object from what might be a fuller and more genuine or adequate encounter. The experience of material objects may not function as evidence in objective judgments unless objectivating conditions, accounted for in Hegel's dialectic, are able to provide the requisite kind of conceptualization. However, as Feuerbach agrees, there are other forms of encounter—not necessarily of an objectivating nature, and not necessarily ensuing in judgments—of equal importance. Such encounters, he claims, are of a sensuous nature, permitting forms of interaction irreducible to, and different from, the formation of objective judgment. Moreover, Feuerbach argues, while individuals exist, the universals we in fact do employ, and the content of universal concepts, rather than, as in Hegel, being constituted dialectically, are created through acts of induction whereby common properties are "abstracted."[10] The ontological primacy, in other words, lies with existing individuals, objects of sensuous awareness, encountered by human

---

9. Hegel, *Phenomenology of Spirit*, 57. Hegel, *Phänomenologie des Geistes*, 78: "Diese *dialektische* Bewegung, welche das Bewußtsein an ihm selbst, sowohl an seinem Wissen als an seinem Gegenstande ausübt, *insofern ihm der neue wahre Gegenstand* daraus *entspringt*, ist eigentlich dasjenige, was *Erfahrung* genannt wird."

10. Of course, a skeptic would want to know how induction is possible without some account of objective judgment.

agents in both contemplation and action. As Marx W. Wartofsky puts it, "Towards a Critique of Hegel's Philosophy" is "neither an abandonment of Hegel's dialectical method nor a rejection of the concrete content of Hegel's applied analysis. It is principally a refutation of the absolutizing of the Hegelian categories, and of the general claim to an 'Absolute' philosophy."[11]

The essay ends on the following somewhat ad hoc but also highly Romantic note:

> Philosophy is the science of reality in its truth and totality. However, the all-inclusive and all-encompassing reality is nature (taken in the most universal sense of the word). The deepest secrets are to be found in the simplest natural things, but, pining away for the Beyond, the speculative fantast treads them under his feet. The only source of salvation lies in a return to nature. It is wrong to look upon nature as contradicting ethical freedom. Nature has built not only the mean workshop of the stomach, but also the temple of the brain. It has not only given us a tongue whose *papillae* correspond to intestinal *villi*, but also ears that are enchanted by the harmony of sounds and eyes that only the heavenly and generous being of light ravishes. Nature opposes only fantastic, not rational, freedom.[12]

The Essence of Christianity, first published in 1841, is Feuerbach's attempt to cash out these ambitious, yet metaphorically formulated claims. What does it take to remain committed to an essentially Hegelian vision of philosophy as a "science of the real" while studying mankind's most exalted achievements in light of a concept of nature? How can the "freedom of fantasy" be

---

11. Marx W. Wartofsky, *Feuerbach* (Cambridge: Cambridge University Press, 1977), 137.

12. Feuerbach, "Towards a Critique of Hegel's Philosophy," 94. For the original, see Ludwig Feuerbach, "Zur Kritik der Hegelschen Philosophie," in *Texte zur materialistischen Geschichtsauffassung*, ed. Helmut Reichelt (Frankfurt: Ullstein, 1975), 131: "Die Philosophie ist die Wissenschaft der Wirklichkeit in ihrer Wahrheit und Totalität; aber der Inbegriff der Wirklichkeit ist die *Natur* (Natur im universellsten Sinne des Wortes). Die tiefsten Geheimnisse liegen in den einfachsten natürlichen Dingen, die der nach dem Jenseits schmachtende phantastische Spekulant mit Füßen tritt. Die Rückkehr zur Natur ist allein die Quelle des Hiles. Falsch ist es, die Natur im Widerspruch mit der ethischen Freiheit aufzufassen. Die Natur hat nicht bloß die gemeine Werkstatt des Magens, sie hat auch den Tempel des Gehirns gebaut; sie hat uns nicht nur eine Zunge gegeben mit Papillen, die den Darmzotten entsprechen, sondern auch Ohren, die nur die Harmonie der Töne, und Augen, die nur das himmlische, selbstlose Wesen des Lichtes entzückt. Die Natur sträubt sich nur gegen die phantastische Freiheit, aber der *vernünftigen* Freiheit widerspricht sie nicht."

countered by "rational freedom"? In particular, what is the meaning and fate of religion given the primacy of finitude?

Like Marx, Nietzsche, and Freud, Feuerbach considers religion—at least in its monotheistic, supersensible form—to be *illusory*: while it does have content, its foundational claims do not refer to anything *real*. However, unlike most atheists, Feuerbach presents an account of what it is to hold religious beliefs, what motivates them, and how they may eventually be overcome. He can, as I mentioned, thus be regarded as a philosophical secularization theorist.

Religion, for Feuerbach, is a species of self-alienation. The believer, he claims, is alienated from her own *essence*. At the beginning of *The Essence of Christianity* he introduces the assumptions on which he bases this view. The first step is to draw a distinction between humans and animals. Animals, he argues, while in many cases conscious, lead lives of immediacy. Not seeing themselves (or their "inner," conscious states) as distinct from the environment, they respond unreflectively to the tasks, dangers, and solicitations at hand. While having a "feeling of self" in the sense of knowing themselves as concrete individuals interacting with the world, they do not have a capacity to sustain a conscious, self-reflective relation to universals, capable of carrying a normative significance. Human agents are self-conscious; they relate to themselves in terms of an understanding of what it is that counts as their "species being" (*Gattungswesen*). In every act of cognitive functioning—indeed in all their intentional engagements with objects—they recognize and consider a concept of human essence, of what it is for beings such as they are to actualize their own purpose. In the exercise of reason and will, and in the capacity for love, agents find the species concept of humanity to be articulated in several ways. The purpose of reason is to actualize reason—to reason to the full; the purpose of the will is to actualize willing—to act freely; and the purpose of love is to love—to experience full satisfaction in one's affective relationship with another being.

Feuerbach's notion of consciousness is of Hegelian descent. As we have seen, Hegel views consciousness as relating apperceptively to the world. Transcending the particularity of mere animal sensibility, it has as its object a universal, a norm—that is, an essence, variably referred to by Hegel as "consciousness's own criterion," "being in itself," and "the True." Thus in knowing, willing, or establishing affective relationships, consciousness, for Feuerbach, takes itself to be constrained by the normative content specified by the universal or essence. Moreover, like Hegel, Feuerbach crucially believes that this essence can appear in an alienated form. Indeed, it can be projected beyond consciousness itself, in which it figures as its other, to become a fully foreign "object." This is what happens in the formation of religious belief. The believer invests her understanding of human essence with the highest possible human ideals. Unable to live up to these ideals herself, the believer then imaginatively creates an illusory object capable of manifesting and actualizing those same ideals. Comparing herself with the ideal, or the essence, the empirical individual cannot help finding herself limited. However, in the divine object—in God, and in particular the figure of Christ, who is supposed to unify humanity with the divine—she finds her own essence objectified and actualized.[13] Thus, while the consciousness of God is originally the self-consciousness of the human agent, in God she finds her own aspirations, her own conception of what she would be if fully actualized, hypostatized as fully authoritative and, in a sense, achievable. The predicates remain the same, yet the object changes. Owing to the imagination, which on Feuerbach's account does the job of presenting the foreign object, the feelings with which one comes to be connected to the object are directed from human to purportedly nonhuman objects (however illusory). The key to religious belief is thus *misapplication*. The predicates associated with humanity's species essence are properly conceived yet misapplied. You believe, Feuerbach writes, in love as a divine capacity only because, as a human being, you accept a normative notion of what would count as true love. You believe in wisdom as a divine capacity only because, as a human being, you accept a notion of what it is that would count as genuine human wisdom. The divine object underwrites and, in the human understanding, actualizes such ideals.

> Now God is the nature of man regarded as absolute truth,—the truth of man; but God, or, what is the same thing, religion, is as various as are the conditions under which man conceives this his nature, regards it as the highest being.[14]

13. Avineri interprets Feuerbach as claiming that, rather than human essence, it is "human wants" that are being projected "on the imagined figure of God." If by "want" he means "desire," then this cannot be an adequate interpretation. What Feuerbach has in mind seems much more akin to an aspiration—to be that which is one's true essence, to become fully actualized. See Shlomo Avineri, *The Social and Political Thought of Karl Marx* (Cambridge: Cambridge University Press, 1968, 10–11.

14. Ludwig Feuerbach, *The Essence of Christianity*, trans. George Elliot (Amherst, NY: Prometheus Books, 1989), 19. See Feuerbach, "Das Wesen des Christentums," in *Texte zur materialistischen Geschichtsauffassung*, ed. Helmut Reichelt, 160: "Gott nun ist das Wesen des Menschen, angeschaut als höchste Wahrheit, Gott aber, oder was eins ist, die Religion, so verschieden wie verschieden die *Bestimmtheit* ist, in welcher der Mensch dieses sein Leben erfaßt, als höchstes Wesen angeschaut."

Feuerbach's account of religious belief is strikingly similar to Hegel's conception of the "unhappy consciousness" in *The Phenomenology of Spirit*. Like Feuerbach, Hegel outlines a formation of consciousness for whom only a "God's eye point of view," a viewpoint external to consciousness and unattainable by it, would suffice to authorize as true and as achievable the vision consciousness has of its own potential. It is also reminiscent of Hegel's more general view of religion in *The Phenomenology of Spirit*—that it is spirit presented to man as an objective universal, an object other than, and radically external to, man considered as a finite being. Although, as we saw earlier, philosophy is able to think and anticipate spirit's return to its finite other (the *kenosis* or exhaustion of spirit in self-conscious, self-reflective agents and their institutions), theology remains stuck with the *representation* (*Vorstellung*) of the spiritual object as foreign and other. Finally, Feuerbach follows Hegel in holding that the alienated essence can be reappropriated. In successful acts of critique and demystification, agents may come to realize that what they had projected into the beyond is in fact their own product, an expression of who they in truth are and therefore their own essence, calling for the epistemically self-assured actualization of its implied normative demands. In both Hegel and Feuerbach, the figure of Christ emerges as a crucial symbol in this regard. Christ, precisely, is the unity of man and God, the finite and the infinite. In Christ, God has become finite while the finite agent has become infinite. The death of Christ is tantamount to God's negation as a transcendent, alien power.

However, while Feuerbach follows Hegel closely in all these regards, he aims to "detranscendentalize" the dialectic of self-differentiation, self-estrangement, and self-appropriation that informs both thinkers' views. On Hegel's idealist account, what is at stake is the absolute Idea, unfolding itself and following a priori, dialectical laws, explored in the *Science of Logic*, of the absolute Idea's diastolic and systolic movement. By contrast, on Feuerbach's account what is at stake is not the Idea but, rather, the concrete human being as an individual and as a species being. As agents reappropriate their species being, rather than seeing the outlines of a world necessarily governed by the demands of reason, they begin singling out capacities that they as finite beings, and in a particular historical formation, have not yet actualized. As opposed to Hegel's idealism, in which the ideal is always supreme, Feuerbach's view is anthropological, aiming to liberate sensuous, finite agents from their self-alienation, thereby paving the way for the realization of an authentic, genuine humanity in every individual.

Considered as a philosophical theorist of secularization, Feuerbach aims to outline and explain both the attraction of religion, the conditions under which it remains attractive, and the process in which it may come to weaken its hold on people's minds and eventually disappear. Religion is mankind's alienated vision of its own objective potential. It is attractive in that human beings, while feeling the distance between themselves and the objective and realizable ideal, seek to close the constructed gap between finite existence and otherworldly promise. It is overcome as agents come to realize that the vision is their own, of themselves, and that as historical beings they may authoritatively aspire to actualize their own potential.

Of course, the idea of God as being man's creation and as embodying man's conception of his own humanity, including his own wishes and ideals, is far from new. In thinkers such as Epicurus, Xenophanes, and Lucretius, it had been clearly articulated, and the demythologizing critique of religious personification had found a number of early modern proponents, including Descartes, Spinoza, and Leibniz. However, unlike many of the leading figures in the tradition, Feuerbach refuses to employ the condescending language of illusion and delusion directly. Drawing especially on Hegel, Feuerbach constructs his account of religion within a complex and ambitious account of human consciousness and its fundamentally intentional nature. Religion, for Feuerbach, is a species of self-misunderstanding, arising not from a theoretical stance—the stance that classical demythologizing accounts would attack—but from human activity: the activity of comporting oneself emotionally, affectively, willingly, or lovingly toward an intentional object.

While his indebtedness to Hegel is explicit, Feuerbach's insistence on sensibility or sensuousness (*Sinnlickheit*) as the primary mode of conscious existence remains at odds with Hegel and situates him more closely to the tradition of British and French seventeenth- and eighteenth-century sensationalism. The emphasis, in particular, on the need for a scientific study of human nature and a reflective elaboration of human need and relations of dependence transforms what structurally was an idealist account into an anthropology of human finitude. Far from simply rejecting religion by referring to its alleged cognitive shortcomings, Feuerbach reveals the limitations of religion from within the framework of speculative idealism. Rather than religion per se, for which Feuerbach has a great deal of sympathy, it seems that the greater enemy of successful modernization is excessive idealism. Even in its alienated form, religion anticipates a more humane and satisfying form of life—the "rational freedom," as he calls it in "Towards a Critique of Hegel's Philosophy," of humans recognizing their real needs as natural creatures as opposed to the "freedom of fantasy" found in the idealist system.

Feuerbach's insistence on conducting his critique of religion within the context of Hegelian speculative idealism and on using his detranscendentalizing of Hegel as a platform for outlining the fate of religion in modernity, while no doubt productive and powerful, comes at a significant price. As the critique of the "left-Hegelian" Feuerbach from "the left" (e.g., by Stirner, Marx, and Engels) quickly started to reveal, his language of consciousness, essence, and species-being remains too much in thrall to the Hegel he seeks to leave behind to constitute a fully successful dismantling of the latter's idealism.

Feuerbach's analysis of consciousness in *The Essence of Christianity* is plagued by a number of shortcomings. He does not offer any compelling reasons for believing that consciousness finds itself relating not only to an essentialist but also to a perfectionist conception of human existence in each act of intentional comportment. It is all very well to hold, as Hegel does, that consciousness exists in relation to a standing conception of its own capacities that normatively constitutes a criterion of successful cognitive, appetitive, and emotional engagement. Yet do individuals, in their thinking and acting, really entertain an implicit vision of their own *perfection*—a vision that can then be projected onto an imaginary other? The argument, after all, about the constitution of religious faith works only based on this assumption. If that claim is called into question, then his account of God remains indefensible. Taking this thought further, it is as though Feuerbach assumes that the human psyche is structured narcissistically. (How else might one account for all his assertions about self-love? "Consciousness is self-verification, self-affirmation, self-love, joy in one's own perfection."[15]) In his writings on narcissism, in particular his metapsychological paper "On Narcissism," Freud argued that the disposition toward "object-love" arises as the result of the displacement of libido from the self toward an external object, and Feuerbach's notion of imaginative projection of a substitute object, attracting human interest and adoration, may seem strikingly similar to Freud's ideas concerning the psychosexual development from aggressive primary narcissism to the more "humble" love of external objects.[16] Yet where Freud provides a proper account, grounded in his metapsychology, Feuerbach resorts to mere phenomenology, doing no more than simply describing, in dogmatic terms, what he takes to be the unavoidable self-centeredness and self-affirmation of consciousness.

Another problem with Feuerbach's position relates to the way it posits human consciousness as a foundation or as something "absolute."

---

15. Feuerbach, *Essence of Christianity*, 6.

16. Sigmund Freud, "On Narcissism," in *On Metapsychology*, trans. James Strachey (London: Penguin, 1984), 80–1: "The sexual instincts are at the outset attached to the satisfaction of the ego-instincts; only later do they become independent of these."

Consciousness relates, as we have seen, to generic conceptions of "humanity" and the like. However, Feuerbach does not inform the reader how norms of this kind can be viewed as *social* achievements. Unlike in Hegel, the generic conceptions, making up what amounts to a constitutive view of the self (in which the self takes itself to exist in relation to normative expectations of what counts as various intellectual achievements and to be constrained by those), are never shown to be elements of collectively achieved mindfulness. Thus it is never made clear what it is that vouches for the authority of these conceptions. The projection onto a divine figure is surely invested with a great deal of authority. However, since the act of projection is that of an individual, and since that individual is taken to be radically nontransparent to itself and its own commitments, it remains unclear what it would mean to claim that it may command any objective or intersubjectively binding authority. As a function merely of individual construction, the normative constraint becomes arbitrary, a mere "This is what counts as X because I say so!"

Finally, as Marx argues in his "Theses on Feuerbach," the notion of essence itself lacks historical specificity and determinacy.[17] While Feuerbach postulates a human essence, it comes across as strangely abstract. In typical cases of philosophical analysis, attribution of essential properties calls for inquiries into apodictic necessity: a property, for example, may be essential to either the existence or the identity of an object if and only if it must be present for the object to exist or be of a particular nature. Feuerbach's notion of essence seems to entail that a set of properties must have been actualized for anyone to *fully count* as a human being. It is supposed to function normatively. However, the account raises a number of questions. Why is it that, for the materialist Feuerbach, anything—an object, an event, an agent—has an essence in the first place, and what does "having an essence or species-being" really mean? Humans love, for example, and employ reason, and from such generic anthropological facts Feuerbach deduces that love and reasoning are of the essence of human life and existence. Yet how people love and reason seems to depend on social context. Can the anthropologist in search for patterns and regularities do more than simply interpret those contexts and employ empirical generalization in standard scientific manner? Feuerbach might reply that since his notion of essence is not necessarily actualized, it would be pointless to look for it empirically.

---

17. Karl Marx, *Early Political Writings*, trans. Joseph O'Malley (Cambridge: Cambridge University Press, 2006), 117: "Feuerbach resolves the essence of religion into the essence of man. But the essence of man is not an abstraction inhering in isolated individuals. Rather, in its actuality, it is the ensemble of social relations."

Indeed, only in cases of complete self-actualization can it be said that a human being *essentially* exists, or has a nature, in accordance with his or her relevant essence. That his epistemology lacks grounding seems evident, however, when considering the foundational role he ascribes to the concept of essence: "That is true which agrees with the nature of the species, that is false which contradicts it."[18] The concept of essence, in other words, since it grounds truth yet is not itself (except on pains of a vicious circle) subject to justification, does not lend itself to rational grounding. Rather, it *is* "the ground." The question, therefore, is whether his view represents much of an improvement on the religious consciousness it aspires to correct. It would hardly be far-fetched to think that Feuerbach replaces a religion of God and the supersensible with a religion of man.[19]

It is in this particular sense that Feuerbach may be said not only to *criticize* religion and identify the self-reflective capacities that would account for secularization (in the restricted sense of overcoming ontotheology), but to *rescue* the elements of religious consciousness that cohere with an exclusive humanism centered on sensuousness and human finitude. Like so many of the other moves in Feuerbach, the speculative structure of this rescuing mission is profoundly Hegelian, inspired by the self-reflective dialectic of consciousness in *The Phenomenology of Spirit*. While religious consciousness takes its objects to be *divine*, the procedure in *The Essence of Christianity* is, as we have already seen, quite simply to demonstrate that consciousness of an object (in this case God) really is *self*-consciousness. The content of religion can, in an anthropological context, be rescued from false hypostatizing simply by attending to religious consciousness as a self-reflexive structure: the "God" it intends is in reality consciousness itself, or feeling itself (insofar as faith was emotionally mediated), and the predicates used to individuate the object (e.g., "perfect" or "infinite" or "pure") characterize nothing but what consciousness, or feeling, actually takes itself to be. As Wartofsky puts it, Feuerbach "aims to bring religion to self-consciousness . . . and, in effect, then, to arrive at *self-conscious self-consciousness*."[20] Immanent critique, in other words, is supposed to be the tool for guiding humanity's search for its own self-actualization; thus, what is rescued in religion is precisely its hidden, unacknowledged preoccupation with ideals that are crucially human,

---

18. Feuerbach, *Essence of Christianity*, 158.

19. As Monod points out, this may also be why Feuerbach cannot fully be classified as a theorist of secularization. If secularization involves, as he puts it, "the liquidation" of the Christian legacy, then Feuerbach's substitution of God for man does not really qualify. See Monod, *La querelle de la sécularisation de Hegel à Blumenberg*, 69.

20. Wartofsky, *Feuerbach*, 275.

able, since they reflect human essence, to stake out emancipatory and self-actualizing courses of action that may allow both individuals and communities to flourish. "Our relation to religion," Feuerbach writes, "is therefore not a merely negative, but a critical one; we only separate the true from the false;—though we grant that the truth thus separated from falsehood is a new truth, essentially different from the old."[21] While the "new" truth can be viewed as essentially different from the unreflective belief it has dialectically superseded, philosophically speaking it is just the "old truth" in its self-conscious, transparent form.

Feuerbach's reading of the Christian Passion reveals how the transformation from "old" to "new" truth, rather than involving a change of content, is supposed to involve a dialectical reversal from unconscious to conscious self-recognition. The "old" truth of what Feuerbach calls "the mystery of the suffering God" is that Christ's suffering for man is an expression of God's love for man. God, the Gospels say, loves humankind so highly that He is willing to let his son suffer and die for its redemption. God's love, in other words, proves itself through suffering, being willing to give up everything for others. In Feuerbach's dialectical reading (or what he calls its "proper translation") of the Passion, the fable it tells is understood as an unconscious form of self-recognition. Rather than a supposed truth about some metaphysical entity, what the fable *really* expresses is something deeply human, namely that love proves itself through suffering—and especially the suffering of the innocent. Christ emblematizes, and elevates into an ideal, the fundamental human propensity to venerate unselfish love and to accept the suffering that potentially comes with such love. Although, as Marx complains, he never manages to justify his essentialism, Feuerbach's method thus reveals an ideal that, on his view, can serve to inform an emancipatory humanism.

Yet to what extent does Feuerbach break with Christianity? In his key writings on religion, it may seem as though he embraces atheism, and that doing so is supposed to bring down the whole religious edifice. However, Feuerbach rescues religion for an age that can no longer accept the old metaphysical beliefs. Rather than the content of religion, he criticizes only the displacements into another world that, in its otherness and alienated form, weakens and confuses humanity in its strivings for self-actualization. In fact, since the attributions with which theology has approached the heavenly God are left unchanged, there is a sense in which Feuerbach remains a Christian thinker, though without its erstwhile hypostatizing. As Ernst Bloch puts it, "the whole apparatus of theology remains intact, it has just

---

21. Feuerbach, *Essence of Christianity*, 270.

moved from its heavenly location to a certain abstract region, with reified virtues of the 'natural basis.'"[22] Feuerbach, to be sure, would not see those virtues as "reified." On his account, they spring directly from the purported essence of humanity. However, once one starts to question the essentialism and, as Marx does, begins looking for ethical ideals within specific constellations of power and socioeconomic division, associating them with ideology and hence with something partial and perhaps even illusory, the Feuerbachian project looks increasingly abstract and unpromising. A quasi-religious ethics devoid of the authorizing capacity of a transcendent God seems at best in need of some alternative source of legitimation. Yet Feuerbach never offers such an account. He addresses the problem of religion from an anthropological viewpoint, attempting both to criticize and to rescue its promise. However, the thinking of finitude that lies at the base of his whole project remains incomplete and too wedded to Hegel's idealist and dialectical view of consciousness to outline the kind of overcoming of religion, and hence of alienation, to which he thinks humanity should aspire.

Finitude and Materialism in Marx

The early Marx shares a number of intellectual concerns with Feuerbach and for a while, in the early 1840s, considered himself completely won over to the position expounded in *The Essence of Christianity*. Like Feuerbach, Marx attempts to replace what he sees as the excessive idealism of Hegel's system with a version of materialism tailored to the articulation of intuitions about human finitude and of a progressive social agenda critically disclosing concrete modes of oppression and injustice. Marx also follows Feuerbach in approaching religion as an illusion generated in various processes of self-alienation. Both are committed to a conception of atheistic humanism in which religion not only is expressive of man's intransparency to himself but manifests commitments—in particular to the actual existence of God—that must be overcome for genuine social progress toward the establishment of a nonalienated society to occur. While subject to philosophical critique, and responsive to it, they think of secularization as ultimately a social process, a task faced by any society in search of a viable determination of itself as modern. That said, Marx's account of religion differs substantially from Feuerbach's, especially with regard to the questions of essence and species being, in response to which Marx calls for a completely different social theory able

---

22. Ernst Bloch, *The Principle of Hope*, vol. 1, trans. Neville Plaice, Stephen Plaice, and Paul Knight (Cambridge, MA: MIT Press, 1986), 267.

to address the hypostatizing of the divine from the standpoint not primarily of contemplation but of human activity or praxis in a concrete societal context. Marx is also considerably more interested in identifying the social conditions that, in his view, motivate agents to engage in religious practice. "Religion," he famously writes in "A Contribution to the Critique of Hegel's Philosophy of Right," is "the sigh of the oppressed creature, the heart of a heartless world and the soul of soulless conditions. It is the *opium* of the people."[23] Both "an *expression* of and a *protest* against wretchedness,"[24] it is—unlike Feuerbach's dialectic of self-alienation, being primarily a cognitive mistake—*ideological*.

The choice of "opium" as the metaphor for religion reverberates with some of Marx's deepest concerns as a social critic. Like religion, opium produces euphoria. However, in its common use, it is taken as a solace or relief from various forms of distress. People consume it in order to escape from a condition they find unbearable. Finally, opium, especially when used regularly, is destructive, incapacitating the individual so that the problems and ills that precipitated taking the drug are not really addressed. Opium, in other words, not only screens reality and its challenges, but it also makes it impossible to face up to them. Its "artificial paradises" (Baudelaire), while expressive of a yearning for happiness, do little more than sustain status quo. Religion, then, is a social construct whose function is to cast a consoling glow over an otherwise miserable and unjust social world. It is an inverted world consciousness, a phantasmagoric realization of human being devoid of true actuality—both an expression of and an attempt to resist wretchedness. Thus,

> The abolition of religion as the *illusory* happiness of the people is a demand for their *true* happiness. The call to abandon illusions about their conditions is the *call to abandon a condition that requires illusions*. Thus, the critique of religion is the *critique* in *embryo of the vale of tears* of which religion is the *halo*.[25]

Marx's engagement with religion found its initial expression in his doctoral dissertation on the ancient Greek atomist Democritus, who, like Epicurus, with whom he is being compared, argued that for men to be free of fear, they must adopt a true, yet also disenchanted, view of the universe

---

23. Karl Marx, "A Contribution to the Critique of Hegel's Philosophy of Right: Introduction," in *Marx: Early Political Writings*, 57.

24. Marx, "Contribution to the Critique of Hegel's Philosophy of Right," 57.

25. Marx, "Contribution to the Critique of Hegel's Philosophy of Right, 57.

as composed exclusively of atoms and the void.[26] While not yet conceived of as a universe that lends itself to human efforts at obtaining control and domination—this would be Bacon's view—it rules out the possibility of evil intentions in nature: without inherent purpose, life *is* what it appears to be and is determined by natural parameters of life itself. The emancipatory potential of this view depends exclusively on the enlightenment project of laying bare cognitive mistakes. While a *critical* approach, its horizon is restricted to *criticism*, the reasoned attempt to substitute a false worldview for one that not only is true but, as true, is better able to satisfy genuine human needs and interests.

Written in a period of German philosophy still in thrall to the great idealist systems of Hegel and Schelling, the interest in Democritus testifies to a predilection for materialism. While the ancient materialism of Democritus shows up few points of convergence with Marx's later dialectical materialism, it is aggressively at odds with theological views emphasizing the presence of divine will in the world. Unlike the typical Greek outlook of the time, divine entities and agents can have no standing in the world; on the contrary, whatever existence they might have must be *beyond being*, or at least beyond known being. The gods have left us, Epicurus claims. They exist in another dimension altogether, uninterested in the fate of mere men.[27] Just as important, classical materialism locates the soul in a physical reality on which it is dependent. While the atoms that supposedly make up the soul are of a special kind (being more "fluid," etc.), there is no deep metaphysical discontinuity between them and other types of atoms. For Democritus in particular, the world is fundamentally *one*, or rather homogeneous, a system of atoms and the void invoking the existence of a plenum governed by uniform laws of movement, attraction, and so forth. That said, ancient cosmological materialism of the kind found in both Democritus and Epicurus has as its ultimate human goal the formation of *ataraxia* (sometimes translated as "equanimity," an untroubled and, as Sextus Empiricus would later put it, "tranquil condition of the soul"). Knowledge of the necessity of all events, and of the timeless laws regulating all (causal or otherwise) interaction between entities, is supposed to help reconcile the thinker with his fate.

---

26. The dissertation, titled "The Difference between the Natural Philosophies of Democritus and Epicurus," was submitted to the University of Jena in 1841. The university awarded the degree.

27. As George K. Strodach puts it in the introduction to his translated volume Epicurus, *The Art of Happiness* (New York: Penguin, 2012), 40, "Epicurus has transported [the gods] to remote interstellar space, where they become beautiful symbols of calm and repose, absorbed in contemplating their own unalloyed perfection and unable to receive human worship or listen to human supplications."

While an enlightened understanding of human existence may call for development and reform, for Democritus the ultimate framework for conceiving of one's relationship to the world is one of acceptance. While the universe is indifferent to men's strivings, a respect for, and understanding of, its modus operandi can lead to joy and liberation—hence the hedonism with which Epicurus, in particular, is associated.

In his extensive comparison between Democritus and Epicurus, Marx finds one decisive difference between the two. Whereas Democritus construes his atomism to preclude any cosmological exception to the principle of strict determinism, Epicurus argues for the existence of a random atomic motion (referred to by his later Roman supporter Lucretius, in *De rerum natura*, as a "swerve") capable, he claims, of accounting for human freedom.[28] Since human action is not entirely governed by deterministic laws, such that everything that will ever occur is determined at the beginning of the universe, it makes sense, Cicero reports about Epicurus's teaching, to deliberate about whether it can be made true that "Milo will wrestle tomorrow." In a completely deterministic universe, in which "Milo will wrestle tomorrow" has been true from eternity, any such deliberation would be absurd.

In a study of the dissertation, Leszek Kolakowski hypothesizes that the contrast between Democritus's strict determinism and Epicurus's notion of freedom may have influenced the later Marx's humanism.[29] On a uniformly deterministic view of the universe such as that of Democritus, there is room neither for emancipatory action nor for the more specifically Marxian notion of dialectical self-appropriation through the overcoming of estranged labor familiar from the *Paris Manuscripts*. Although formulated in metaphorical terms and without much argument, Epicurus's view would be compatible with, and perhaps underwrite, Marx's interest in liberation and its conditions. It would also provide a necessary (though hardly sufficient) condition for leading the kind of life free of metaphysically motivated fear that Epicurus proposes as an ideal for human beings. As in the later Marx, notions of materialism, humanism, critique, and emancipation would interrelate to inspire action. To be sure, nothing in Epicurus suggests anything like a social and historical account of religious faith. Nor does he propose, as Marx later does, that the concept of labor should be viewed as the key to understanding human essence and its potential for full self-actualization.

---

28. For an imaginative take on Lucretius's notion of the swerve and its implications for modernity, see Stephen Greenblatt, *The Swerve: How the World Became Modern* (New York: W. W. Norton, 2012).

29. Leszek Kolakowski, *Main Currents of Marxism*, trans. P. S. Falla (New York: W. W. Norton, 2005), 83–88.

The dissertation sets the stage for Marx's critical engagement with alienation and religion; it hardly informs us of his subsequent view.

However, in the early 1840s, having been exposed to Feuerbach's theory of religion, Marx begins to develop an account that situates religious yearnings, beliefs, and imagery in a social space structured by ideology and ridden with social tensions—a space emerging from the, in his view, decisive contradiction between labor and capital. Responding directly to Feuerbach in the fourth thesis of the 1845 "On Feuerbach," he writes the following:

> Feuerbach's point of departure is the fact of religious self-estrangement, the duplication of the world into a religious and a secular world. His work consists in dissolving the religious world into its secular basis. But the fact that the secular basis becomes detached from itself and established as an independent realm in the clouds can be explained only by diremption and self-contradiction in the secular basis. This basis, therefore, must be understood in itself, in its self-contradiction, and be revolutionised in practice. Thus, for instance, once it is discovered that the earthly family is the secret of the Holy Family, it is the former that must then be nullified both in theory and in practice.[30]

"Feuerbach," he adds in the next entry, "not satisfied with *abstract* thinking, wants perception; but he does not comprehend the perceptible as *practical*, human-sensible activity."[31]

Marx's critique is well known. Feuerbach's notion of essence unwittingly reintroduces the abstraction requirement that he himself had targeted in Hegel. To escape Hegel's idealism and attain a genuinely materialistic standpoint from which to address the vexing question about the fate of religion, one must not only juxtapose reason to sensuousness by defining human existence in material terms but must situate individuals in a social and historical space. Moreover, this social and historical space must be interpreted in terms of collective activity or praxis. Feuerbach, Marx contends, "does not see that 'religious disposition' is itself a social product and that the abstract individual he analyses belongs to a specific form of society."[32] As a result, Feuerbach remains a prisoner of the "bourgeois" position from which he seeks to extricate himself. Whereas Marx invokes the historical totality of human self-production, considering social relations to be central to his *explanans*, Feuerbach begins and ends his investigation with the individual

---

30. Marx, *Early Political Writings*, 117.
31. Marx, *Early Political Writings*, 117.
32. Marx, *Early Political Writings*, 118.

and arrives, as we have seen, at a mystified, indeterminate notion of essence. Ultimately, Marx submits in the sixth thesis, Feuerbach is obliged "to abstract from the process of history . . . , and to assume an individual who is only abstractly—*in isolation*—human."[33] By viewing the real—even in materialist terms—objectively, as a set of finished data, Feuerbach does not manage to go beyond the horizon of abstract thinking. As Marx puts it in *The German Ideology*, Feuerbach "posits '*the* Man' instead of 'real, historical man.'"[34] Although he manages to escape the abstractions produced by idealist thinking, his materialism restricts itself to a view of the real in terms of what it "naturally" or "essentially" is for an item to be. However, while natural items may in some cases be approached along such lines, human beings are *active*. Not only do they change both ontogenetically and phylogenetically, but they initiate change and rationally see it through in the light of heteronomously or autonomously set goals. According to Marx, for the complete overcoming of abstract thought to be possible, both materialism and an understanding of history in which man is considered to be active and self-producing will be required. Man is a thoroughly temporal being, existing in history as a being mediated by history itself.[35] However, man is also a *creator* of history—its true yet unacknowledged subject.

Whether implicitly or explicitly, both Feuerbach and Marx conceive of human existence in terms of a conception of finitude. As a theorist of religion (and, related to that, as a critic of absolute idealism), Feuerbach sees the main marker of finitude as materialism—a stance that, for him, includes a commitment to a naturalistic ontology, a detranscendentalized understanding of reason and *Geist*, and to viewing sensuous nature as the primary source of our cognitive, practical, and emotional orientation. Marx's understanding, however, involves *two* main markers of finitude: the ontological primacy of material reality (entailing both anti-idealism and an understanding of human orientation as structured around needs and need-interpretation rather than pure reasoning) *and* the fact that humans exist in a historically constituted social space characterized not by cooperation but by class division under conditions of scarcity. Religion misrepresents

33. Marx, *Early Political Writings*, 118.

34. Marx, *Early Political Writings*, 142. See also Marx, *Early Political Writings*, 145: "Insofar as Feuerbach is a materialist, history plays no role with him, and insofar as he considers history, he is no materialist. With him materialism and history are mutually exclusive, which is already obvious from what has been said."

35. For my own thoughts regarding the temporal implications of modern man's historical existence, see Espen Hammer, *Philosophy and Temporality from Kant to Critical Theory* (Cambridge: Cambridge University Press, 2011).

human life not only because it contraposes the real secular/material world to the illusory divine world, but because it ties human self-interpretation to an illusory point of view detached from the vicissitudes and constraints of sociohistorical existence. By promising salvation, the hope of a final or absolute justice, capable of redeeming all earthly misery, casts a conciliatory glow over conditions that, if viewed exclusively on their own terms, should not be accepted. While motivated by the hope of happiness, by precluding the formation of genuine social consciousness, it is essentially affirmative. It follows that, for Marx, secularization involves more than overcoming self-alienation as consciousness retrieves its hypostatized other. Genuine secularization ultimately depends on social transformation. A society in which there is no alienation or injustice would neither need nor produce ideology. It would view itself in terms of its actually existing conditions and accept atheism. What Marx calls "communism" is thus a system of socialized labor and material equality in which projections of a happy, just, and fulfilled state of humankind into the beyond would serve no social function and for this reason would disappear.[36]

This, at least, is the bare outline of Marx's view. Yet how does he justify such a perspective on secularization? Can the achievement of finitude become an authoritative form of collective self-interpretation? There are many texts one might consult. Remarks on religion are scattered across all of Marx's work from the early writings in the 1840s to the 1860s *Capital* and beyond. However, the most interesting and valuable ones are to be found in the early phase, which includes the *Critique of Hegel's Philosophy of Right*, *On the Jewish Question*, *On Feuerbach*, and *The German Ideology*.

An early yet forceful sketch of something like a theory of the mystifications that prevent agents from realizing their true conditions and hence achieving a sense of their own finitude appears in the 1843 critique of Hegel's *Elements of the Philosophy of Right*. In line with other left-Hegelian thinkers, Marx claims that Hegel *mystifies* the nature and potential of modern social life. His deduction of the rational state, being derived from the purportedly rational movement of his dialectical logic (the "Idea") without proper grounding in concrete social analysis and historical understanding, is, Marx argues, "abstract." By interpreting not only the ideal but also the existing state of reformist Prussia in line with his dialectic, and hence in an a priori

---

36. Of course, religious belief continued to exist in twentieth-century communist states such as the Soviet Union and China. This could mean that Marx's prediction is false (and that his premises are false). Yet it could also mean that these states never managed to attain the level of development that Marx associated with the idea of communism.

fashion, Hegel inadvertently condones and indeed glorifies contemporary political arrangements. In Marx's formulation, "it makes a deep mystical impression to see a particular empirical existent posited by the Idea, and thus to encounter at all levels an incarnation of God."[37] The Hegelian process of spirit's self-objectification and concurrent self-appropriation, Marx argues, is ultimately to be interpreted as "*God, absolute spirit,* the *self-knowing and self-manifesting Idea.* Actual man and actual nature become mere predicates, symbols of this hidden, unreal man and this unreal nature."[38]

On Marx's account, which aspires to be materialist, the actually existing state is a thoroughly historical product, reflecting the interests of the bourgeoisie; and civil society, rather than being ordered along Hegelian lines, is organized around the opposition between capital and labor, creating vast and inexorable asymmetries of wealth, power, and freedom. Religion—not just in liberal-bourgeois, capitalist society, but in all historical conditions, including ancient and feudal ones—belongs, together with law, art, and culture in its most general sense, at the level of the superstructure, which for Marx is also the level of ideology. The superstructure contrasts with that of the "base," which, according to Marx, it reflects. While the base is made up of the conglomerate of relations of production (including class as defined by economic parameters) and means of production (including technical means of production and their organization), the ideological superstructure is generated by the base as well as providing a justification for its very existence and modes of social organization.

While common at the time and still accepted by some Hegel scholars, Marx's ascription to Hegel of a neo-Platonic account of dialectical spirit as the driving force (and animating, generative "producer") of empirical history is highly questionable. A closer look reveals that, in the "Preface" to his *Elements of the Philosophy of Right,* Hegel makes it clear that he wants to avoid putting forward what he sees as an "empty ideal" of the kind found in Plato's *Republic.* Plato's ideal state, he maintains, lacks proper dialectical grounding. Hegel, however, is equally uninterested in offering an empirical account of the kind found in the historical school of Friedrich Karl von Savigny and Gustav Ritter von Hugo. Rather, his ambition—as expressed in the famous *Doppeltsatz* "What is rational is actual; and what is actual is rational"—is to show what *Wirklichkeit* (actuality) requires, where *Wirklichkeit* is the full development of a potential according to its corresponding idea of rationality.[39] *Wirklichkeit,* Hegel is at pains to express in later expositions

---

37. Marx, *Early Political Writings,* 22.
38. Marx, *Early Political Writings,* 93.
39. Hegel, *Elements of the Philosophy of Right,* 20.

of the *Doppeltsatz*, should not be confused with *Existenz* or *Dasein*, the existence of some entity.[40] Thus the state whose essential features he develops may very well be *wirklich* without being real in the sense of existing: whatever it is, it should not be confused with Prussia, even as it was to have become under the reform administrations of Chancellor Karl Freiherr von Stein and Hardenberg, had they been successful.

While Hegel cannot be said to have conflated the ideal state of *Elements of the Philosophy of Right* with the empirical state of Hegel's Prussia, it remains that he derives the categories of his political theory from the a priori movements of his dialectics. From immediacy to mediacy and ultimately the complete articulation of the Idea qua absolute and self-mediated, Hegel's *Science of Logic* sets forth the idealistic yet also ontological conditions of all his other material accounts or *Realphilosophien*. According to Marx, this elevation of the dialectical logic to a universally foundational status for the system as a whole means that Hegel is prevented from approaching society theoretically except through categories that are abstract, grounded in the dialectical account of the absolute Idea, and therefore unable to engage with the actual finitude of empirically existing agents in a historically real political society. Thus Hegel, Marx writes,

---

40. G. W. F. Hegel, *Hegel's Logic*, trans. William Wallace (Oxford: Oxford University Press, 1975), § 6: "But if I have spoken of *actuality*, then it is self-evident that you are to think of the sense in which I use this expression, since I have treated of actuality in a worked-out *Logic*, distinguishing it precisely not only from the contingent, which has existence, but also from [two senses of] existence (*Existenz, Dasein*) and other determinations. . . . When [the understanding] with its 'ought' turns to trivial, external and transitory objects, institutions, conditions, etc., which perhaps may have a great relative actuality for a certain time and in a certain sphere, it may be right and in such cases it may find much which does not correspond to universally correct determinations. For who is not clever enough to see much in his environment which is not in fact as it ought to be? But this cleverness is wrong to imagine that such objects and their 'ought' have any place within the interests of the philosophical science. For science has to do only with the Idea, which is not so impotent that it only ought to be without actually being; hence philosophy has to do with an actuality of which those objects, institutions, conditions, etc. are only the superficial exterior." See also Robert Pippin, *Interanimations: Receiving Modern German Philosophy* (Chicago: University of Chicago Press, 2015), 130–31: "It is extremely important that Hegel never says that it is the content of metaphysics, some doctrine of substance, that requires an unusual or new logic for its expression, but that logic *itself*, a theory of thinking properly understood, *is* metaphysics. And it is absurd to attribute to him the position that this is so because reality is actually composed of thoughts, or divinely mental entities. He also says several times that the *Logic* does not concern thought about any empirical object but concerns what he calls the 'actuality' of objects, not their existence or any matter of fact about them."

develops merely a *state formalism*. For him, the actual *material* principle is the *Idea*, the abstract thought-*form* of the state as a subject, the absolute Idea which has in it no passive or *material* moment. In contrast to the abstraction of this Idea the determinations of the actual, empirical state formalism appear as the *content*; and hence the *actual* content (in this case actual man, actual society etc.) appears as a formless inorganic matter.[41]

At this point the challenges Marx faces in developing his own account are considerable. He sees the task of philosophy as breaking through mystification, abstraction, and ideology. He aspires to understand the actual or real world of actual people. Central to such an undertaking is Marx's *materialism*, which branches out in a number of directions.

There is, as I already mentioned, the classical—"Democritean" and "Epicurean"—materialist side of Marx, emphasizing the ontological primacy of matter over mind or spirit. According to this view, man is a natural being, and ideas of mind or spirit as existing sui generis, emerge as mystifications. With ideas of the primordiality of nature there follow ideas of radical finitude, including Marx's highlighting of man's sensuous nature, his fundamental and constitutive embodiment, itself generating ideas of man's proneness to suffer, the vulnerability and brevity of individual lives, as well as neo-Epicurean ideas of happiness. Marx's materialism also entails ideas of man's concrete dependence on the nature and quality of his immediate material surroundings. The need for food, water, air, health, and such, makes a mockery of the exalted visions of absolute or self-sufficient human subjectivity familiar from German idealism.

Just as important, Marx's materialism demands that humans are considered as standing in concrete relation to fellow human beings in a society organized along certain lines. In a class-ridden society, these relations, while appearing formal, based on freely endorsed, contractually regulated exchange between persons endowed with particular roles (to which are associated duties and entitlements), are in the Marxian scheme relationships of domination and inequality, including asymmetrical distributions of property and power as well as material and symbolic resources. Indeed, freedom, on this materialist view, effectively equals power: the power or ability to get something done.[42] Those without power are radically unfree, incapable of bringing about change.

41. Marx, *Early Political Writings*, 26.

42. At this point I follow Raymond Geuss, *Politics and the Imagination* (Princeton, NJ: Princeton University Press, 2010), 57.

Thus, as his critique of Feuerbach makes clear, a materialist worldview is at best necessary but not sufficient for the formulation of an account of finitude. Just as crucial for Marx's conception of finitude is his positioning of man in history, generating not only a materialist view but what Marx calls historical materialism. Yet why is a materialist account of the type outlined above, and defended by Feuerbach, not able to inform us of what it is to exist historically? And why is existing historically a necessary dimension of the theoretical achievement of finitude?

Western ideas of historical existence range from early medieval, essentially Augustinian, notions of linearity and teleology, according to which the individual's fate is ultimately decided by God's design, to modern visions of radical contingency, according to which an individual's fate is largely intransparent, the result only of contingent causes devoid of purpose or meaning.[43] In the former models, individual action becomes understandable and transparent to the extent that it is a function of, and serves to bring forward, history's macrolevel development. In the latter models, it is made sense of in light of causal explanations. In both cases the individual, rather than being endowed with a concrete historical existence, is either subsumed by history or eliminated qua agent by interpretating action in causal terms only.

When Marx seeks to locate humans concretely in "the process of history," he tries to avoid both pitfalls. There is no extra-empirical, "universal history" that, as Marx interprets Hegel, somehow serves as the engine of empirical history, driving it relentlessly forward toward a predetermined goal. On the other hand, to be concretely situated in history is not simply to be pushed along by causes over which the individual has limited or no control. Rather, to exist concretely as a material being is to be a historically mediated being who also is the source or origin of history itself.

It may seem counterintuitive to hold that individuals are both produced, as it were, by history and producers of it. However, this is Marx's view,

---

43. Saint Augustine, *City of God*, trans. Henry Bettenson (London: Penguin Books, 2003), 176: "It is therefore this God, the author and giver of felicity, who, being the one true God, gives earthly dominion both to good men and to evil. And he does this not at random or, as one may say, fortuitously, because he is God, not Fortune. Rather he gives in accordance with the order of events in history, an order completely hidden from us, but perfectly known to God himself." Richard Rorty, *Contingency, Irony, and Solidarity* (Cambridge: Cambridge University Press, 1989), 22: "The line of thought common to Blumenberg, Nietzsche, Freud, and Davidson suggests that we try to get to the point where we no longer worship *anything*, where we treat *nothing* as a quasi divinity, where we treat *everything*—our language, our conscience, our community—as a product of time and chance."

which he develops and defends in key early writings such as the *Paris Manuscripts* and *The German Ideology*.

The following passage from *The German Ideology* offers a good sense of how Marx conceives of this concreteness:

> [Feuerbach] does not see that the perceptible world around him is not something given from eternity and always the same, but is rather the product of industry and of social conditions, and indeed, in the sense that it is an historical product, the result of the activity of a whole series of generations, each one of which stood on the shoulders of its predecessor, improved further its industry and its commerce, and modified its social order according to altered needs. Even the objects of the most simple "sense certainty" are given to him only through social development, industry, and commercial trade. The cherry tree, like almost all fruit trees, was planted in our latitude only a few centuries ago, as a result of *commerce*, and thus *through* this action of a certain society in a certain time given to Feuerbach's "sense certainty."[44]

Marx criticizes Feuerbach's dialectic of sensuousness, which identifies needs and dependencies rooted in man's material existence yet fails to embed them in the historical world of praxis.[45] Yet he also continues his dialectical and critical *Auseinandersetzung* with Hegel. Central to this undertaking is the notion of labor, which Marx, in the *Paris Manuscripts* and elsewhere, claims to be appropriating from Hegel.

Hegel's notion of labor is for Marx a shot at the important dimension of activity and praxis lacking in Feuerbach's materialism. Not surprisingly, however, the Hegelian account of labor is, according to Marx, itself estranged: "Hegel knows and acknowledges only labor of the abstractly spiritual kind."[46] Again, this critique is targeting what Marx sees as Hegel's fetishizing of spirit, the account of spirit as essentially sui generis, which in practically all the early Marx's writings gets interpreted as ideological. By putting the various pieces together, it can now be conjectured that Marx's discovery of the importance of activity, together with his claim that

---

44. Marx, *Early Political Writings*, 143.

45. Wartofsky, *Feuerbach*, 21: "Marx's critique of Feuerbach is not that Feuerbach's intentions are wrong, or that the dialectic is wrongly grounded. Rather, it is that the sensibility, which Feuerbach takes as the domain of the dialectic, remains an abstract sensibility: It remains, for all Feuerbach's protestations, a reflected-upon praxis, or a praxis within reflection, a praxis of belief and of thought. It remains *philosophy*."

46. Marx, *Early Political Writings*, 87.

a genuine historical materialism must combine the idealist emphasis on activity with the insights of classical materialism, represents his attempt to situate man as a finite creature in a concrete historicity. For Marx, concrete historicity and activity are two sides of the same coin. The one could not exist without the other.

Via labor, human beings produce the conditions of their own existence. They collectively transform the external world in light of self-chosen plans, values, and commitments, thereby actualizing themselves as free. Moreover, in doing so they also transform themselves, turning the mere instinctual nature of their subjectivity into self-conscious proficiency. Labor humanizes the world while also naturalizing the subject.

However, since labor under capitalism is alienated, the activity of self-production remains both intransparent and incomplete. In Marx's analysis of alienation, wage labor involves separating the worker from his own product, from the very process of producing it, as well as from the collective species-being of his existence. The worker does not control the product, which is expropriated and sold for profit by the owner of capital. Moreover, working on the assembly line or at a machine, he relates to only a fragment of the total production process. Finally, rather than being a member of a class united by a common interest in overthrowing capitalism, the worker finds himself represented as an individual employee in competition with other potential or actual employees.

What is concrete, then, namely the collective endeavor of actualizing human freedom via laboring self-externalization, is under capitalism represented as abstract; thus Hegel's philosophy, and indeed all "bourgeois thinking" from Locke and Kant to Fichte and beyond, which focuses on social relations as constituted by unconstrained, rational agreements among rights-bearing individuals, is for Marx made to look plausible by the real (yet *ultimately* illusory) presence of such abstraction. Marx, in other words, only indirectly situates man in a concrete historicity. Modern, laboring agents are self-actualizing beings, and laboring is a necessary component of historical existence. In this, albeit philosophical sense, they are free. They create their own historical conditions and therefore create history itself. However, since labor is alienated, the very situatedness in history of concrete agents achieving self-actualization through labor appears incomprehensible or simply not in view.

At this point it is worth asking what the achievement of human finitude really means for Marx. I mentioned that Marx responds to Hegel's rationalism by attempting to situate human beings in a concrete historicity. We have now seen that that situatedness is neither epistemologically available to the agents themselves nor in fact even fully evident. The lives of modern agents whose labor power is commodified are indeed thoroughly abstract. How can I then claim that Marx manages to break through to such a view?

Marx is dismissive of any view, such as Hegel's, that abstractly determines man's existence. As we have seen, his materialism entails both the primacy of material reality and an emphasis on man's social existence in an empirical social arrangement. It is true that the world of exploited, alienated labor is such that central social categories appear timeless and fixed. Labor itself appears as a commodity, to be quantified and exchanged for a wage presented as freely agreed to by the worker. Property is viewed not as grounded in a factual relation of exploitation between human beings, but as a right seized upon by industrious individuals. Individuals are endowed with supposedly inalienable rights guaranteed by the state. Indeed, the complete ideological superstructure of liberal, capitalist society appears to be timeless and immediately valid, devoid of any genetic dimension or internal contradictions. However, according to Marx the abstract appearance of society may be challenged at two central levels.

First, it is challenged by social criticism, the self-reflection of bourgeois society. Social criticism is fundamentally (though of course not exclusively) a matter of retrieving a sense of the historical nature of what otherwise appears to be timeless and fixed. By such a sense I mean an understanding of the emergence and dynamics of social forms, how such forms have come into being, what kind of social relations they reflect, and how the practices they are composed of are grounded in asymmetrical distributions of power, resources, and entitlements. The critique of ideology, for example, in the way Marx outlines it in *The German Ideology*, is supposed to show how consciousness is determined by life, where life is the "real life process of men," the way men produce their means of life "conditioned by a definite development of their productive forces and by the relations that correspond to these forces."[47] As social criticism and ideology critique proceeds in this way ("empirically and without any mystification and speculation"[48]), it aims to show that

> The shadowy pictures in the human brain are also necessary sublimations of men's material life process, empirically verifiable and tied to material presuppositions. Consequently, morality, religion, metaphysics, and the other ideological constructs and forms of consciousness that correspond to them no longer retain the appearance of independence.[49]

47. Marx, *Early Political Writings*, 124.
48. Marx, *Early Political Writings*, 124.
49. Marx, *Early Political Writings*, 125.

As the "appearance of independence" fades away, Marx thinks that history itself comes into view: "As soon as this active life process is represented, history ceases to be a collection of dead facts, as it is with abstract empiricists, or an imagined action of imagined subjects, as it is with the idealists."[50] Ideology, which in the way it is presented "has no history, no development," starts to be viewed as the product of actual living individuals with a particular history.

It is important to note that Marx thinks not only that ideology critique of this kind is indeed available, but that it may also succeed in actually breaking through the mode of appearance of social forms.[51] In this way critique is aligned with the effort to think human finitude by placing agents concretely in history as finite, sensuous beings.

The second sense in which the inert social forms of capitalist society may be challenged centers on the experience of the proletariat. More than any other class or social group, the proletariat, according to Marx, incorporates the contradiction between alienation and self-actualization. Being exploited, the proletariat experiences immiseration; indeed, devoid of property and of anything except its own labor power, it has nothing to lose and everything to win in the event of an overthrow of capitalism.[52] On the one hand, therefore, the proletariat, with its universal interest, is the universal class. On the other hand, however, it finds itself in an alienated state, as a particular class with apparently particular interests, unaware of itself as universal.

The key sense in which alienation is experienced as unreal relates to suffering. The proletariat's dissatisfaction with existing social forms is not primarily epistemically based. Rather, dissatisfaction, for Marx, is experienced as suffering—physical suffering, to be sure, but suffering more generally at "not being at home in the world." Marx's analysis of alienation can thus be viewed as a phenomenology of human nonactualization, experienced as physical and psychic suffering. It is ultimately Marx's view that

50. Marx, *Early Political Writings*, 125.

51. The problem of self-reference has plagued Marxist ideology critique from the early Frankfurt School to Althusser and beyond. How can ideology critique achieve objectivity? How can it escape ideology? Does it have to escape ideology in order to succeed? Does it really purport, as Althusser suggests with his distinction between science and ideology, to do so? These are no doubt important questions that I am not able to deal with in this book.

52. Hence the final sentences of the *Manifesto of the Communist Party* in Karl Marx, *Later Political Writings*, ed. and trans. Terrell Carver (Cambridge: Cambridge University Press, 1996), 30: "Let the ruling classes tremble at a communist revolution. Proletarians have nothing to lose in it but their chains. They have a world to win."

suffering and social discontent tie the worker to his historical fate; indeed, the fact of systemically induced suffering is incompatible with standard self-interpretations of liberal, bourgeois society. It thus has at least the potential to escape ideology and alert the proletariat to its role as the exploited class.

So what is left of Hegel's program in the philosophy of the early Marx? The answer, especially since the 1932 publication of the *Paris Manuscripts*, has tended to be that Marx retains, or at least formulates, a conception of *humanism*. To be sure, attributing humanism to Marx has always implied an emphasis on finitude. Unlike Hegel, Marx does not view human beings as *geistige*: they neither express divine spirit nor carry it forward. However, the rejection of Hegel's concept of spirit does not entail that Marx has a completely nominalist view of the human predicament. What made the writings of the young Marx so exciting to the interwar generation of Marxists was that he seems to establish an account of human *essence*. Man's alienation is to be understood in terms of estrangement from one's own essence. Thus Marx should be viewed as a theorist of self-actualization.

As I have already indicated, a true self-actualization would involve a state (communism) where man produces himself as well as his products, and where nature is humanized and man naturalized: a true speculative identity of naturalism and humanism, materialism and idealism. The communism in which private property has been fully superseded, Marx writes in one of his most speculative passages, "equals humanism, and as fulfilled humanism equals naturalism; it is the *genuine* resolution of the conflict of man with nature and of man with man, the true resolution of the conflict between existence and essence, objectification and self-affirmation, freedom and necessity, individual and species. It is the solution of the enigma of history and knows itself to be that."[53]

At odds with the familiar Althusserian reading, however, Marx never argues that man possesses any *pregiven* essence.[54] He at no point refers to man's nature in abstraction from his material existence. Nor does he ever purport to offer any kind of analysis in terms of necessary and sufficient criteria for man to be fully real, or having actualized himself. Although his

---

53. Marx, *Early Political Writings*, 79. This is a complex passage that is difficult to translate. See Karl Marx, *Ökonomisch-philosophische Manuskripte* (Frankfurt: Suhrkamp, 2009), 116: "Dieser Communismus ist als vollendeter Naturalismus = Humanismus, als vollendeter Humanismus = Naturalismus, er ist die *wahrhafte* Auflösung des Widerstreits des Menschen mit der Natur und d[em] Menschen, die wahre Auflösung des Streits zwischen Existenz und Wesen, zwischen Vergegenständlichung und Selbstbetätigung, zwischen Freiheit und Notwendigkeit, zwischen Individuum und Gattung. Er ist das aufgelöste Räthsel der Geschichte und weiß sich als diese Lösung."

54. Louis Althusser, *For Marx*, trans. Ben Brewster (London: Verso, 2005), 226.

account of self-actualizing reveals traces of an Aristotelian *dynamis* and *energeia* approach, and at times is couched in unmistakably Hegelian terms (in particular as *an-sich-sein* and *für-sich-sein*), he squarely rejects any natural rights theory.

It remains, however, that Marx, especially in the *Paris Manuscripts*, employs the term essence (*Wesen*) in what seems like a distinctly Hegelian manner. However, one should also note that the central term in this regard is *labor*—man's self-production as a free and fully socialized being—hence a dynamic, open self-relation mediated by one's engagement with the object. Man's nature cannot be pinned down to something pregiven or extratemporal. On the contrary, the essence of man is whatever he makes of himself; it is the very process of determining oneself as that laboring being Marx thinks one is.

It is now possible to see that, while responding to the excesses of Hegel's idealism, Marx largely succeeds in providing a coherent philosophy of radical finitude. While active and self-producing (albeit in an alienated manner), man is a material being, living in a material world, delivered to a temporality that is both secular and suggestive of indefinite progression.

If Marx outlines a philosophy of history according to which religion was always illusory and fated to go away once humankind overcomes the hypostatizings and modes of alienation that prevent it from recognizing its own finitude (and reality), then not only does he *critique* religion, but he also situates it within a framework of progressive secularization. Religion is destined to disappear as bourgeois society fades away owing to its inner contradictions. Yet to what extent, if any, does he *rescue* religion? Is he not the thinker of an uncompromising, unyielding atheism, for whom religion not only was an illusion, keeping people in thrall to false and alienating promises of salvation, but preventing them from taking the kind of action that supposedly is necessary to overcome alienation? Is he not a prophet, as it were, of what Taylor calls an age—a *secular age*—"in which the eclipse of all goals beyond human flourishing becomes conceivable,"[55] and in which religion has been deprived of precisely the features that motivated people to accept it? I have argued that he was, and that, with Marx, the possibility of exclusive humanism emerges with unparalleled consequence. That said, while the anticipation of such a state of affairs seems fully authentic in both the early and the late Marx, there are other dimensions of his teaching, especially those that address the structure of historical development (and with that, the process of secularization as he sees it), that do not so easily fall in line with the exclusive humanism of his anticipatory view of full human

---

55. Taylor, *Secular Age*, 19.

self-actualization. No reader of Marx may have gone further in revealing those strands than Löwith, who in *Meaning in History* claims to see in Marx a full-fledged messianic thinker.

Löwith's evidence for this reading points in several directions and presupposes a number of contentious hermeneutic claims. Marx, he maintains, "sees in the proletariat the world-historical instrument for achieving the eschatological aim of all history by a world revolution."[56] A chosen people, the proletariat, prompted by its prophet Marx, undergoes a series of hardships before finally triumphing in some redemptive state of ultimate transformation from necessity to full freedom. Moreover, echoing the movement from the *civitas Terrena* to a *civitas Dei*, history itself is viewed as a providential advance toward this final goal. Finally, Marx even had an equivalent of Judeo-Christian original sin: exploitation. "As a supreme and all-pervading evil, exploitation is far more than an economic fact."[57] The guiding idea behind these attributions is that what presents itself as the discontinuity of secularization actually possesses internal continuity; indeed, secularization is in fact a repetition of certain structures that, according to Löwith, must be deemed more or less ahistorical.

Following Blumenberg, I think one should be skeptical of this view, which lends itself to a number of interpretations. On a particularly strong interpretation, Löwith introduces what Blumenberg calls "constants in history," structures that remain completely unchanging over time. However, in Löwith's exposition there is no evidence of a commitment to such constants, and it is far from clear what such evidence would involve. At the

---

56. Karl Löwith, *Meaning in History* (Chicago: University of Chicago Press, 1949), 37. See also Monod, *La querelle de la sécularisation*, 70, who sees Marx's position as at best unstable: "Tantôt la politique marxienne se voit versée du côte de la *sécularisation absolue*, comme l'expression politique accomplie d'une pensée radicalement athée; tantôt (en convergence avec l'identification nietzschéenne du socialisme comme rejeton du christianisme), la pensée de l'histoire qui accouche de la révolution prolétarienne est versée du côte d'une *forme sécularisée de messianisme*." Leszek Kolakowski takes a slightly different approach. He sees Marxism not only as showing structural similarities with key Judeo-Christian ideas of history, but as "performing the function of religion." See his *Main Currents of Marxism*, 1208: "Almost all the prophecies of Marx and his followers have already proved to be false, but this does not disturb the spiritual certainty of the faithful, any more than it did in the case of chiliastic sects: for it is a certainty not based on any empirical premises or supposed 'historical laws,' but simply on the psychological need for certainty. In this sense Marxism performs the function of a religion, and its efficacy is of a religious character. But it is a caricature and a bogus form of religion, since it presents its temporal eschatology as a scientific system, which religious mythologies do not purport to be."

57. Löwith, *Meaning in History*, 43.

very least, if such constants do exist, then it would follow that all belief systems are repetitions, and that history is some sort of eternal return of the same. Yet such a view would be highly implausible. A weaker interpretation, reminiscent of Habermas's reconstruction of the role of Christianity in accounting for modern beliefs and commitments, would consist in the entirely uncontroversial claim that Marxism would be inconceivable without Christianity.[58] Admittedly, though in a materialist and less teleological framework, it does seem to repeat some of the historical elements of interpretation that shaped the Christian tradition after Origen and Augustine. Yet a similar claim could be presented about the modern age in general; thus the "inconceivable without" thesis does not seem specific enough to contribute to an understanding of Marxism as such. Leaving aside the various interpretations of the secularization theorem, Löwith's interest in the supposed eschatology of Marxism, and hence in the Judeo-Christian origin of its philosophy of history, echoes the kinds of claims one sometimes hears from people who dismiss Marxism completely. In their estimation, if Marxism can be shown to incorporate an eschatological view of history, then it follows that the entire doctrine, insofar as it is predicated on a rejection of religion in general, must be incoherent.

It stands to reason that the idea of progress reverberating in Marxist hopes for an end to systemically generated injustice cannot be viewed simply as a repetition of Judeo-Christian hopes of salvation. As Ernst Bloch points out, while Marxism admittedly has had many religious precursors, including the Exodus (with its promise of collective liberation) and the Gospels (with their promise of universal justice grounded in visions of compassion and equality), the hope it projects is predicated not on possibilities associated with a world other than this one but, rather, with life in this world.[59] If Marxism desublimates the idea of heaven, then it does this so

---

58. Habermas, *Auch eine Geschichte der Philosophie*. See also Shmuel N. Eisenstadt, "Religious Origins of Modern Radicalism," *Theoria: A Journal of Social and Political Theory* 106 (2005): 51, who claims that "that many central and continual dimensions and tensions of the cultural and political programme of modernity and of modern political dynamics are deeply rooted in the religious components of the civilization which they developed, and that these dimensions and tensions constitute in many ways the transformation, even if in secular terms, of some of the basic religious orientations and the tensions that have been constitutive of these civilizations. This is especially true of the Jacobin component of the cultural and political programme of modernity—a component which is at the root of what is probably the most continual dramatic confrontation in the modern political discourse and dynamics—namely, the confrontation between pluralistic and totalistic and totalitarian ideologies, movements and regimes."

59. Ernst Bloch, *Principle of Hope*, vol. 3.

radically, so entirely without accepting the religious impulse with its wish for escape from mortal existence and from what I have called finitude, that any attempt to see it as Messianic seems ill founded.[60] If anything, the idea of utopia as tied up with nature and the pacification of humanity's natural tendencies toward violence and oppression is a modern invention, one that, as T. J. Clark has argued, may have come into existence around the time of the early Renaissance.[61]

Even if all of this is true, its vision of a genuinely nonalienated human community does resonate with certain strands of Judeo-Christian thought.[62] To be sure, Marx did not say much about social relations under communism. His rejection of "blueprint" socialism—socialism prescribed abstractly and in the absence of attention to its historical conditions, which would have to be actualized—led him to focus his research on the nature and contradictions of liberal capitalist systems. What he does say, though, indicates that he follows especially the Christian tradition in viewing *status gratiae* to involve (a) an overcoming of abstract individualism (setting the individuals against each other), (b) a view of self-actualization as being fully dependent on successful participation in a community, and (c) some notion of happiness or flourishing such that individuals may satisfy all their real needs and do so not at the expense of other individuals' need satisfaction but in a state of cooperative self-reproduction. The fully socialized individual finds self-actualization in and through the community, which is the highest and most authoritative reality. All forms of alienation,

---

60. For a discussion of this kind of atheism, see Martin Hägglund, *This Life: Secular Faith and Spiritual Freedom* (New York: Pantheon Books, 2019).

61. T. J. Clark, *Heaven on Earth: Painting and the Life to Come* (New York: Thames and Hudson, 2018). In paintings by Giotto and Bruegel, Clark (17) finds displayed "the idea that the world we inhabit might open onto another—be interrupted by it, or called to it, or visited by it and make sense at last in the light of the visitation. Call it the image of the earthly giving way to the heavenly, the miraculous, the truly revolutionized. The second is the idea, close to the first but distinct from it, that the world we know might be raised to a higher power, 'deified' by an energy that, though it may ultimately be a gift of God, is manifest here and now in a quickening, an intensifying, an overflowing, a supercharging of altogether human powers—be they imaginative, erotic, ecstatic, intellectual, irenic or jihadist, possessed by an exceptional individual or created by a fused group."

62. According to Alasdair MacIntyre's *Marxism and Christianity* (Notre Dame, IN: University of Notre Dame Press, 1984), Marxism adopts yet modifies Christianity's deification of history grounded in an anticipatory vision of justice and nonalienation. Like Christianity, Marxism offers a conception of community integrated through love and solidarity.

dehumanization, and reification associated with the commodification of labor would be overcome.

In this redeemed social space there would be no need for divinities. The community and what it offers would make superfluous any appeal to the supersensible. There would, however, be a "conscience social" in Durkheim's sense: a communal mindedness that individuals would find authoritative and meaningful. Moreover, as Marx suggests especially in the *Paris Manuscripts*, the very relationship with nature would be transformed. Unlike the relationship with nature under conditions of capitalist exploitation, which is abstract and objectifying, the transformed relationship would "resurrect" nature and bring about, Marx writes, a "naturalism of man and the accomplished humanism of nature."[63] In the most general terms available, the Marxian "heaven on earth" vision seems to be aspiring to bring about a materialist version of Hegelian reconciliation: the successful overcoming of all oppositions, including not only the fundamental Marxian one of capital versus labor but of the opposition between subject and object, mankind and nature. However, unlike the relationship found in Hegel, which is set to take place at the level of *Geist*, Marx's *Versöhnung* belongs within the "finitist" tradition of criticism of Hegelian rationalism begun by Schelling and taken up by the left-Hegelians, Kierkegaard, and Nietzsche. The next chapter will analyze Nietzsche's more distinctly anti-Hegelian contribution to this tradition.

63. Marx, *Early Political Writings*, 80.

[CHAPTER FIVE]

Nietzsche and the Overcoming of Christianity

While each of the philosophers I have focused on in this book sees the concept of divinity in ontotheology as in need of radical rethinking, no nineteenth-century thinker has been more emphatically associated with the idea of the death of God than Nietzsche. In the well-known 125th entry of the 1882 edition of *The Gay Science*, Nietzsche lets "the madman," one of his numerous figures, run into a marketplace crying "Where is God?" and proclaiming that "*We have killed him—you and I.*" "This tremendous event," he continues, "is still on its way, wandering; it has not yet reached the ears of men. Lightning and thunder need time; the light of the stars needs time; deeds need time, even after they are done, in order to be seen and heard. This deed is still more remote to them than the remotest stars—*and yet they have done it themselves.*"[1]

The despair and confusion over the death of God is posed as a challenge, something that has to be accepted in its finality. While promising collective self-transformation and self-overcoming ("Do we not have to become gods merely to appear worthy of it?"), the process of secularization has already begun, Nietzsche tells us, and is in its final stages, being brought about by human agents, first unreflectively but later as an ideal. Included in the vision of deicide is the view that the death of God must be an act of self-interpretation, eventually initiating a secular order in which values are explicitly understood to be human products. Indeed, as the following quotation from the early writings makes plain, Nietzsche is taking himself to be a witness to a process of secularization, one that inevitably, he argues, will lead to the end of Christianity.

> I note a weariness *in regard to religion*: people have finally grown tired of and exhausted by the weighty symbols. All possible forms of Christian

---

1. Friedrich Nietzsche, *The Gay Science*, trans. Josefine Nauckhoff (Cambridge: Cambridge University Press, 2001), 119–20.

life have been tried: the strictest and the most lax, the most harmless and thoughtless and the most reflective. It is time to discover something new, or else one must fall back into the same old cycle over and over again. Of course it is difficult to emerge from the whirlpool after it has spun us around for a few thousand years. Even mockery, cynicism, and hostility toward Christianity have run their course. What one sees is an icefield in warming weather: the ice is everywhere broken—dirty, lusterless, dotted with puddles of water, dangerous. A considerate and seemly abstention seems to me to be the only appropriate attitude: I thereby honor religion, though it is dying. Our job is to assuage and soothe, as in the case of the grievously, hopelessly ill. All we must protest against are bad, thoughtless, and bungling physicians (which is what most learned persons are). Christianity will very soon be ripe for critical history, i.e. for dissection.[2]

Despite the image of an icefield in warming weather, inevitably coming to an end, however, Nietzsche does not end up indifferent to religion. His attitude is vastly different from post–World War II pragmatist thinkers such as Richard Rorty, who (in my view falsely) took Nietzsche to have asked his readers simply to leave religion behind and, in a true enlightenment spirit, "become adults."[3] As I will argue in this chapter, he closely follows the "critique and rescue" formula that we have seen is operative in Kant,

---

2. Friedrich Nietzsche, *Philosophy and Truth: Selections from Nietzsche's Notebooks of the Early 1870's*, ed. and trans. Daniel Breazeale (Amherst, NY: Humanity Books, 1979), 103. The quotation is from Nietzsche's abandoned *Philosophenbuch*.

3. See Richard Rorty's essay "Anticlericalism and Atheism," in *The Future of Religion*, by Richard Rorty and Gianni Vattimo, ed. Santiago Zabala (New York: Columbia University Press, 2005), 29–42. Rorty is by no means completely dismissive of religion. He argues that "love" is a component of Christian teaching that ought to survive secularization and remain a public metanorm. However, while allowing for religion as a private mode of self-interpretation, he criticizes all forms of foundationalism and metaphysics. At best, religion is private storytelling. In his *Late Notebooks*, Nietzsche, in the true spirit of classical enlightenment thinking, will sometimes, though not very frequently, simply consider Christianity as "immature," something childish that humanity, for this very reason, ought to leave behind. See Nietzsche's entry from the fall of 1885, *Writings from the Late Notebooks*, trans. Kate Sturge, ed. Rüdiger Bittner (Cambridge: Cambridge University Press, 2003), 41: "It may be hoped man will raise himself so high that the things previously highest to him, e.g., the belief in God he has held up to now, appear childlike, childish, and touching: indeed, that he will do again what he did with all the myths—turn them into children's stories and fairy-tales." See also the following semibiographical remark from the winter of 1887–88 (*Writings from the late Notebooks*, 234): "Not for a single hour of my life have I been a Christian: I regard everything I have seen as Christianity, as a contemptible ambiguity of words, a real cowardice towards all the powers that otherwise rule."

Hegel, Feuerbach, and possibly even Marx. Nietzsche offers a number of arguments to cast doubt on the very existence of God. Just as important, he symptomatically reconstructs the ideals and evaluations that he sees informing faith and devotion. In both these regards, Nietzsche consistently targets Christianity, claiming that its conception of a transcendent God means it is dismissive of life as it is, instead cultivating a life-denying ethic of humility and idealism. In the following I reconstruct and discuss these arguments. However, I also take Nietzsche to move beyond the exclusive commitment to critique. From his earliest writings, including *The Birth of Tragedy*, to the very latest, written in a frenzy before his collapse in 1889, he calls for a radical transformation of contemporary culture guided by ideals associated with the ancient Greek demigod Dionysus and the figure of Zarathustra, his own invention, who not only challenge the values associated with Christianity but call for the cultivation of an entirely new attitude, radically self-transformative, toward life and human existence. Nietzsche sees Christianity as undergoing an internal process of secularization, culminating with "the death of God." Yet does he propose that his fellow Europeans introduce a successor religion? Or is the cult surrounding the charismatic authorities of Dionysus and Zarathustra, in that they so adamantly reject all appeals to transcendence, of some postreligious kind? I will claim that Nietzsche ends up calling for a reinstatement of religion. As such, he calls for an antimodern version of modernity, at odds with the enlightenment ideals that guide the other thinkers whose writings on religion I analyze in this book.

Nietzsche's Enlightenment Criticism

In his writings from the late 1880s, including *Twilight of the Idols*, *The Genealogy of Morality*, *The Anti-Christ*, *Thus Spoke Zarathustra*, and sections from his unfinished manuscript *The Will to Power* (recently gathered in English as *Writings from the Late Notebooks*), Nietzsche directs his antireligious sentiments toward Christianity, whose influence and significance he both criticizes and historically reconstructs. For considering Nietzsche as a contributor to the discourse of secularization, it is mainly his historical narrative, the genealogy he presents, that is of interest. However, since that narrative can hardly be distinguished rigorously and systematically from the critique, I will start by discussing the latter.

Some of Nietzsche's objections to Christianity are undeniably of enlightenment origin, reflecting his appreciative attitude, especially in the middle period, toward thinkers such as Voltaire, Diderot, and materialists such as d'Holbach. In *The Anti-Christ*, section 15, for example, he presents a direct cognitive attack, claiming that "In Christianity, morality and religion are completely out of touch with reality."[4] Immediately upon making this statement, he lists a number of supposedly "imaginary" entities and phenomena associated with Christian dogma and practice. In this religion, he writes, there are imaginary *causes* such as "God," "soul," and "spirit" and imaginary *effects* such as "sin," "redemption," and "grace." Christians, he claims, imagine the existence of an anthropocentrically formulated "natural science" of metaphysical entities; and neither their "psychology" (with its concepts of repentance, humility, temptation, etc.) nor their soteriological and eschatological "teleology" (involving claims about "the kingdom of God," "the Last Judgment," and "eternal life") is anything but "fictitious." Unlike dreams, Nietzsche adds, which while fictitious when considered as narratives at least mirror some features of reality, the Christian imaginary (and imagery) just "falsifies, devalues, and negates actuality."[5]

While the claims in this section of *The Anti-Christ* are largely left unsupported by arguments and evidence, Nietzsche elsewhere provides a number of strategies for supporting them argumentatively. One of the most frequent, introduced as early as in the abandoned *Philosophenbuch* of the early 1870s, refers to a purportedly deep-seated anthropological tendency to draw inferences based on epistemological principles and categories to which no corresponding reality *an sich* can justifiably be said to correspond, yet which, by creating order in an otherwise unruly and heterogeneous universe, serve individuals' needs to obtain mastery over their surroundings.[6] For example, in the interest of making reality appear intelligible and therefore manageable, humans believe that every event has an identifiable cause, at least in principle, and that the same cause always produces the same effect. Beliefs of this kind, functioning as epistemic principles, provide pragmatic frameworks within which agents may explain and predict phenomena, and on that basis may be able to make rational plans and, in general, motivate rational decisions and actions. In *Twilight of the Idols*, Nietzsche returns to these reflections, though in a more overtly psychological manner, emphasizing not only pragmatic but emotional commitments. There exists, he claims, a deep-seated anthropological tendency to seek out causes capable of explaining the occurrence of desired emotional

---

4. Nietzsche, *The Anti-Christ, Ecce Homo, Twilight of the Idols, and Other Writings*, trans. Judith Norman (Cambridge: Cambridge University Press, 2005), 13.

5. Nietzsche, *Anti-Christ, Ecce Homo, Twilight of the Idols, and Other Writings*, 13.

6. Nietzsche, *Philosophy and Truth: Selections from Nietzsche's Notebooks of the Early 1870's*.

responses. "*The entire realm of morality and religion belongs to this concept of imaginary cause.*"[7] One places one's trust in God, for example, because of a feeling of plenitude and strength that gives rise to hope; hence God is mistakenly viewed as the cause of something that can actually be explained by the contingent, or at least mundane, existence of particular conscious states. In other words, it feels good to believe in God; thus, we like to think of God as an existing causal power. Like Hume, Nietzsche dismisses any appeal to natural necessity, claiming instead that humans *project* regularity into nature, thereby falsely yet unavoidably imputing to events explanatory causes so as to experience (in however an illusory fashion) order, stability, and predictability.

In writings from the same period, he speculates that language helps to generate and sustain this tendency. In simple attributions, we say that "this happened *because* of that," implying not only that one event happens after another (perhaps, as Hume argued, in spatiotemporal contiguity with it), but that a necessary connection exists between them, however invisible and intangible it may seem. Against the physicotheological arguments of natural religion, familiar from much enlightenment thinking, according to which God is considered the ultimate cause not only of the very existence of the world but of its apparently inherent order as well, Nietzsche's considerations may well be considered powerful. He manages to throw doubt on our tendency to want to find uncaused causes, and indeed on causal explanations in general. He critiques our tendency to hypostatize conceptions of substantiality and essence. However, their full power and consequence do not become apparent until the anthropological framework within which Nietzsche frames his critique of religion is made evident.

It is, Nietzsche argues, in the interest of naturally self-preserving animals such as human beings not only to search for causes that may explain events but, more generally, to minimize complexity by projecting onto reality a system of universals. In several of his writings, Nietzsche speculates about the possible connection between such behavior and the structure of language. The predicative structure of simple indicative judgments such as "The grass is green" makes agents prone to believe in some underlying substance, metaphysically different from its shifting attributes, able to account for the unity of an object as well as its predicted causal efficaciousness. We think of the grass as displaying a certain essential unity, and of its greenness as being uniform, corresponding to the apparent essentiality suggested by the concept of greenness. Indeed, the very mastery of the first-person pronoun, as in the expression "I drink water," insinuates, he claims,

---

7. Nietzsche, *Anti-Christ, Ecce Homo, Twilight of the Idols, and Other Writings*, 180.

the existence of an unchanging ego, capable of initiating and completing an action. Moreover, the employment of general nouns lulls us into believing that they refer to something real. Thus, when perceived by an agent, a tree is more than a multiplicity of appearances, presented temporarily and to the senses; rather, it instantiates *treeness*, the essence of what being a tree involves. "I am afraid," Nietzsche writes, "that we have not got rid of God because we still have faith in grammar."[8] Finally, in a critique of physico-teleological arguments, he notes that conventional linguistic performance includes being able to draw inferences. However, from p implies q, it does not follow that q implies p. "If God exists, his creation would be orderly" does not mean that whatever order we may find in the cosmos licenses us to infer a divine origin or principle.

The enlightenment aspiration informing these kinds of critical statements is evident. Nietzsche unquestionably understands the ontotheological views of Christian thinking to be largely false or without reference, fabrications brought about through the structure of ordinary language combined with an inborn anthropological desire for order, meaning, and predictability. However, unlike Hume, in the *Dialogues concerning Natural Religion*, or Kant, in the transcendental dialectic of the *Critique of Pure Reason*, he does not primarily conduct his critique of Christianity in a cognitive vein. Indeed, his attitude toward the idea that religious faith can be treated cognitively seems to have been predominantly negative: religion, for Nietzsche, is ultimately to be theorized as a lived practice and not just a set of beliefs purporting to be true of given domain.[9] Thus the focus, at least in the middle and late writings, is on what it may be that, independent of epistemic reasons, *motivates* agents to become religious (and especially Christian). Whereas Hume and Kant sought to criticize the exalted role of reason in much of Christian thinking, paving the way in Hume's case for agnosticism and in Kant's case for an autonomous and principled account of *Glaube*, Nietzsche provides his own secularization narrative grounded in a concept of value.

---

8. Nietzsche, *Anti-Christ, Ecce Homo, Twilight of the Idols, and Other Writings*, 170.

9. For another expression of this approach, see the following passage in Raymond Geuss, *Changing the Subject: Philosophy from Socrates to Adorno* (Cambridge, MA: Harvard University Press, 2017), 183: "So although it is not completely false to say that Nietzsche thinks he has 'refuted' Christianity, this is also not really the way he would think about it. The reason for this is that Christianity is not primarily a sequence of propositions; rather, it is a historically complex conjunction of habits, dispositions, beliefs, values, and practices which is directed at giving structure to human life and dealing with some of its less palatable aspects. So the question is less Is it true? than Does it work?"

The shifting of attention from truth to value—and the attendant viewing of truth-claims in light of their value—constitutes one of the truly innovative and original moves in Nietzsche's work. Christianity, he claims, while giving believers an imaginary metaphysics, is rooted in, and expressive of, a specific set of values. These values, moreover, are mainly negative or, as Nietzsche often puts it, "reactive." They include a hatred of everything "natural" or "earthly," a hatred of "strength" and of "life" (*Leben*) in general, of the body and its functions, of sexuality, play, and joy, while favoring the ideal, the transcendent, the soul, with all of this being accompanied or complemented by such attitudes as humility and ultimately a celebration of weakness. Christians, he claims, react to life and its conditions with a resounding No! Christianity, he submits in *The Anti-Christ*, "has taken the side of everything weak, base, failed, it has made an ideal out of whatever *contradicts* the preservation instincts of a strong life."[10]

Nietzsche grounds the strength/weakness distinction in his doctrine of the will to power (*Wille zur Macht*), inherited from Schopenhauer's notion of the will to life yet transformed in a number of consequential ways. Where Schopenhauer sees the will as a fundamentally metaphysical and supersensible type of striving, divorced from empirical existence while nevertheless determining and objectifying itself in it, Nietzsche understands it as operative *in nature itself* as a plurality of different and opposing desires for expansion, domination, self-assertion, self-transformation, and freedom. The will to power, being in living beings akin to an instinct or unreflective drive, makes itself felt in every individual. It even dominates the human intellect, influencing its end-setting and interpretive strategies. Indeed, life (*Leben*) itself, Nietzsche claims, is permeated and even constituted by the will to power. While actively searching for modes and methods of self-overcoming, rejoicing in its own creations while always seeking to disclose new opportunities for engagement, life "stamps" everything around it with significance and meaning, presenting the world primarily in evaluative rather than cognitive terms.

In his 1887 *On the Genealogy of Morality*, Nietzsche employs his psychology and ontology of the will to power to construct a genealogy of what he thinks of as Christian (but also fundamentally modern) morality.

---

10. Nietzsche, *Anti-Christ, Ecce Homo, Twilight of the Idols, and Other Writings*, 5. See Nietzsche, *Der Antichrist*, in *Friedrich Nietzsche: Sämtliche Werke, Kritische Studienausgabe in 15 Bänden*, ed. Georgio Colli and Mazzimo Montinari (Berlin: De Gruyter, 2014), 6:171: "Das Christentum hat die Partei alles Schwachen, Niedrigen, Missrathnen genommen, es hat ein Ideal aus dem Widerspruch gegen die Erhaltungs-Instinkte des starken Lebens gemacht."

Combining reflections on etymology, history, religion, and psychology in what is more of an associative than an explicitly argumentative text, the details of this genealogy are not always persuasive. However, its main structure carries a lot of conviction.

Just as Hegel followed Gibbon in seeing the fall of the Roman Empire as having been in central respects caused by the rise of Christianity, so in the First Essay of *On the Genealogy of Morality* Nietzsche associates a fundamental historical change of mentalities and cultural forms with the late Roman period. To be sure, the significance of this change, which he deems "the slave's revolt in morality," consists in its coinciding with, and involving, the rise to hegemony of Semitic and Christian patterns of evaluation and interpretation, effectively bringing the ancient pagan world to an end. On Nietzsche's account, the victory of especially Christianity brings about a self-negating, self-vitiating form of nihilism that in modernity has come to dominate virtually all forms of thinking.

The ancient world, Nietzsche claims, was dominated by a certain warrior ethic in which the fundamental evaluative contrast was between "good" and "bad" (*gut und schlecht*). This "noble" morality was founded on the affirmation of oneself as an aristocratic, strong, and courageous being, taking satisfaction in one's challenging yet essentially healthy and happy life form while aspiring to be loyal, ruthless, impressive, and playful. Although these nobles could dismiss their enemies or those they deemed weak or inferior, rather than hating them, they would fight them or, if possible, remain indifferent to them. The concern of a warrior centered on being creative, and on living so as to be able to say yes to whatever life brings. This included hardships and sufferings, which the warrior should be able to welcome as inevitable elements of a life well lived. According to Nietzsche, the noble person would be uninterested in considering his own value compared with others.' Instead, he would derive his evaluation of others from the standard he spontaneously applied to himself: thus, to the extent that the other fell short of the expectations expressed by that standard, he represented "the bad" and acted "badly." Such "slaves" or, as he calls them, "inferiors," were, in one of Nietzsche's many etymological inferences, *schlecht* (bad) simply because they were *schlicht* (low, plebeian). The noble person might love his enemies out of respect. Yet he might also find himself prey to more barbaric impulses against which he would marshal no moral qualms. The Nietzschean noble can act like a "blond beast avidly prowling for spoil and victory."[11] Or he can he be more high-minded, the Athenian warrior singled

---

11. Friedrich Nietzsche, *On the Genealogy of Morality*, trans. Carol Diethe (Cambridge: Cambridge University Press, 2007), 23.

out by Pericles for his "unconcern and scorn for safety, body, life, comfort" but also, Nietzsche adds, displaying a "shocking cheerfulness and depth of delight in all destruction, in all the debauches of victory and cruelty."[12]

Somewhat surprisingly given the prevailing interest in Christianity, Nietzsche does not say much about the nobleman's religion. However, if he does have anything like religious beliefs and sentiments, it is likely that Nietzsche would associate those with the disposition, explored as early as in *The Birth of Tragedy*, to affirm and endorse life as it is, regardless of what it brings the individual in terms of hardship and suffering. A precursor to the *Übermensch*, the nobleman of *On the Genealogy of Morality* exists within a world of sacred immanence: spiritually he is a child—innocent, cruel, and joyful, though with no outside or transcendent perspective on himself and his actions.

Nietzsche's famous "slave revolt" is not primarily understood as a revolt executed by slaves (although the implication no doubt is that it arises from within subjugated, "inferior" groups). Rather, what it signifies is the introduction of an entirely new system of evaluation, one that Nietzsche views as decisively structuring slave or plebeian *mentality*. As the original representative of this new mentality, he singles out a "priestly people," the Jews, who especially in their Babylonian exile are said to have developed *ressentiment* against their masters. Too weak to obtain physical revenge, they would compensate for their weakness by what Nietzsche calls an "imaginary revenge" consisting of a radical redescription and reorganizing of the complete system of value interpretations characteristic of the traditional warrior culture.[13] While the nobleman would fundamentally distinguish between good and bad (*gut und schlecht*), the burgeoning slave morality would be based on an evaluative distinction between good and evil (*gut und böse*). According to the latter binary, what the noble morality would deem to be good would now, in a complete reversal, be evil, and what was once bad would now be deemed good. Thus the noble virtues of courage, self-confidence, and heroism would in the new valuation become the vices of cruelty, arrogance, and pride, while the low character traits (when seen from the noble perspective) such as impotence, timidity, fawning, and sheepishness would be valorized as the virtues of humility, patience, friendliness, and solidarity

---

12. Nietzsche, *On the Genealogy of Morality*, 23.

13. Nietzsche, *On the Genealogy of Morality*, 20: "The beginning of the slaves' revolt in morality occurs when *ressentiment* itself turns creative and gives birth to values: the *ressentiment* of those beings who, denied the proper response of action, compensate for it only with imaginary revenge."

with one's neighbor.[14] Viewing the figure of Christ as the embodiment of these virtues and dispositions, and calling for the complete downfall of the old pagan order, Christianity continued what the Semitic peoples had begun: it created a brand-new social order structured around a rejection of the older expressions of strength. From now on the meek shall inherit the earth.

Not only do the noble and slave attitudes differ in their systems and categories of valuation, there is an equally important contrast between activity and reactivity or reaction. As I already mentioned, the noble morality affirms itself and its virtues—saying, as Nietzsche puts it, yes to itself both "thankfully and exultantly."[15] While it does contain negative valuations such as "low," "common," and "bad," these are just "pale contrasts" to its own positive self-valuation and do not seem to play much of a role in the nobleman's thinking except to affirm him in his own sense of glory and greatness. The slave morality, by contrast, understands itself fully in light of negation, of being different from or other than the hated object. Even in its destructive moments, noble morality is inherently creative and life-enhancing. Slave morality, by contrast, is creative only in its *cleverness*, the passive and, according to Nietzsche, mainly intellectual rejection of what is other than itself. While the nobleman immediately seeks to destroy his enemies, the slave condemns his enemies for falling short of expectations that can be articulated in abstract terms: one should not be or do *x*, *y*, or *z* (where *x*, *y*, and *z* represent ways of being that the slave considers to be other than what he himself represents as morally valid).

It follows that slave morality sets up transcendent ideals that, rather than emerging from some spontaneous process of self-affirmation that calls for action, universally condemn the purportedly unjust. Owing to his subjectivism about value and his naturalistic belief that behind any act of valuation stand "instincts" or "will to power," Nietzsche rejects from the outset the notion that these ideals are able to reflect any deeper reality: "To talk of 'just' and 'unjust' *as such* is meaningless; an act of injury, violence, exploitation or destruction cannot be 'unjust' *as such*, because life functions *essentially* in an injurious, violent, exploitative and destructive manner, or at least these are its fundamental processes and it cannot be thought of without these characteristics."[16] God, the ultimate principle and agent of justice, is invented by the weak, by the priestly communities, so as to be able to condemn life itself and valorize the weak over the strong. It is the ultimate expression of *ressentiment*.

---

14. Julian Young, *Nietzsche's Philosophy of Religion* (Cambridge: Cambridge University Press, 2006), 149.

15. Nietzsche, *On the Genealogy of Morality*, 20.

16. Nietzsche, *On the Genealogy of Morality*, 50.

Virtually all of Nietzsche's scathing criticisms of modernity follow from this one idea. Christianity has remained the dominant symbolic form in Western history since the fall of the Roman Empire. For Nietzsche its triumph was never in question. However, Christianity harbors within itself a hatred of life that as such qualifies as *nihilistic*. Indeed, Christianity can be considered one long and continuous battle against the kinds of dispositions, actions, and virtues that, since they permit what Nietzsche thinks of as genuine flourishing, a life of freedom and self-actualization, ultimately make life worth living. As this battle is waged by Christian culture and, in modernity proper, by its various ideological avatars (Kantianism, liberalism, socialism, and all other ideologies of "equality," "justice," and, effectively, "weakness"), Nietzsche claims to detect a progressive onset of weakness that undermines its own ability to create value. The nobleman created value spontaneously. We need to imagine him as having been spontaneously creative. Modern agents manage at best no more than to condemn and reject: turning weakness into an accomplishment while rejecting all forms of genuine human excellence, all they can ultimately do is concentrate on their own well-being. They are atheists not from an inability to justify their religious beliefs but from no longer having the strength to sustain complex value projections.

Like Weber, the late Nietzsche's understanding of secularization focuses on tendencies and pressures inherent in Christianity itself. While the madman in section 125 of *Gay Science* cries out that "we have killed God," apparently meaning that the death of God is an event in, and within the framework of, human history, Nietzsche seems to resist appeals to some outside *explanans*. The Christian God (and with that, as Heidegger puts it, "the highest values") has lost all authority, all plausibility, because the religion of Christianity, owing to its value system, has suppressed all spontaneity, creativity, and claims to genuine freedom in favor of a one-sided celebration of weakness. As Christianity underwent various purifying measures such as the Reformation, its rejection of strength and self-affirmation was exacerbated, intensifying the steady progress of autosecularization.

In the second and third chapters of *On the Genealogy of Morality*, Nietzsche adds further arguments about how the supposed self-dissolution of Christianity has taken place. One such argument explores the Christian internalization of guilt in acts of confession and expressions of remorse. The Christian sees himself as someone in dire need of forgiveness. While the noble person turned his instincts outward, actively responding to the world and the challenges it presents, the slave/Christian internalized his sense of debt and, while understanding himself as a sinner, directed aggression not against some outside enemy but against himself, thereby creating what Nietzsche calls "conscience." The account is largely psychological, anticipating ideas of the superego in Freud and Foucault's various stories of the historical transformation of punishment from being exterior to being, with "humanism," an interior event. However, Nietzsche frames his account within an extended reading of the debtor-creditor relation that shows it to be a complex, social event as well. In noble societies members were, through religion and other symbolic practices, made aware of their indebtedness to the community and their ancestors, and the more powerful and victorious the community, the greater the debt of the individual. While a breach of tribal expectations would incite the need for sanctions, unlike the arrangements existing in societies dominated by "slave morality," those sanctions would not appeal to the perpetrator's purported sense of guilt and responsibility. Rather, like animals that are bred, their main purpose would be to inflict pain with a view to disciplining and reintegrating the individual. Indeed, Nietzsche's noble society is not unlike Durkheim's tight-knit religious communities. By paying one's respect to gods and ancestors through, for example, sacrifice, the social bond was affirmed. The stronger the community, the more powerfully one would have to express one's sense of debt. With the intensifying of the debt, the ancestors and spirits to whom one sacrifices, and for whom one feasts, would take on greater authority and importance. At some point these objects of veneration, made possible by active expressions of a commitment to social cohesion, turned into gods. In Nietzsche's account, this may be how transcendent gods came into being: they satisfied the need for a symbolic order capable of expressing the strength of the community and the obligations it imposed on individual members.[17]

While the noblemen articulate their sense of indebtedness to the social order by projecting figures of undisputable, absolute authority, the slaves start concentrating that authority in a single entity, the Christian god, to whom no debt can ever be repaid through human efforts. The slaves, then, are inherently sinful, saturated with a sense of guilt and separated by an abyss from God's infinite demands. And since, according to their understanding, they cannot themselves do anything to repay debt, the only way it could be paid would be through God's own intervention and mercy. This, to be sure, goes a long way toward explaining the figure of Christ, whose suffering and crucifixion as the Son of God means that God is the one who in the final instance pays the debt man has accrued. Thus, with Christianity comes a peculiar form of *Schuld*, a form of moralized debt that not only calls for a payment in a legalistic sense (in the German sense of being a *Schuldner*,

---

17. Nietzsche, *On the Genealogy of Morality*, 60–61.

of owing somebody something) but that combines debt and guilt. Not only does the Christian feel infinitely indebted, but being indebted is as such something that condemns him to being inferior, indeed, to being a "sick" individual. The appropriate response to this predicament, Nietzsche avers, is to cultivate an attitude of humility and to "torment" oneself.

The important theme of asceticism completes both the genealogical account of morality and Nietzsche's story of secularization. While asceticism is normally understood as a religious practice, in the third chapter of *On the Genealogy of Morality*, Nietzsche takes a much wider view of it, considering asceticism as an ideal that has played a defining role not only in Christianity (from the medieval period and beyond) but also in much of modern culture. The ascetic ideal, Nietzsche claims, "*springs from the protective and healing instincts of a degenerating life*, which uses every means to maintain itself and struggles for its existence."[18] Asceticism disciplines, setting up prohibitions where the noble ideal would call for self-affirmation. On that basis, and as Freud would later argue in *Civilization and Its Discontents*, it contributes to the building of civilization despite its unprivileged starting point. Yet rather than affirming life and the will, the ascetic ideal prefers "nothingness," the negation of life that is emblematically expressed through the desire for transcendence. According to Nietzsche, contemporary European culture is saturated with asceticism.

Thus Richard Wagner, who in the name of music had promised cultural renewal, incorporated ascetic elements in his late operas, especially *Parsifal*, in which the longing for redemption overshadows the more "manly" knightly virtues known from his other operatic productions. Likewise, Schopenhauer constructed his vision of liberation from suffering, the resignation characterized in the fourth book of *The World as Will and Representation*, around an account of ascesis, the denial of the will. Even Kant, with his valorization of duty over inclination and his many idealistic dualisms, was for Nietzsche an ascetic thinker, one who praised everything that is conducive to "purity" and, at least implicitly, viewed human embodiment as a threat to universality and truth. Addressing his moral theology, Nietzsche goes so far as to mock Kant's claim to have overcome "theological conceptual dogmatism ('God,' 'soul,' 'freedom,' 'immortality'),"[19] suggesting that it never weakened the role of the ascetic ideal in his thinking. Kant's denial of knowledge for the sake of making room for faith amounts to little more than a return to Christianity and its ascetic ideals: "'There is no knowing: *consequently*—there is a God': what a new *elegantia syllogism!* What a *triumph* for the ascetic ideal!"[20]

---

18. Nietzsche, *On the Genealogy of Morality*, 88.
19. Nietzsche, *On the Genealogy of Morality*, 115.
20. Nietzsche, *On the Genealogy of Morality*, 116.

One might think that the emergence of natural science, which can be said to be predicated on the rejection of transcendence and a commitment to curiosity and openness to existence and life as they really are, would fall outside the purview of Nietzsche's conception of asceticism. However, the will to objectivity and truth, he argues, is itself a symptom of weakness: it implicitly yet significantly rejects the strength and will to power associated with interpretation, the capacity to impose value and order, that Nietzsche sees in "healthy" and "strong" civilizations. As he puts it,

> science rests on the same base as the ascetic ideal: the precondition of both the one and the other is a certain *impoverishment of life*,—the emotions cooled, the tempo slackened, dialectics in place of instinct, *solemnity* stamped on faces and gestures (solemnity, that most unmistakable sign of a more sluggish metabolism and of a struggling, more toiling life). Look at the epochs in the life of a people where scholars predominated: they are times of exhaustion, often of twilight, of decline,—gone are the overflowing energy, the certainty of life, the certainty as to the *future*. The preponderance of the mandarins never indicates anything good: any more than the rise of democracy, international courts of arbitration instead of wars, equal rights for women, the religion of compassion and everything else that is a symptom of life in decline.[21]

Science, in other words, rather than being a cause of secularization, is one of its symptoms. The main driver is always Christianity itself.

The notion of culture as having been saturated with scholarly commitments—a culture in which scientific rationalism with its exclusive demand for fact-gathering, objectivizing, and causal explanation has come to dominate at the expense of a more vital ability to create form—remains central in much of Nietzsche's writing, including the *Untimely Meditations*, in which he criticizes historicism, as well as the early *Birth of Tragedy*, in which he develops his critique of rationalism from the vantage point of an interpretation of Greek tragedy. Attacking modernity, the enlightenment critique of religion is couched in skeptical and genealogical terms aimed at problematizing and ultimately dissolving the appeal of nihilist and ascetic ideals. If the efforts associated with these two strategies had concluded Nietzsche's engagement with Christianity, then viewing him as a straightforward atheist, committed in some at least partial manner to the secular ideals of a modern liberal order, might have been possible. *The Birth of Tragedy*, however, complementing these efforts, introduces a rather different set of ideas. At center stage here

---

21. Nietzsche, *On the Genealogy of Morality*, 114.

is a demigod, Dionysus, a figure of sacred transcendence and metaphysical unity, who in the *Late Notebooks* and elsewhere is put forward as the antithesis of Christ. To obtain a more complete picture of Nietzsche's struggle with Christianity, it is therefore necessary to look closer at this early work.

"Have I Been Understood?" Dionysus against the Crucified

Kant and Hegel employ the critique/rescue dialectic to defend Christianity from the onslaught of enlightenment criticism and ongoing secularization. In both thinkers, the remaining religious aspirations are intimately tied up with accounts of human ideals as defined, whether in terms of morality or spirit, through reason. While Kant, despite his strong commitment to rational self-determination, formulates an abstract conception of transcendence, viewing God as a transcendent moral lawgiver, Hegel seeks to mediate the absolute with history, thereby threatening, as we have seen, to make his own view indistinguishable from the traditional secularization narratives that focus exclusively on disenchantment and rationalization. Attempting to overcome religious alienation while arguing that humankind may, in a meaningful way, aspire to the ideals hitherto ascribed to God, Feuerbach makes use of a similar dialectic to establish a robust, unambiguous humanism. Following Feuerbach yet radicalizing his emphasis on finitude, Marx critiques religion while also purporting to rescue elements of religion in his quasi-eschatological vision of a liberated humanity at the end of history. Unlike all these thinkers, Nietzsche does not try to show how religion may be sublated along idealist lines or transformed along humanist lines. Rather, Nietzsche uses the critique/rescue strategy to actually rescue religion—and in some primordial sense he wants to rescue religious experience as well. Kant and Hegel purport to rescue Christianity. By contrast, Nietzsche's religion—if that is the right word—is pagan.

That, at least, is a widespread view among Nietzsche scholars. In *Nietzsche's Philosophy of Religion*, for example, Julian Young, having analyzed his critique of Christianity, interprets Nietzsche as calling for a "new faith," one based on adherence to the values and philosophy associated with the ancient Greek demigod Dionysus. Far from being an a-theist, as a superficial reading of such writings as *Anti-Christ* and *Thus Spoke Zarathustra* might suggest, Nietzsche, he thinks, was a pantheist for whom the world itself is wholly perfect, enabling a supreme affirmation of life that eventually abolishes all guilt, justifies all suffering, and makes human existence perennially joyful.[22] In a similar vein, Michel Haar refers to Dionysus as being, for

---

22. Young, *Nietzsche's Philosophy of Religion*, 199.

Nietzsche, "a divinity still to come and a sacred form, both surprising and beyond classification, ever abounding and beyond limit."[23] Yet the views on this score are very divided. Many commentators have seen Nietzsche as being radically opposed not only to Christianity but to all forms of religious belief and practice. In his genealogy of nineteenth-century nihilism, for example, Michael Gillespie takes such a view.[24] According to Gillespie, rather than responding to the implicit nihilism of Christianity by advocating a different religion, Nietzsche radicalizes nihilism by championing a Promethean vision of humans as omnipotent, endowed with an infinite will by which the world, or at least our view of it, can be reordered. Whereas enlightenment criticism and disenchantment owing to rationalization had generated a crisis of meaning, leaving the purportedly autonomous subject of contemporary bourgeois society without the existential orientation needed to make meaningful ethical decisions, Nietzsche is upping the ante by creating the *Übermensch* as a figure of pure creation, destruction, and the general exercise of will. The *Übermensch* continues the modern drive toward viewing the subject as the source and originator of all value (and concomitantly toward viewing the universe itself as wholly disenchanted), and the figure of Dionysus, far from being a significant *religious* source of inspiration for Nietzsche, is cast as carrying mythological meaning relevant for the construal of the *Übermensch*.

In the hope of arriving at a settled view of this complicated theme in Nietzsche's writings, it is necessary to analyze those of his conceptions that most obviously seem to address the prospects for a new religion. Among those are the late yet unsystematic remarks on the eternal return, the attempt to bring about a new mythology based on the figure of Zarathustra and, most important, the appeal to the figure of Dionysus, who precisely is considered to pose the relevant counterclaims to Christ and Christianity. Is Dionysus a religious figure, and does Nietzsche by invoking him constitute himself as a religious follower? In one sense the answer is evident: the Dionysus he keeps coming back to in both the early and the late writings (though hardly in the writings from the middle period) is a figure of extraordinary charismatic power, able, as Euripides portrays him in the late tragedy *The Bacchae*, to present his followers with transgressive experiences of unquestionable divine authority. Dionysus, however, is a demigod, an offspring of Zeus's illicit tryst with the woman Semele, who in

---

23. Michel Haar, *Nietzsche and Metaphysics*, trans. Michael Gendre (Albany: State University of New York Press, 1996), 143.

24. Michael Gillespie, *Nihilism Before Nietzsche* (Chicago: University of Chicago Press, 1996), xxiii.

Nietzsche's interpretation, especially after his break with Wagner and his rejection of Schopenhauer's metaphysics, increasingly is associated with a certain amoral, aesthetic, and ecstatic affirmation of the world as it is, a space of immanence that, far from being contrasted with some transcendent externality, becomes an arena of both creation and destruction. Thus Dionysus, while a religious figure, and the new mythology grounded in deference to this figure and what it signifies, almost paradoxically seem to point beyond religion.

In an entry from the *The Late Notebooks*, Dionysus is seen *both* as a religious figure *and* as someone who incorporates the kind of radically life-affirming stance with which Nietzsche confronts Christianity. The religious man (if Christian) may well be a decadent, someone who rejects life. However, in the "pagan cult" (obviously the cult of Dionysus) based on "thanking and affirming life" and the "vindication and deification of life," Nietzsche claims to have discovered an exception to religious decadence.[25] He continues: "This is where I set the *Dionysus* of the Greeks: the religious affirmation of life, of life as a whole, not denied and halved."[26]

Suffering, a theme of considerable importance to Nietzsche's thinking, permits us to distinguish in a preliminary fashion between the two contrasting ways of being religious. Whereas the Christian considers suffering a path toward redemption, Dionysian or "tragic" man sees existence as "*blissful enough* to justify even monstrous suffering. The tragic man says Yes to even the bitterest suffering: he is strong, full, deifying enough to do so. The Christian says No to even the happiest earthly lot: he is weak, poor, disinherited enough to suffer from life in whatever form. . . . Dionysus cut to pieces is a *promise* to life: it will eternally be reborn and come home out of destruction."[27] It appears, in other words, as though Nietzsche endorses a stance that, despite its wholesale rejection of Christian values and the Christian desire for transcendence, he himself does not hesitate to call religious. However, it is not that he either embraces a radical atheism or calls for a continuation of anything that his German audience at the time would be able to recognize as religious. Rather, amid what he interprets as cultural decline and decadence, Nietzsche seeks to *rescue* a form of religiousness that, in his view, has been buried under two thousand years of Christian dominance. The question, of course, is whether any such rescue effort is even conceivable.

25. Nietzsche, *Late Notebooks*, 249.
26. Nietzsche, *Late Notebooks*, 249.
27. Nietzsche, *Late Notebooks*, 249.

Kant's, Hegel's, Feuerbach's, and even Marx's rescue efforts made sense *within* a Judeo-Christian horizon. While criticizing Christianity, they also retrieved elements of it. Nietzsche, by contrast, calls for a cultural revolution, and as such for a transformation of the fundamental parameters within which human value can be assessed. At the end of *The Anti-Christ* he refers to it as involving "a revaluation of all values." As such it is an experiment with a forgotten or at least repressed form of meaning-making, capable of subverting and overturning existing practices of evaluation and interpretation.

Nietzsche frequently points to *The Birth of Tragedy* as the work in which, for the first time, he fully discovered the phenomenon and implications of the Dionysian. The late *Ecce Homo*, for example, composed some months before Nietzsche's collapse in January 1889, refers to this book as one in which the reactualization of "the Dionysian state" was supposed to usher in a "*tragic* age," an age in which life is supposed to be affirmed "even in its strangest and harshest problems."[28] Likewise, the 1886 "Attempt at a Self-Criticism," written in Sils-Maria on the occasion of the reissue of his first work, points to the immense importance of Dionysus for his own thinking, how this figure made him overcome pessimism, and how it anticipates his own figure of Zarathustra.[29] In view of the religious dimensions of Dionysus, however, *The Birth* poses a number of challenges for its interpreters. For one thing, what Nietzsche, as the title indicates, purports to do in this work is to provide an account of how Attic tragedy came into being. It hardly seems designed to address the questions of religion that kept haunting him in the 1880s. For another, while *The Birth* assigns Dionysus a crucial role in accounting for the origin of Greek tragedy, taking this figure (and the cult surrounding him) to be its decisive forerunner, the interpretation of this demigod appears to be obscured to a considerable extent by the many layers of philosophical and cultural ideas through which Nietzsche views both Dionysus and tragedy itself. Not only does Nietzsche reflect on the empirical facts surrounding the development of this literary form, but he invokes the dualistic metaphysics of Schopenhauer's *The World as Will and Representation*, mapping the key deities of Dionysus and Apollo as well as various accounts of the interconnections between music, drama, stage, experience, and audience onto the fundamental metaphysical duality of "world-will"

---

28. Nietzsche, *Anti-Christ, Ecce Homo, Twilight of the Idols*, 109–10.

29. Nietzsche's *Twilight of the Idols* ends with some, for him, fairly characteristic references to the Dionysian as encompassing "joy" and "joy in destruction," referring to *The Birth of Tragedy* as his first "revaluation of all values," with which "I am back on that soil where my wants, my *abilities* grow—I, the last disciple of the philosopher Dionysus,—I, the teacher of eternal return."

and "representation" (*Vorstellung*). Also, in addition to being an *altphilologisch* tract (one that, as such, was severely criticized by, among others, the philologist Ulrich Wilamowitz-Möllendorff), *The Birth* offers a critique of contemporary society and culture, holding up Wagner as the hero of a reimagined future for Germany and as an authentic representative of the spirit of ancient Greek tragedy. Behind the deceptive simplicity of this first major writing by Nietzsche lurk such a large number of complex and interweaving motivations that teasing out the meaning of any one set of them easily risks oversimplification and misunderstanding.

To approach the religious significance of the figure of Dionysus in *The Birth* more specifically, the most useful place to start may be its convoluted and scattered remarks on modernity. It is in response to the assessment of modernity that he formulates his view of the implications of the Dionysian.

In his account of the downfall of tragedy as a dominant cultural form in ancient Greece, Nietzsche invokes "Socratic rationalism." According to Nietzsche, human life is subject to the inherently indifferent and amorphous, individuality- and form-denying incursions of the world will, and therefore also to suffering and death. Since it never seriously addresses this tragic reality, Socratic rationalism can never be anything but shallow. Initially introduced into tragedy by Euripides's character-driven and discursive dramas, it finds its emblematic literary expression in the naive moral didacticism of Aesopian fable and sets the stage for what Nietzsche calls Alexandrian culture, in which "theoretical man" has fully destroyed "Dionysiac wisdom and art."[30] In modernity, however, this rationalism translates into the view, familiar from Weber's theory of secularization, that science and technological rationality must (and indeed will) replace myth, and that all human problems, including existential ones, permit a rational answer. Nietzsche's early vision of modernity is almost completely predicated on the idea of the abiding triumph of Socratic rationalism. Surprisingly, given its leading role in the later writings, the supposed nihilism of Christianity plays no role in *The Birth*. According to Nietzsche in this work, the crucial problem of modernity is not that Judeo-Christian religious practice has inculcated modern agents with a "hatred of life" and a valorization of weakness for its own sake, but that the ideal of rational explanation, and of the "theoretical man," has come to dominate all manner of orientation and meaning-making and become the exclusive source of ethical advice, undermining the sacred and immediately authoritative power of myth and pagan religious practice, leaving people with no sense of meaning, orientation, or identification: "Our whole modern world is caught in the net of Alexandrian culture, and the

---

30. Nietzsche, *Birth of Tragedy*, 109.

highest ideal it knows is *theoretical man*, equipped with the highest powers of understanding and working in the service of science, whose archetype and progenitor is Socrates."[31]

The yearning in Germany for a new mythology and its complex history from Schelling to Wagner, Nietzsche, Mann, and beyond has been documented in painstaking detail by Manfred Frank.[32] As Frank points out, myths serve to integrate communities: by accompanying cultic practice, and by referring the members to their sacred origins, they make up a central part of the foundation on which authentic communal life depends. Endowed with an authority provided and guaranteed by their taken-for-granted relationship to the sacred, they provide existential orientation and stake out essential value orientations. In modernity, in which that deep sense of unity and participation has been lost, since agents lack a sense of themselves as belonging to a mythically founded social order, they inevitably have to represent themselves in terms of individualism—the abstract individualism, roughly speaking, of political liberalism, but also the relativistic individualism of mere subjective preference-formation. Rather than being communally sanctioned, life plans and self-interpretations become something for which the individual stands responsible. Thus, in *The Birth*, Nietzsche alludes to the *Gemeinschaft/Gesellschaft* contrast, arguing that all levels of a "*Volk*," including the state apparatus itself, tend to be affected by the loss of myth.[33]

In addition to the existential superficiality of theoretical and scientific explanations, and the loss of a mythically integrated community, the early Nietzsche detects in modernity a triumph of technology. Not only does the consideration of "theoretical man" never transcend the level of appearance (in the Schopenhauerian sense), but his understanding of how the world might be "corrected" is inherently technological and pragmatic. In place of "metaphysical solace," Nietzsche writes, the theoretical man offers

---

31. Nietzsche, *Birth of Tragedy*, 110.

32. Manfred Frank, *Der kommende Gott: Vorlesungen über die neue Mythologie I* (Frankfurt: Suhrkamp, 1982); and Frank, *Gott im Exil: Vorlesungen über die neue Mythologie II* (Frankfurt: Suhrkamp, 1988).

33. Nietzsche, *Birth of Tragedy*, 108–9: "Now place beside this type of mythical culture abstract man, without guidance from myth, abstract education, abstract morality, abstract law, the abstract state; consider the rule-less wandering of artistic fantasy, unbridled by an indigenous myth; think of a culture which has no secure and sacred place of origin and which is condemned to exhaust every possibility and to seek meagre nourishment from all other cultures; that is the present, the result of Socratism's determination to destroy myth."

a form of earthly harmony, indeed its very own *deus ex machina*, namely the god of machines and smelting furnaces [*den Gott der Maschinen und Schmelztiegel*], i.e., the energies of the spirits of nature, understood and applied in the service of higher egotism; it believes in correcting the world through knowledge, in life led by science; and it is truly capable of confining the individual within the smallest circle of solvable tasks, in the midst of which he so cheerfully says to life: "I will you: you are worth understanding."[34]

Nietzsche, of course, views the attitude expressed in this quotation as naive. It demonstrates no interest in the fundamental questions of life and is satisfied with technological solutions in cases where metaphysical insight (mediated, in particular, by art) would have been more appropriate and fulfilling. However, the technoscientific orientation (and the intellectualizing that goes with it) also serves to *disenchant* the world. As quoted earlier, Weber defines disenchantment as the notion that "we are not ruled by mysterious, unpredictable forces, but that, on the contrary, we can in principle *control everything by means of calculation*."[35] In almost exactly the same way, Nietzsche considers modern life devoid of magic. It offers its members a world in which nothing "shines" any longer and where even art, which for the ancient Greeks was always tied up with a mythical horizon that would generate charismatic authority, is reduced to information or mere entertainment.[36]

In matters of aesthetic concern, Nietzsche places special blame on what he sees as the loss of the Apollonian *Kunsttrieb* (art drive). Symbolized by the figure of Apollo, this is associated with a yearning for form, individuation, and beauty, but also for embodying communal ethos and endowing it with expressive and motivational power. Nietzsche's modernity, in other words, seems incapable of glorifying itself. While it takes immense pride in scientific and technological progress, and in its respect for the moral sanctity of the individual person, it contains no resources, whether theoretically or practically, for generating a sense of genuine and deep meaning. The inevitable human suffering that once, due to the institution of tragedy, had

---

34. Nietzsche, *Birth of Tragedy*, 85.

35. Weber, *Vocation Lectures*, 12–13.

36. For a wide-reaching account of the contrast between Greek paganism and modernity in terms of the metaphor of "shining," see Hubert Dreyfus and Sean Dorrance Kelly, *All Things Shining: Reading the Western Classics to Find Meaning in a Secular Age* (New York: Free Press, 2011).

been met with a certain tragic acceptance and even affirmation of life, cannot be addressed—or even expressed—other than as a scientific problem.

I have already hinted at what is generally accepted as the central, organizing question raised in *The Birth*, namely the problem of suffering and death.[37] While both Schopenhauer and Nietzsche purport to explain the perpetuity of suffering with reference to the metaphysical thesis of the *Wille*, The *Birth* abounds with references to how, in their myths, the ancient Greeks, despite entertaining no such view, envisioned life as inherently absurd, tragic, and, in the final instance, perhaps not worth living. Thus, upon being asked by King Midas what the best and most excellent thing for human beings might be, the forest daemon Silenus, "companion of Dionysus," replies that "The very best thing is utterly beyond your reach: not to have been born, not to *be*, to be *nothing*. However, the second best thing for you is: to die soon."[38] The fate of such figures as Oedipus and Prometheus testifies precisely to this sense of tragic inevitability: in spite of their supreme greatness and excellence as characters, they undergo the most extraordinary horrors—Oedipus unknowingly kills his father and sleeps with his mother and then, having solved the riddle of the Sphinx, eventually tears out his own eyes; Prometheus, on account of his love of mankind is condemned to be bound to a rock while an eagle feeds on his liver. In their splendor and luminosity, Nietzsche argues, the Olympian gods were largely created to help the Greeks survive and overcome the terror and disgust associated with human existence.

Among the responses to suffering being presented in *The Birth*, we have already encountered "Socratism," the view that reason, and in modernity technology, has in principle the capacity to solve every human problem, which Nietzsche sees as inadequate. Some cultures, such as that of the Fijian Islanders, have presumably not disposed of any such collective solution to the problem of suffering, and have been led to such levels of despair as to see

---

37. In his Introduction to the Cambridge University Press edition of *The Birth of Tragedy*, xxii, Raymond Geuss takes this to mean that *The Birth* "is intended as a contribution to philosophical theodicy." Insofar as Nietzsche expressly wants to show that the world is worthy of human approbation, despite appearances to the contrary, and that a thoughtful consideration of human existence is able to sustain an optimistic attitude toward life and the world as a whole, this attribution may seem justified. However, as Geuss himself points out, Nietzsche's theodicy is at odds with much of the theological tradition. Philosophical theodicies in the West, while complex, have typically appealed to the existence of an omnipotent God who, based on a rational plan, has benevolently arranged history to maximize human flourishing and happiness. There is nothing of that in Nietzsche's thinking.

38. Nietzsche, *Birth of Tragedy*, 23.

no alternative but to adopt "an ethic of genocide out of pity."[39] The Greeks, though, invented three mythically shaped ways to handle their pessimism. All of these, Nietzsche argues, were able to turn the collective from a pessimism of resignation to a pessimism of strength. The first, associated with Apollo and yielding an "Apollonian" outlook on life, centered on the projection of beautiful illusions, the dreamlike and tranquil perception of beautiful forms of the kind found in Doric art. At least according to Nietzsche's characterization, the Apollonian view seems removed from the intense encounters with the sacred associated with Dionysus. Modeled on Schopenhauer's account of the *principium individuationis*, providing the conditions (space, time, and causal determinacy) under which entities can appear to human cognition, it involves no claim to metaphysical reality and nothing but a superficial delight in the mere appearance of things. As such it bears greater similarity to the nineteenth-century cult of *l'art pour l'art* that Nietzsche was familiar with than to ancient religious practice. Still, the aestheticizing, idealizing attitude of the Apollonian is not without value. It offers its supporters a means to "justify" human life.[40] (By "justification" Nietzsche obviously does not have in mind some merely rational activity such as providing reasons. No reason or principle could prompt an individual to find joy and existential endorsement in art. The Apollonian *Rechtfertigung* of life is better thought of as a worldview, a way of viewing and evaluating the world involving an unstable combination of perceptual, emotive, and rational powers.) The Olympian gods are made in the image of humans; in short, they present glorifying "mirror images" of human life, ideals to identify with, and as such they are able to make human life seem worth living.

Nietzsche's attempt to provide a "justification" of life is relevant to his assessment of the Apollonian orientation. The cult of beauty and divine radiance reflected in classical Doric art does, he thinks, go at least some way toward reconciling people to suffering and death. (At least it seems to have done so during a certain phase of ancient Greek history.) However, the Apollonian strategy is not without shortcomings. It seems fleeting, more or less wholly indexed to exceptional experiences that do not easily carry over into the sphere of everyday life. Also, as Nietzsche himself points out, it faces a metaphysical challenge. The works of art in which the proponents of Apollonian culture see themselves reflected and idealized fall short of reality. Indeed, the "justification" of life is precisely illusory: the gods are

---

39. Nietzsche, *Birth of Tragedy*, 74. Nietzsche's claim about the Fiji islanders seems entirely unwarranted.

40. Hence Nietzsche's famous theodiciacal remark in *The Birth of Tragedy*, 33: "—for only as an *aesthetic phenomenon* is existence and the world eternally *justified*—"

creatures of human dreams, masking reality more than they reveal it. We have seen how the later Nietzsche claims to detect a life-negating tendency in Christianity. Although the Apollonian orientation does not negate life but claims to endorse and affirm it, it does so in a way that, by idealizing and aestheticizing, evades its actual nature.

While also meant to provide existential solace, Dionysian culture is much closer to the kind of religiousness that continues to attract Nietzsche throughout his career. It is true that he does not return to the figure of Dionysus until the final years before the collapse, and that the figure of Apollo, "the god of all image-making energies,"[41] eventually starts to dominate much of his thinking, especially about art and the form-giving conditions of culture. However, to the extent that Nietzsche indeed can be said to claim to rethink and even reactualize a form of pre-Christian religiousness, the Dionysian impulse must be viewed as the more central of the two "drives."

Considered as philosophical notions, both the Apollonian and the Dionysian are complicated by the fact that, semantically, they harbor both metaphysical, aesthetic, cultural, social, religious, and psychological elements, each associated with a specific set of defining experiences suggestive of something like a phenomenology. In terms of the latter, we have seen how the Apollonian is related to dreams. However, since the early Nietzsche has in mind collective achievements, the emphasis on the dream image may be misleading.[42] Dreams seem eminently tied to individuals and the phenomenal content of individual experience. Yet in focusing on the dream image Nietzsche hardly has individuals in mind. Indeed, just as the experience of viewing a work of art in a museum or a gallery can be said to be collective, affecting every member of the audience, so contemplating the image of the god in the beautiful sculpture is common and available to everyone and, as such, constitutive of the community's self-understanding. The Dionysian, however, is much more overtly collective, focused on experiences of transgression, bliss, and terror that the community undergoes not as the result of its individual members' receptiveness but as a unity or totality irreducible to the sum of its elements. Being exposed to the Dionysian, Nietzsche writes, "is best conveyed by the analogy of *intoxication* [*Rausch*]."[43] And by intoxication, he clearly means activities and states involving communities: then this, involving sex and drugs, is about revelry, though in a cultic form of the kind that supposedly existed around the figure of Dionysus.

41. Nietzsche, *Birth of Tragedy*, 16.

42. Andrew Huddleston, *Nietzsche on the Decadence and Flourishing of Culture* (Oxford: Oxford University Press, 2019).

43. Nietzsche, *Birth of Tragedy*, 17.

The complexities surrounding this demigod are considerable. The myths through which Dionysus has become known and celebrated come in different versions, each with its associated cultic practices. Also, while Nietzsche may be the most influential exponent of the Dionysian in modern European culture, reflections on the social, cultural, and existential implications of this figure precede Nietzsche by more than half a century, starting with Schelling and several of the most prominent German Romantics, who viewed Dionysus as a figure of the deep integration, authority, and meaning that they typically believed modern Europe had lost. Dionysus, of course, is well known to modern audiences from Euripides's tragedy *The Bacchae*, a play Nietzsche repeatedly praises despite his otherwise negative view of this tragedian as elsewhere having introduced "Socratism" on stage, owing to his emphasis on dialogue and psychological character study. In *The Bacchae*, Dionysus is portrayed as endowed with boundless charismatic authority, capable of seducing his followers (mainly women, the "maenads") into relinquishing all forms of moral prohibition and sense of separateness in favor of being submerged into an irresponsible and ultimately dangerous crowd of revelers. As Frank points out, the version of Dionysus to which Nietzsche pays the most extended attention seems to be "Dionysus-Zagreus," the demigod who as a young boy was torn to pieces by the Titans as punishment for his illicit existence as the love child of Semele's tryst with Zeus.[44] Thus the myth of Dionysus/Zagreus places the suffering of the individual at center stage. However, in the mystery cults surrounding this figure, the focus is equally on Dionysus/Zagreus as a figure who *overcomes* suffering, who after being transformed into air, water, earth, and fire returns, promising a renewed unity of all that exists, and especially between man and nature. In the conclusion to Nietzsche's reflections on Dionysus/Zagreus, he sees the myths surrounding him as offering "the fundamental recognition that everything which exists is a unity; the view that individuation is the primal source of all evil; and art as the joyous hope that the spell of individuation can be broken, a premonition of unity restored."[45]

As with the Apollonian, the Dionysian solution to suffering finds its ultimate explanation within the framework of Schopenhauer's metaphysics. Since, on this view, suffering is restricted to individuated beings with constantly frustrated desires, unification with primordial being (the "*Ur-Eine*") puts an end to suffering. Rather than being exposed to the contingency that comes with individuation, the human being relinquishes its claim to individuality, and as a result becomes part of a vast, profound wholeness.

44. Frank, *Gott im Exil*, 53.
45. Nietzsche, *Birth of Tragedy*, 52–53.

The immediate problem with this view, of course, if construed along Schopenhauerian lines, is that metaphysical transgression of this kind would not be compatible with any form of recognizable human experience and indeed would involve an extinction of the individual qua individual. How can that affirm life? Also, since it breaks away from the epistemic conditions of experience in general, it is far from clear how such an act may count as an experience of identification—and if it cannot be experienced, what would identification amount to? Indeed, Nietzsche refers to a "breakdown of the *principium individuations*," and he also speaks of how "we catch a glimpse of the essence of the *Dionysiac*," causing "subjectivity to vanish to the point of complete self-forgetting."[46]

Nietzsche's solution to the seemingly intractable problem of bringing his vision of Dionysian bliss so close to what we ordinarily would think of as death consists, one might argue, in seeing Dionysianism as akin to an encounter with the sublime. In the well-known accounts in Longinus and Kant, while the sublime terrifies, it does permit some form of controlled spectatorship, allowing for pleasure and enjoyment. Many of Nietzsche's passages describing the encounter with the Dionysian go in this less metaphysically charged direction. While the following passage contains several references to the Schopenhauerian metaphysics of phenomenon and the thing-in-itself (or *Wille*), it also provides a powerful description of how Nietzsche envisions an encounter with the sacred that does not presuppose any elements of Schopenhauer's idealism.

> In the same passage Schopenhauer has described for us the enormous *horror* which seizes people when they suddenly become confused and lose faith in the cognitive forms of the phenomenal world because the principle of sufficient reason, in one or other of its modes, appears to sustain an exception. If we add to this horror the blissful ecstasy which arises from the innermost ground of man, indeed of nature itself, whenever this breakdown of the *principium individuationis* occurs, we catch a glimpse of the essence of the *Dionysiac*, which is best conveyed by the analogy of *intoxication*. These Dionysiac stirrings, which, as they grow in intensity, cause subjectivity to vanish to the point of complete self-forgetting, awaken either under the influence of narcotic drink, which all human beings and peoples who are close to the origin of things speak of in their hymns, or at the approach of spring when the whole of nature is pervaded by lust for life.[47]

46. Nietzsche, *Birth of Tragedy*, 17.
47. Nietzsche, *Birth of Tragedy*, 18.

Through this drug-induced and sexually charged intense combination of "horror," blissful "ecstasy," and "lust for life," the participant in Dionysian revelry experiences a deep sense of unity, uniting not only humans but all of nature.

> Not only is the bond between human beings renewed by the magic of the Dionysiac, but nature, alienated, inimical, or subjugated, celebrates once more her festival of reconciliation with her lost son, humankind. Freely the earth offers up her gifts, and the beasts of prey from mountain and desert approach in peace. Singing and dancing, man expresses his sense of belonging to a higher community; he has forgotten how to walk and talk and is on the brink of flying and dancing, up and away into the air above. His gestures speak of his enchantment.[48]

While Nietzsche's Romantic rhetoric may, as he later recognized, strike us as overblown and flowery, it definitely characterizes a deep sense and understanding of the power of the sacred.[49] Dionysus is a god of music, song, dance, intoxication, and eroticism. Drawing support from all levels of society and thereby undermining social differences, and even the difference between living and dead, thereby reconstituting the community to itself in its immediacy and capacity for self-authorization, his presence both equalizes and unifies. As historian of religion Mircea Eliade puts it, "Intoxication, eroticism, universal fertility, but also the unforgettable experiences inspired by the periodic arrival of the dead, or by *mania*, by immersion in animal unconsciousness, or by the ecstasy of *enthousiasmos*—all these terrors and revelations spring from a sole source: *the presence of the god*. His mode of being expresses the paradoxical unity of life and death. This is why Dionysus constitutes a type of divinity radically different from the Olympians."[50]

Is Nietzsche referring to a *religious* experience? About that there can be no question. The theme of Dionysus that keeps emerging throughout Nietzsche's writing entails an unmistakable commitment to the idea that, if

---

48. Nietzsche, *Birth of Tragedy*, 18.

49. Nietzsche's self-criticism is no less than brutal. See the 1886 "An Attempt at Self-Criticism," in *The Birth of Tragedy*, 5: "I repeat: I find it an impossible book today. I declare that it is badly written, clumsy, embarrassing, with a rage for imagery and confused in its imagery, emotional, here and there sugary to the point of effeminacy, uneven in pace, lacking the will to logical cleanliness, very convinced and therefore too arrogant to prove its assertions."

50. Mircea Eliade, *A History of Religious Ideas*, vol. 1, *From the Stone Age to the Eleusinian Mysteries*, trans. Willard R. Trask (Chicago: University of Chicago Press, 1978), 372.

interpreted correctly, what we know about the cult of Dionysus may in fact provide a complex set of ideals with which Christianity can be confronted. While implicit in *The Birth*, Nietzsche pits one religion against another.[51] Does he manage to show that Dionysian culture is able to provide existential solace? I have argued that the Schopenhauerian interpretation in which the Dionysian encounter is supposed to involve a loss of individuality and the "suspension of the *principium individuationis*" seems unpromising. However, if the Dionysian festival is interpreted in its proper religious framework, and in terms of its psychological impact, then another Nietzschean claim, central to his late interest in Dionysus, can be shown to be important. While difficult to characterize properly, the claim, as in the long-standing philosophical discourse on the nature of the sublime, focuses on an exposure (no doubt psychologically regressive), up to the point of identification, to heterogeneity and chaos, followed by an experience of inevitable regeneration, differentiation, and creation. The rites surrounding the figure of Dionysus/Zagreus mimic very primitive celebrations of natural cycles, ranging from death to rejuvenation. The Maenads, enacting the dismembering of Dionysus in the hands of the Titans, would hunt wild animals, kill them, and eat them raw. Not only would they take pleasure in the act of destruction, they would also feel connected to a larger unity in which individual suffering may be overcome. The unity, forged and guaranteed by the presence and authority of Dionysus, is both communal, promising equality and reciprocity, and natural, promising enjoyment and pleasure.

The theme of affirmation (for the late Nietzsche so central) plays into the account—and this is one point of difference between Nietzsche and Schopenhauer, for whom the most adequate response to the pervasiveness of the will is resignation. The Dionysian revelers do not respond to suffering with a demand for idealization or transcendence. Instead, they endorse, up to the point of rejoicing in it, the playful and decidedly amoral becoming of the world, including the kinds of transformations that, as in Dionysus's case, bring about hardship and physical challenge. Moreover, the rites of Dionysus rejuvenate and strengthen communal bonds, expressing, in terms anticipating Durkheim's social interpretation of religion, the ultimate power of social cohesion. The universal "brotherhood" they speak of also finds

---

51. I thus agree with Haar, *Nietzsche and Metaphysics*, 131: "[Nietzsche's] 'atheism' is not concerned with the simple possibility of God, but rather asserts a distinction between a heavily conceptualized and domesticated God and a divinity free from the conceptual weight of metaphysical theology. Nietzsche initiates a questioning, which makes him, as Heidegger wrote, 'the last German philosopher who was passionately in search of God.'"

expression in "dithyrambic" music, performed in a state of rapture. (Despite the forced comparison, of which *The Birth of Tragedy* contain so many, Nietzsche hears a similar call for the destruction of all the "rigid, hostile barriers" between human beings in Beethoven's [and Schiller's] *Hymn to Joy*.)

This vision of unity may seem like a model of genuine cultural achievement. Invoked as a counterweight to the purported nihilism and exhaustion of modern, Christian and post-Christian, culture, it may, as Nietzsche believes, serve as a potent ideal for critics calling for radical cultural transformation. However, the Dionysian state is unstable and harbors a potential for cruelty and moral regression. Just as Kant's and Schiller's sublime objects justifiably provoke fear, and lest one is willing to be exposed to serious, and sometimes lethal, risk should only be beheld at a safe distance, so the promise of existential solace via some form of active participation in the ever-changing forces of nature may quickly become a real threat to the individual (as indeed it was to Pentheus, who, at the end of *The Bacchae*, is decapitated by the frenzied maenads).

According to Nietzsche, the Greeks eventually rejected Dionysian culture for precisely this reason. For a while it was replaced by Apollonian culture and its promise to veil the terrible aspects of existence. However, a more coherent and more effective solution to the challenge of suffering and finitude came with the cultural achievement of tragedy and with "tragic culture." Combining the chorus and the individual characters on stage, the tragedy unites both Dionysian and Apollonian elements. The music provided by the chorus transports the spectator into an ancient Dionysian world of continuity, transgression, play, and cruelty. However, thanks to the beautiful Apollonian veil created by the vision of heroic individuals on the stage, the suffering of the hero can be beheld as something palatable and indeed even aesthetically enjoyable and glorious. While Dionysian culture invites the individual to experience an ambivalent and potentially dangerous identification with existence in both its enchanting and its terrible aspects, Apollonian culture idealizes and ultimately veils reality. Only tragic culture contains the kind of cult that will successfully synthesize sublime transgression with the distance and tranquility that Apollonian viewership provides.

In his middle period—from the mid-1870s to the mid-1880s—Nietzsche proved decidedly skeptical regarding the kind of cultic, pagan religious practices he highlighted and endorsed in *The Birth of Tragedy*. Reasons for this are multiple and are certainly related to his eventual rejection and breakup with Wagner and his followers, for whom the idea of reconstituting German culture through music and opera, conceived along lines similar to Nietzsche's metaphysical interpretation of Greek tragedy, had been central even before the publication of this early work on tragedy. In works such as

Human, All Too Human (1878), "Assorted Opinions and Maxims" (1879), "The Wanderer and His Shadow" (1880), *Daybreak* (1881), and the first four books of *The Gay Science* (1882), Nietzsche develops his genealogical method, starts taking a rather positive view of science and even sees himself as a "psychologist," completely dismisses Schopenhauer's metaphysics (and indeed all forms of metaphysics, espousing instead a version of naturalism), and seems to valorize individualism and personal autonomy to an extent that would have been impossible during the early period.[52] During this middle period, while Nietzsche continues his crusade against central features of modern life, including its supposed failure to value strength and creativity in favor of generalizing to ever more areas of human involvement a quasi-Christian emphasis on pity and benevolence, we find a thinker at least in partial acceptance of modernity. Perhaps the most overt expression of this newfound belief in the superiority of select features of modern existence is his repeated praise for certain thinkers of the French Enlightenment, including Voltaire and Diderot. Nietzsche of the middle period seems far removed from the Romanticism of his youth.

The moment, at the end of book 4 of *The Gay Science,* when he suddenly introduces the figure of Zarathustra (about whose peregrinations, prophecies, and ideals he immediately goes on to compose *Thus Spoke Zarathustra*) is thus, to say the least, perplexing. Not only is Zarathustra's name taken from a Persian religious thinker of the sixth/seventh century BC (known to the Greeks as Zoroaster) who propagated fanciful metaphysical doctrines and a radical distinction between good and evil, but Zarathustra, who refers to the sun as an "over-rich heavenly body" and speaks in the prophetic language of an Abraham or a Moses, seems to occupy a highly enchanted and indeed religiously charged space. His "service of God," we learn in book 5 of *The Gay Science*, composed in 1887, consists not in the intellectual activities of the scholar or the philosopher but in "dance." Dance, Nietzsche writes, is Zarathustra's "only piety."[53] And in the high-strung rhetoric of the late, autobiographical reflections in *Ecce Homo*, Nietzsche returns to the characterization of Zarathustra as "a dancer," claiming to see in him "someone with the hardest, the most terrible insight into reality, who has thought 'the most abysmal thought,'" and who, rather than "objecting to existence," finds "one more reason in it for *himself to be* the eternal yes to all things, the incredible,

---

52. For an excellent overview of Nietzsche's middle period, see Ruth Abbey, *Nietzsche's Middle Period* (Oxford: Oxford University Press, 2000).

53. Nietzsche, *Gay Science*, 246.

boundless yes-saying, amen-saying into all abysses." Then, completing the paragraph, he writes: "*But this is the concept of Dionysus once more.*"[54]

I agree with Robert Pippin's insistence that whatever Zarathustra is a prophet for, it cannot simply be a "replacement" religion.[55] The fervor that animates this very strange writing from Nietzsche's hand is too much tinged with a vision of what it would mean to *overcome* religion for Zarathustra's affirmative philosophy to count as just "one more way of being religious." One of the first things we learn about Zarathustra, after all, is that he thinks, and is ready to proclaim, "that *God is dead!*"[56] Upon meeting an old, worshipping hermit in the woods on his way down from the mountains, he mocks the man's reverence while soon after proclaiming the coming of the overman, "the meaning of the earth," and saying that nothing is more valuable than remaining "faithful to the earth."[57] However, as with the figure of Dionysus and the cult surrounding his existence, there can be no question that Zarathustra engages deeply with the needs that have motivated religious attitudes and behavior, and also that his teaching of radical affirmation reverberates with experiences that can be said to have a religious significance, although obviously not in a Christian, ontotheological sense. Like Dionysus (in Nietzsche's reading), Zarathustra portrays himself as responding to a version of the problem of theodicy. The version cannot be the narrow one handed over from Leibniz, namely how God's infinite goodness and benevolence can be vindicated in view of the existence of evil. Rather, it must be a wider form of theodicy (expressed in manifestly Schopenhauerian form in *The Birth of Tragedy*) of how life in general can have any value despite the prevalence in it of suffering, contingency, and disappointment—in short, how the recognition of human finitude can be accommodated and accepted without losing the will to live and, in an even more general sense, the capacity to entertain value. Rather than arising from a metaphysical deficit of the kind that the early Nietzsche ascribed to the world will, "the terrible insight into reality" that Nietzsche in *Ecce Homo* ascribes to Zarathustra seems to reflect an acknowledgment of suffering and death, but also of the numerous responses that Zarathustra identifies as being detrimental to human flourishing. As humans search for an otherworldly solution to their woes, they tend to debase and demean themselves while failing to seek out the opportunities that life, when fully affirmed, holds in store for them. They suffer

---

54. Nietzsche, *Anti-Christ, Ecce Homo, Twilight of the Idols, and Other Writings*, 131.

55. Robert Pippin, "Introduction," in Nietzsche, *Thus Spoke Zarathustra*, trans. Adrian del Caro (Cambridge: Cambridge University Press, 2006), ix.

56. Nietzsche, *Thus Spoke Zarathustra*, 5.

57. Nietzsche, *Thus Spoke Zarathustra*, 5–6.

from their own lack of enjoyment, their many refusals and rejections, their negativity. The list of figures in *Thus Spoke Zarathustra* who can be said to incorporate some such way of self-depredation is long and includes "the dwarf," "the priests," "the Hinterworldly" (*den Hinterweltlern*), and literally a host of skeptics for whom the world, and the conditions of human existence (as they see them), do not deserve our approbation.

How, in view of the acknowledgment of suffering, can Zarathustra's joy be expressed? Indeed, exactly what does affirmation (*Bejahung*) mean and involve? Especially toward the end, *Thus Spoke Zarathustra* abounds with passages that, in terms reminiscent of certain forms of religious discourse, are suggestive of reverence before the world itself. In the "Sleepwalker's Song," which Zarathustra teaches his followers at midnight, pain is overcome by joy as its implicit narrator is overcome with a sense of mystery and awe that makes him admonish "mankind" to pray.[58] However, according to Nietzsche's self-evaluation in *Ecce Homo*, the "basic idea of the work" is the thought of the eternal return.[59] While versions of this idea, with which Nietzsche seems to have been obsessed, occur frequently in the late work and include quasi-scientific, hypothetical, and mythological accounts, the most influential statement may be the one at the end of book 4 of *The Gay Science*. Here the topic of eternal recurrence becomes a question, posed by a "demon," of how one would respond to the prospect of an eternal repetition of one's own life: "—What if some day or night a demon were to steal into your loneliest loneliness and say to you: 'This life as you now live it and have lived it you will have to live once again and innumerable times again; and there will be nothing new in it, but every pain and every joy and every thought and sigh and everything unspeakably small or great in your life must return to you, all in the same succession and sequence— even this spider and this moonlight between the trees, and even this moment and I myself.'"[60] One response, Nietzsche indicates, would be to see this endlessly repetitive movement as entirely meaningless since it would lack any final goals: whatever the fixed sequence of events amounted to, there could be no ultimate or external purpose (it would not be *for* anything); and everything that is possible would already have been reached. Despite its internal movement and endless repetition, it would be a static world, one without promise

---

58. Nietzsche, *Thus Spoke Zarathustra*, 264: "O mankind, pray! / What does deep midnight have to say? / From sleep, from sleep—'From deepest dream I made my way:—/ The world is deep, / And deeper than the grasp of day. / Deep is its pain -, / Joy—deeper still than misery: / Pain says: Refrain! / Yet all joy wants eternity—/— Wants deep, wants deep eternity.'"

59. Nietzsche, *Anti-Christ, Ecce Homo, Twilight of the Idols*, 123.

60. Nietzsche, *Gay Science*, 194.

and hope. In an entry from *Writings from the Late Notebooks*, Nietzsche thus characterizes this version of eternal recurrence as "the most extreme form of nihilism: nothingness ('meaninglessness') eternally!"[61]

One might think that the fatalistic reading of the thought-experiment exhausts all relevant possibilities. However, Nietzsche provides another interpretation, centered no longer on its ontological implications but on what it would mean for an individual to accept the doctrine. Fundamentally, what the statement now involves is whether an individual can find it in herself to affirm life as it is, both here and now, in the past, and in the future. Since every single moment will have to be accepted as forever repeating itself, it will become eternal, calling for an unconditional endorsement: *this* is your life, and if you are willing to accept it as forever recurring, it follows that even its most negative aspects, the suffering and pain, the meaninglessness and resentment, the boredom and misery, are equally perfect, or at least beyond possible improvement. Indeed, as Nietzsche describes it, the achievement of affirmation within the terms set by such a scenario transforms everything, all manners of existence, into something divine. It is worth noticing that as the world appears "perfect, divine, eternal,"[62] the result may be thought of as a form of pantheism. Comparing his own affirmative stance to Spinoza's claim to see every moment as having a "*logical* necessity" (presumably because, in *The Ethics*, Spinoza arrives deductively at a radically deterministic view of reality), Nietzsche admits to "a sense of triumph about the world's being constituted *thus*."[63]

As Michel Haar points out, the implicit reference to pantheism—that the world is divine—should not be understood literally.[64] Unlike Spinoza, Nietzsche never identifies the world with some new god; there is no Deus sive Natura, nor is there a panentheism according to which the world somehow is in, or an aspect of, God, a part, as it were, of God's body. While the affirmation at every moment of the world implied by the doctrine of the eternal return is supposed to make us see the world in each of its moments as divine, there is no divine totality present within existence, nor does Zarathustra include any divine intentions or purposes. The world of Zarathustra's imagination is not that of a fairy tale: it can include wars, wounds, and earthquakes. It is, however, transfigured.

---

61. Nietzsche, *Writings from the Late Notebooks*, 118.
62. Nietzsche, *Writings from the Late Notebooks*, 118.
63. Nietzsche, *Writings from the Late Notebooks*, 118.
64. Haar, *Nietzsche and Metaphysics*, 142.

The idea of the eternal return runs up against some fairly obvious challenges. On the one hand, construed as an ontological doctrine, Nietzsche's doctrine seems woefully unsupported by evidence. On the other hand, considered as a mere thought experiment, it raises some very thorny questions. What if the world (as we know it) does not "deserve" to be affirmed—or only in a limited and perhaps attenuated sense? While most people find something in life they deeply cherish, few or no one could see themselves esteeming *everything* unconditionally. Indeed, certain things seem for perfectly acceptable reasons impossible to value positively and see as good: unjustified suffering, unmitigated ugliness, immorality. Of course, if the series of events that make up one turn of this cosmological wheel is in some way bad or evil, then the perfection Nietzsche has in mind must *exclusively* be a function of the act of affirmation, and at this point one may wonder whether affirmation could be a form of self-delusion: I am in hell but keep telling myself that things are great. Does this make them good?

For Nietzsche, affirmation is an act of the will; it is something one decides to do, in a supreme act of self-overcoming, regardless of evidence. Affirmation is not blind to the world. It is, though, indifferent to all value except its own self-created value—and, by implication, indifferent to the value of moral responsiveness, the experience of being called upon by some moral authority different from one's own will to do or value the good. The overt amoralism implied by the doctrine threatens to make the agent of affirmation cold, stoic, and self-centered, though without the redeeming features of stoic reliance on natural law. Zarathustra asks his followers to celebrate the world yet hardly gives them a reason to do so. The reasons for doing so, which would be evaluative, are supposed to be generated and then imposed on reality only by the subject itself. As a result, it is hard to see how his preachings and prophecies, despite their celebration of life and promises of personal and cultural rejuvenation, can form the basis for a new faith.

As was the case with Dionysus, the tropes used to characterize Zarathustra are to a considerable extent drawn from the tradition of aesthetic and philosophical thinking about the concept of the sublime. Zarathustra's preferred abode is high in the mountains, making it necessary for him to *descend* in order to find human beings; and he enjoys wandering either in stark sunlight or in dark nights lit only by the stars and the moon. In *Ecce Homo*, Nietzsche famously remembers how, in Sils Maria, during the writing of *Thus Spoke Zarathustra*, one day in August 1881 he found himself "6,000 feet beyond people and time."[65] In Longinus, Kant, and Schiller, whose writings on this subject Nietzsche is likely to have

---

65. Nietzsche, *Anti-Christ, Ecce Homo, Twilight of the Idols*, 123.

read, the experience of the formless and overwhelming (in terms of both magnitude and power), if taking place from a safe distance, can give rise to a unique feeling of bliss and joy even if the content of the experience gives rise to concern. As long as one is safely ensconced on a cliff high above the roaring ocean, it is possible, Longinus claimed, to enjoy the spectacle of a shipwreck.[66] For Kant and Schiller, we enjoy such a spectacle because the envisioning of the sublime hints at the exalted grandeur and power of our own nature as creatures not just of nature but of reason and morality. If indeed—with a number of qualifications—Zarathustra, with his claim to be able to find joy in even the most adverse circumstances, incorporates and expresses a view of the world as sublime, then it should not come as a surprise that the involvement with reality he recommends can seem detached, predominantly imaginary (a "display"), and without the ability to acknowledge pregiven value.

As I mentioned, the Dionysus of *The Birth of Tragedy* can also be viewed as a figure of the sublime—and, as such, being juxtaposed to the beautiful forms of the Apolline, Dionysus represents the formless, transgressive qualities of nature; and, indeed, Nietzsche refers several times to the Dionysian satyr as sublime. Yet unlike Zarathustra, for whom sublimity is fundamentally a lonely experience, brought about through acts of existential affirmation, Dionysus promises unity and participation, the overcoming of separation within an enchanted space of the sacred. Confronted with Dionysus (as Nietzsche construes him), the onlooker does not need to actively affirm anything in order to find meaning. On the contrary, the Dionysian is characterized as a wave that just washes over people, eliminating their sense of separation and their insight into the prevalence of negativity and suffering. The Hamlet of Nietzsche's *The Birth of Tragedy* is portrayed as having succumbed to a nauseating feeling of the impossibility and meaninglessness of all action. Like the "hinterworldlings" of *Thus Spoke Zarathustra* who feel nauseated by the world, calling it "a filthy monster," Hamlet has had insight into "the terrible truth."[67] Yet if faced with the satyr chorus of the dithyramb, a figure like Hamlet would instantaneously be healed.

> Art alone can re-direct those repulsive thoughts about the terrible or absurd nature of existence into representations with which man can live; these representations are the *sublime*, whereby the terrible is tamed

---

66. For an elegant and effective exploration of this imagery as a metaphor, see Hans Blumenberg, *Shipwreck with Spectator: Paradigm of a Metaphor for Existence*, trans. Steven Rendall (Cambridge, MA: MIT Press, 1997).

67. Nietzsche, *Thus Spoke Zarathustra*, 164; Nietzsche, *Birth of Tragedy*, 40.

by artistic means, and the *comical*, whereby disgust at absurdity is discharged by artistic means. The dithyramb's chorus of satyrs is the saving act of Greek art; the attacks of revulsion described above spent themselves in contemplation of the intermediate world of these Dionysiac companions.[68]

In *Thus Spoke Zarathustra*, we find very little of this spontaneous, celebratory, and totemistic collectivity. There are followers and prophets, animals and children, but hardly any attempt to zero in on the kind of collective effervescence that, in *The Birth of Tragedy*, is supposed to abolish the individual's experience of suffering. The collectivities that do occur are predominantly viewed as sterile, offering no space for creation and meaning-making.

The "Land of Education," for example, on which Zarathustra offers his opinions, seems to present a version of the enlightened community of scholars that Nietzsche criticized in the *Untimely Meditations*. While "educated," they have no beliefs and hence no commitments and are, in short, *incapable of faith*. Owing to an excess of historical knowledge, they are cognizant of all human possibilities, yet only as somebody else's. Their ironical detachment paralyses action, and, as Young suggests, devalues all value along the lines of the "nihilism of postmodernity."[69] Another and considerably more mysterious moment when, in *Thus Spoke Zarathustra*, something like a community is gathered involves the "Ass Festival," briefly interrupting the ecstatic sections toward the end of work when Zarathustra starts articulating his vision of "the eternity of all things" in the concluding "Sleepwalker's Song." As a model for the Ass Festival, Nietzsche may have had in mind the medieval Feast of Fools with its remnants of archaic religious practice. Organized by the clergy, the Feast of Fools contained carnivalesque elements, men dressing up as women or animals, and, at the center, an ass that was led up the church aisles covered in a golden cloth. Not only did this ritual parody the Eucharist and even Calvary, but it also performed a subversion of social and cultural hierarchy.

Is the Ass Festival some kind of Zarathustrian analogue to the Dionysian cult? The overall sentiment at the festival (and indeed also when heard through the narrating voice) seems to be one of silliness, leading Zarathustra to speak in terms that indicate ridicule and contempt: '"They've all gone *pious* again, they're *praying*, they're mad!'—he said and

---

68. Nietzsche, *Birth of Tragedy*, 40.
69. Young, *Nietzsche's Philosophy of Religion*, 111.

he was amazed beyond measure."[70] Pretty soon Zarathustra, who is not typically disposed to humor, can "no longer control himself" and starts crying "Hee-yaw himself even louder than the ass."[71] By holding that the Ass Festival in fact alludes to the Saturnalia of ancient Rome, thereby representing "the subterranean survival of pagan Dionysianism into the Christian era,"[72] Young claims that it should be taken seriously as an expression of something that Zarathustra ought to, and in fact does, endorse. Indeed, at the end of the section on the *Ass Festival*, Zarathustra seems to take some inspiration from the spectacle, pointing to the need, in his view, for *"new festivals,"* festivals for the sake of the participants but also for Zarathustra himself.[73] However, the Ass Festival itself is a caricature of religious worship. What should be eternal, or at least should express some kind of relation to the divine, turns out to be an adorned animal, effectively a symbol of stupidity and narrow-mindedness.

However, the pathos of Zarathustra's "prayer" cannot be denied. Zarathustra gets portrayed as being moved by an affirmation of life strong enough to overcome Christian *ressentiment* and to enable a life-enhancing celebration of one's existence even in its most painful moments. Yet it is Dionysus (in Nietzsche's reading) who makes it possible to see Nietzsche as genuinely searching for a contrast to Christianity that is not simply atheistic in some straightforward sense. Nietzsche opposes Dionysus to Christ, and, as Reginster points out, while both of these are figures of suffering, they stand radically opposed in how they evaluate their suffering: Dionysus affirms, Christ negates.[74] Yet Dionysus functions as an emblem not only of affirmation but of cultic unity and the dispossession of selfhood. In a late note from spring 1888, Nietzsche explicitly identifies the Dionysian (now understood more directly and not, as in *The Birth of Tragedy*, primarily in conjunction with the aestheticizing and form-giving capacities of Apollonian sublimation) with paganism and the "pagan cult."[75] The highest "thanking" and "affirming" of life, he writes, includes, in its "highest representative," not just a "vindication" but a "deification" of life. In Dionysus, he continues, one finds "the religious affirmation of life,

70. Nietzsche, *Thus Spoke Zarathustra*, 254.

71. Nietzsche, *Thus Spoke Zarathustra*, 255.

72. Young, *Nietzsche's Philosophy of Religion*, 116.

73. Nietzsche, *Thus Spoke Zarathustra*, 257–58.

74. Bernard Reginster, *The Affirmation of Life: Nietzsche on Overcoming Nihilism* (Cambridge, MA: Harvard University Press, 2006), 229.

75. Nietzsche, *Writings from the Late Notebooks*, 249.

of life as a whole."⁷⁶ Unlike the more "aesthetic" affirmation of life with which he interprets Greek tragedy, the Dionysus of these late passages is truly a figure of what Otto would call *das Heilige*. It is perhaps in this sense that Dionysus is proclaimed to be Zarathustra's teacher. Far from just being a function of human projection, his authority is supposed to be wholly self-constituted, capable of casting a spell on his followers that allows for no hesitation or rational consideration. What Nietzsche calls for is nothing less than a complete reanimation of the world. Responding to the death of the god of transcendence, of ontotheology, he offers a god of radical immanence, able to overcome nihilism and create nothing but joy. While purporting to critique and help destroy Christianity, he rescues a more original experience of the divine.

---

76. Nietzsche, *Writings from the Late Notebooks*, 249.

Concluding Remarks

"God is dead!"—the assertion resonating throughout so much of nineteenth-century intellectual life brings up a number of complex issues related to the implications of secularization. In particular, the assertion generates questions about what it means to achieve a modern form of life. Does such a life necessarily involve a complete break with religion, or only some transformation or reinterpretation of it? By following the trajectory starting with Kant and ending with Nietzsche, I have explored how key thinkers in this tradition have both criticized their religious backgrounds and attempted to rescue elements of them.

I have argued that traditional secularization theory, according to which the process is carried forward mainly by the triumph of reason, the rationalization of society, especially in science, but also in law, morality, statecraft, and everyday life, not only fails to do justice to the real nature of religion, which is mistakenly treated as centered on belief, but is also set up to misrecognize, and ultimately reject, the critique/rescue dialectic itself. On the view associated with secularization theory, there is quite simply nothing to rescue once the epistemic claims contained in religious faith have been shown to be without merit. Against such an approach, I have examined philosophical enterprises that, by refusing to see faith in exclusively epistemic terms, have located religious belief within various ethical models. And by demonstrating how these models, even in circumstances of rapid modernization, permit the continuation or, in some cases, transformation of commitments previously associated with religion, I have considered their interest in religion to provide determinate content to their own philosophical accounts of meaningful contemporary aspirations.

I have attempted to map this dialectic. Kant envisions the achievement of a genuinely modern culture in light of his conception of a community undergoing a transition from revealed (or ecclesiastical) religion to a religion rooted in participation in an ethical community for whom God mainly plays a moral role as a stipulated condition enabling the practical employment of reason. For Kant this transition involves a transformed self-understanding whereby the full implications of what was merely implicit in revealed religion becomes explicit and guides action in the ethical community. However, while collectively committed to the laws of virtue and to the freedom the exercise of such virtue is predicated on, such a community must also be a juridical one, joined by constitutional laws. In this way Kant claims to be pointing to the potential, inherent in Christianity, for a form of self-overcoming that is more a form of full self-actualization than a step in an entirely new direction. The hitherto unacknowledged telos of Christianity is fundamentally moral and rational, structuring a life that, for Kant, comes to define what it truly is to be modern.

Kant both criticizes religion and rescues it, though in a form that may seem unrecognizable to traditional believers. What makes his complex assessment of faith, rationality, and the culture of modernity particularly interesting hinges not only on the moral interpretation of religion but also on his insistence on the inescapable need for an evidence-transcending supplement to autonomous morality. By claiming that moral life cannot be viewed as complete without reference to the concept of the Highest Good, motivating the stipulation of metaphysical entities such as God and immortal lives, Kant effectively admits that the reigning and defining principles of rationality in modernity, emphasizing demands of strict universality and abstraction, may be insufficient or, when considered in isolation, even incoherent or stultifying. Kant, in other words, reminds us not only of the potentials and prospects of enlightenment but also of its limits. From his interpretation of religion, he gathers ideals meant to be valid both for a rational secular order and for aspirations that cannot fully be fitted within such an order. Included in those aspirations is a desire for what Kant calls happiness, but also a desire for meaning—for a form of justice that goes beyond human law, and for a connection with the world that is richer and more assured than that of mere concept-mongering and subsumption.

In his early writings, Hegel introduces a retrograde vision of ethical life (*Sittlichkeit*) designed to incorporate elements of participatory religious practice while adhering to Kant's wish to consider religion mainly in moral terms. In the *Volksreligion*, as he calls it, members of the community find themselves motivated to act morally not only by the commands of reason itself but by "the heart"—the emotionally charged dispositions they inculcate and integrate as they partake in the community's self-authorizing practices. The early Hegel's understanding of the fate of religion (and more specifically Protestant Christianity, of course) thus anticipates Durkheim's approach: Religion is best theorized in its social aspect and as a social practice. As such it aspires to unite otherwise disunited agents, provide a sense of authority able to overcome the abstractions associated with Kant's moral rigorism, and transcend the Kantian split between empirical inclination and purely rational lawgiving. While being more attentive than Kant to the actual needs satisfied by religious practice—the needs, say, for a sense of belonging and community, for a visible emergence of authority, and for a more integrated sense of selfhood than that of the Kantian divided self—the upshot of Hegel's stipulations regarding the *Volksreligion* is that the purportedly one-sided rationalization of Enlightenment universalism must be rejected. The early Hegel of the *Tübingen Essay*, though hardly a reactionary, looks for an alternative to modernity (most likely to be found in the ancient Greek polis). A society entirely without the ability to project what it sees as the contours of a meaningful way of life would suffer anomie and nihilism.

The mature Hegel from the 1807 *Phenomenology of Spirit* onward takes a different and less nostalgic view of religion. He situates religion as an expression of the absolute and defines spirit as divine, while historically situated. However, since spirit is inextricably linked to the space of historical self-understanding, dialectically articulating that understanding in both social and symbolic forms, its erstwhile and long-standing existence as the transcendent, essentially reified entity of traditional theology and belief gives way, over the course of history, to an interpretation according to which spirit is mediated with the world itself, most strikingly with the state, which Hegel ultimately comes to see as "divine." Throughout this process of spirit's articulation in otherness, religion loses its authority, paving the way for philosophy to be recognized as the most adequate articulation of the absolute. In much of Hegel's reconstruction of the history of spirit one may detect elements of secularization. From the "unhappy consciousness" of early Christians, for whom the finite and the infinite are radically separated, Hegel's *Geistesgeschichte* moves forward to the onset of modernity when enlightenment criticism and Pietist rejection of both enchantment and every external manifestation of religious practice combine to introduce conditions whereby the state itself, as articulated philosophically, may arrive as the objective expression of spirit and the absolute. While Hegel retains a conception of God and even can be said to keep a quasi-Thomistic belief in His rational articulability, the overcoming of the division between God and world (made symbolically available in the figure of Christ) means that religion sheds every sense of the sacred, of mystery, of transcendence, and of a personal God. The implication is not that religious practice will disappear completely. Rather, it is that religion will no longer prove authoritative. For Hegel, modernity is an epoch of rationalization, rationally articulated freedom, and disenchantment. As opposed to his early dreams of a republican reconstitution of something like the ethical and spiritual community of the ancient Greeks, the mature Hegel purports to reconcile himself to a prosaic world of bourgeois equality and bureaucratic statehood. He rejects Kant's insistence on the need (at least for our moral lives to be intelligible) to rescue some conception of transcendence.

Feuerbach's projection theory finds religion to be a false projection of human essence. The critical project thus hinges on retrieving the alienated essence, showing it to be human, a vision of what humans may meaningfully aspire to. As the ontological framework for his investigations, Feuerbach adopts a version of materialism that emphasizes the finitude of human existence. Although Feuerbach constructs a conception of human selfhood that incorporates central elements of Hegel's view of normatively engaged self-interpretation—that is, of thinking and acting according to shared yet ideally self-chosen norms and standards that direct and regulate one's efforts at sense-making—he understands human existence in terms of a conception of sensuousness and embodiment. Unlike his idealist predecessors, Feuerbach theorizes human aspiration in terms of satisfying empirical, sensuous need. Being liberated from purportedly false forms of self-alienation makes it possible for such aspirations to be embedded in concrete human efforts and undertakings. If only, Feuerbach seems to say, we can figure out what kind of beings we really are, it will become clear to us what genuine self-actualization would involve. Indeed, despite our finitude, we can meaningfully aspire to be all the things that for a thousand years an alienated humanity associated exclusively with the divine.

Although Feuerbach goes further than both Kant and Hegel in criticizing religion (neither Kant nor Hegel would ever see religious belief as a mere illusion), like them he finds a way of rescuing its key elements. On Feuerbach's view, the alienated aspects of human selfhood can be retrieved and reappropriated, and, to the extent that they are, they are able to form the basis for a humanism that seeks to replace faith in God with faith in humanity. Marx's response to this strategy is ambivalent. While endorsing Feuerbach's view of religion as a species of self-alienation and accepting what he sees as the progressive potentials embedded in his materialism, he articulates a different view of human finitude. Adding a historical perspective yet rejecting Hegel's idealist construction of progress in favor of a socioeconomic understanding of social development and transformation, Marx interprets religious belief as ideological, reflecting and affirming the social system and the social divisions it has grown from. Having arrived at the well-known conclusion that religion is "opium for the people," offering illusory prospects of happiness in an oppressive reality while screening real opportunities for social change, Marx retains nothing whatever of classical religious ontotheology. However, as many commentators, including Löwith, have noted, he does construe history in ways that seem analogous to features of Judeo-Christian eschatology. Marx's historical-dialectical materialism promises its own kind of salvation; it sets up an ideal of justice that is supposed to supersede and overcome all previous social arrangements and finally liberate all individuals from oppression; and in the name of this ideal it views all individuals not only as having equal dignity but as deserving the same possibilities of self-actualization and an equal share of the outcome of production, which for Marx should be wholly socialized. While religion and historical-dialectical materialism show certain undeniable analogies, Marx consistently dismisses the appeal to otherworldly experiences, realities, or states. He unflinchingly holds on to the promise of earthly happiness. What remains is a vision involving compassion, solidarity, radical equality, and communal co-operation.

Nietzsche differs completely from the other thinkers whose views regarding the fate of religion I have examined in this volume. His response to what he sees as the impossibility of rationally defending ontotheology and what he presents as his diagnosis of Christianity's exhaustion is to call for a form of reenchantment of the world. Nietzsche's procedure is complex, moving through at least two steps: one that, in the spirit of the Enlightenment, criticizes Christianity from an epistemic and a genealogical point of view, and another, associated with his abiding preoccupation with the figure of Dionysus, in which he explicates and defends, both historically and philosophically, what such a reenchantment would involve and how it would qualify as a proposal for cultural reform and even revolution. The first step—especially the genealogy of Christian (slave) morality and its ideal of ascesis and self-abnegation—seems to funnel into a wholesale rejection of religion. This is the Nietzsche of "God is dead" who does not see any viable ideals for the future culture of modernity other than atheistic, exclusively humanistic, ones. Indeed, in *On the Genealogy of Morality* he considers the rejection of the vitality associated with life itself to have undermined Christianity and destroyed it from within. As Heidegger would later argue, the ontotheological versions of Christianity harbor within themselves a commitment to nihilism: there is no desire other than to negate.

In view of Nietzsche's almost visceral skepticism of everything to do with religion, it is intriguing yet also fascinating to discover that he proposes a set of ideals grounded in what I interpret as a religious sensibility, albeit not the one he finds in Christianity. Dionysus, with his promise of ecstatic self-transformation, is unquestionably a religious figure, and so was the cult surrounding this figure from which Nietzsche derives his conception of the origin of Greek tragedy. However, when viewed through the lens of the late invention of Zarathustra, it becomes evident that, while religious in a manifestly pagan sense, these ideals also align with Nietzsche's quest to articulate a position of radical affirmation in which the material world itself and our earthly conditions of existence are being elevated to the point of being holy and worthy of worship. For Nietzsche, the human being is "a bridge," a transitional entity, able to pave the way for the Overman, the figure of unrestricted self-affirmation and innocent life, who is supposed to transcend all the ideals of Christian, nihilist culture.

Hegel's effort to articulate secularization in terms of the emergence of a both liberating and self-actualizing form of ethical life (including the modern state and its both historical and conceptual presuppositions) continues to set the stage for both the Left Hegelians and Nietzsche. When compared with Feuerbach and Marx, however, Nietzsche is the one who most consistently breaks free of Christianity. Both Feuerbach and Marx hold on to at least certain key elements of a Christian worldview. Feuerbach does so with his anticipation of a community that retains, as Löwith puts it, "the Christian predicates while discarding their subject."[1] Although Marx manages to call Feuerbach's ahistorical, anthropological abstractions into question by situating them within a historical and materialistic framework, many of his key ideas, including the inevitability of class division and the anticipation of a reconciled state beyond history, remain in debt to a Judeo-Christian framework. Despite its thinking of radical finitude, it is hard not to agree with Joseph Schumpeter, who in *Capitalism, Socialism, and Democracy* writes that "In one important sense, Marxism *is* a religion. To the believer it presents, first, a system of ultimate ends that embody the meaning of life and are absolute standards by which to judge events and actions; and, secondly, a guide to those ends which implies a plan of salvation and the indication of the evil from which mankind, or a chosen section of mankind, is to be saved."[2] Nietzsche not only shares these thinkers' emphasis on human finitude and their rejection of all philosophical accounts of ontotheology, including that of Hegel, he launches a critique of the system of values that has underpinned the development of Christianity so powerful that his "rescue" attempt no longer carries any overt Judeo-Christian overtones. He recognizes the dangers of "nihilism"—how the loss of organizing, authoritative values and value judgments goes hand in hand with a diminished capacity to orient oneself ethically and act in decisive, creative ways, reflective of one's

---

1. Karl Löwith, *From Hegel to Nietzsche: The Revolution in Nineteenth-Century Thought*, trans. David E. Green (New York: Columbia University Press, 1964), 340.

2. Joseph A. Schumpeter, *Capitalism, Socialism, and Democracy*, 3rd ed. (New York: Harper, 2008), 5. To these points Schumpeter adds Marx's role (within Marxism) of being a prophet.

"power" and "vitality." However, by locating "the will to nothingness" of nihilism within the Christian worldview and attitudes more generally, he is precluded from following Hegel and the Hegelian tradition in viewing the promises of modernity in terms of a "translation" of Christianity into a secular register. For Nietzsche, the only form of modernity worth having will be one that has shed every vestige of Judeo-Christian belief and attitude. It is therefore interesting to note that, with the realization of the promises contained in Nietzsche's social philosophy, most of the commitments we would normally associate with modernity—liberal freedom, scientific reason and technology, consumerism, bureaucratically organized statecraft—are being squarely rejected as expressive of weakness and reaction. What makes Nietzsche unique is that he, in effect, completely condemns modern life as we know it. Nietzsche's modernity is countermodern, and in several key respects socially regressive.

In *The Birth of Tragedy*, the cultural rejuvenation being promised is intimately connected to the aesthetic cult surrounding Wagner at Bayreuth. Nietzsche sees Wagner as the contemporary forerunner of a revolution that ultimately would carry political implications. However, as Nietzsche came to realize that Wagner's operas—largely because of their Schopenhauerian and, in the final instance, Christian quest for redemption—may themselves be viewed as implicated in the history of Western nihilism, he gradually detaches his Dionysianism from any vestige of metaphysical dualism, attempting instead to understand it in terms of a philosophy of radical affirmation. Rather than a figure of metaphysical ambiguity, able to unite his followers within some deeper unity associated with the Schopenhauerian *Weltwille*, the Dionysus of the late writings, especially after the invention of the figure of Zarathustra, is a figure of uncompromising, unconditional acceptance and affirmation of the conditions of human existence, representing a vision of ecstatic self-overcoming. While the theodiciacal themes of suffering and how to flourish despite risk and finitude remain constant, the kind of authority assigned to Dionysus changes. It is no longer metaphysically founded. Instead, it is based on the attraction associated with Dionysus's innocence and playfulness, his childlike existence "beyond good and evil."

All this, of course, is heady stuff. Historically, it has also been dangerous. While the ideals projected by Marx's battle with religion became the basis for much of the totalitarian politics in the twentieth century (though one could argue forever about how much of it *really* served as justification), there can be little doubt that Nietzsche's version of this battle helped set the stage for much of the steely right-wing politics that culminated in fascism. To be sure, Hitler and his acolytes knew how to couch politics in neopagan forms. With its highly studied intimations of sacredness, the Führer cult offered its own communal spaces of collective self-dissolution and heteronomy—different, no doubt, from Nietzsche's Dionysian revelers, but also historically and ideologically similar in their rejection of morality, idealism, transcendence, autonomy, and individualism in favor of merging one's sense of selfhood with a collective social organization and unconditionally accepting some founding past and sovereign, charismatic force.

Although the progressive secularization of liberal societies returns its members to the agonizing questions of selfhood, meaning, and contingency to which religion for thousands of years provided answers, the legacy of this nineteenth-century debate is still with us, shaping the accounts we may manage to give of ourselves. If anything, I hope in this book to have shown that it is worth revisiting.

Bibliography

Abbey, Ruth. *Nietzsche's Middle Period*. New York: Oxford University Press, 2000.
Adorno, Theodor W. *Metaphysics: Concepts and Problems*. Translated by Edmund Jephcott. Stanford, CA: Stanford University Press, 2001.
———. *Negative Dialectics*. Translated by E. B. Ashton. New York: Continuum, 1973.
———. *Negative Dialektik*. Frankfurt: Suhrkamp, 1982.
Adorno, Theodor W., and Max Horkheimer. *Dialectic of Enlightenment: Philosophical Fragments*. Translated by Edmund Jephcott. Stanford, CA: Stanford University Press, 2002.
Allison, Henry E. *Kant's Transcendental Idealism: An Interpretation and Defense*. New Haven, CT: Yale University Press, 1983.
Althusser, Louis. *For Marx*. Translated by Ben Brewster. London: Verso, 2006.
Aristotle. *The Complete Works of Aristotle*. 2 vols. Princeton, NJ: Princeton University Press, 1984.
Armstrong, Karen. *Fields of Blood*. London: Bodley Head, 2014.
Augustine. *City of God*. Translated by Henry Bettenson. London: Penguin Books, 2003.
Avineri, Shlomo. *The Social and Political Thought of Karl Marx*. New York: Cambridge University Press, 1968.
Beck, Lewis White. *A Commentary on Kant's "Critique of Practical Reason."* Chicago: University of Chicago Press, 1996.
Beck, Ulrich. *Risk Society: Towards a New Modernity*. Translated by Mark Ritter. Washington, DC: Sage, 1992.
Beiser, Frederick C. *German Idealism: The Struggle against Subjectivism, 1781–1801*. Cambridge, MA: Harvard University Press, 2008.
Bellah, Robert. *Religion in Human Evolution: From the Paleolithic to the Axial Age*. Cambridge, MA: Harvard University Press, 2011.
Berger, Peter L. *The Sacred Canopy: Elements of a Sociological Theory of Religion*. New York: Anchor Books, 1990.
Bloch, Ernst. *The Principle of Hope*. 3 vols. Translated by Neville Plaice, Stephen Plaice, and Paul Knight. Cambridge, MA: MIT Press, 1986.
Blumenberg, Hans. *The Legitimacy of the Modern Age*. Translated by Robert M. Wallace. Cambridge, MA: MIT Press, 1991.
———. *Shipwreck with a Spectator: Paradigm of a Metaphor for Existence*. Translated by Steven Rendall. Cambridge, MA: MIT Press, 1997.
Casanova, José. *Public Religions in the Modern World*. Chicago: University of Chicago Press, 1994.

Cicero. *On the Nature of the Gods (De natura deorum)*. Translated by H. Rackham. Cambridge, MA: Harvard University Press, 1933.

Clark, T. J. *Farewell to an Idea: Episodes from a History of Modernism*. New Haven, CT: Yale University Press, 1999.

———. *Heaven on Earth: Painting and the Life to Come*. New York: Thames and Hudson, 2018.

Comte, Auguste. *Introduction to Positive Philosophy*. Translated by Frederick Ferré. Indianapolis: Hackett, 1988.

Crane, Tim. *The Meaning of Belief: Religion from an Atheist's Point of View*. Cambridge, MA: Harvard University Press, 2017.

Dawkins, Richard. *The God Delusion*. London: Bantam, 2006.

Dennett, Daniel C. *Breaking the Spell*. London: Allen Lane, 2006.

Derrida, Jacques. "Christianity and Secularization." *Critical Inquiry* 47, 1 (2020): 138–48.

Dreyfus, Hubert, and Sean Dorrance Kelly. *All Things Shining: Reading the Western Classics to Find Meaning in a Secular Age*. New York: Free Press, 2011.

Durkheim, Émile. *The Division of Labor in Society*. Translated by W. D. Halls. New York: Free Press, 2014.

———. *The Elementary Forms of Religious Life*. Translated by Carol Cosman. Oxford: Oxford University Press, 2001.

Dworkin, Ronald. *Religion without God*. Cambridge, MA: Harvard University Press, 2013.

Eco, Umberto. *The Name of the Rose*. Translated by William Weaver. Boston: Mariner Books, 1994.

Eisenstadt, Shmuel N. "Religious Origins of Modern Radicalism." *Theoria: A Journal of Social and Political Theory* 106 (2005): 51–80.

Eliade, Mircea. *A History of Religious Ideas*. 3 vols. Translated by Willard R. Trask. Chicago: University of Chicago Press, 1978.

Epicurus. *The Art of Happiness*. Translated by George K. Strodach. New York: Penguin Books, 2012.

Erasmus and Luther: The Battle over Free Will. Edited by Clarence H. Miller. Translated by Clarence H. Miller and Peter Macardle. London: Hackett, 2012.

Fackenheim, Emil L. *To Mend the World: Foundations of Post-Holocaust Jewish Thought*. Bloomington: Indiana University Press, 1994.

Feuerbach, Ludwig. *The Essence of Christianity*. Translated by George Elliot. Amherst, NY: Prometheus Books, 1989.

———. *The Fiery Brook*. Translated by Zawar Hanfi. London: Verso, 2012.

———. *Principles of the Philosophy of the Future*. Translated by Manfred Vogel. Indianapolis: Hackett, 1986.

Fichte, J. G. *Werke*. Edited by F. Medicus. Leipzig: Felix Meiner, 1910.

Frank, Manfred. *Gott im Exil: Vorlesungen über die neue Mythologie II*. Frankfurt: Suhrkamp, 1988.

———. *Der kommende Gott: Vorlesungen über die neue Mythologie I*. Frankfurt: Suhrkamp, 1982.

Freud, Sigmund. *Civilization and Its Discontents*. Translated by James Strachey. New York: W. W. Norton, 1989.

———. *On Metapsychology*. Translated by James Strachey. London: Penguin, 1984.

Gauchet, Marcel. *The Disenchantment of the World: A Political History of Religion*. Translated by Oscar Burge. Princeton, NJ: Princeton University Press, 1997.
Gehlen, Arnold. *Man: His Nature and Place in the World*. Translated by C. McMillan and K. Pillemer. New York: Columbia University Press, 1988.
Geuss, Raymond. *Changing the Subject: Philosophy from Socrates to Adorno*. Cambridge, MA: Harvard University Press, 2017.
———. *Politics and the Imagination*. Princeton, NJ: Princeton University Press, 2010.
Gillespie, Michael Allen. *Nihilism Before Nietzsche*. Chicago: University of Chicago Press, 1996.
———. *The Theological Origins of Modernity*. Chicago: University of Chicago Press, 2008.
Gilson, Étienne. *The Philosophy of St. Thomas Aquinas*. New York: Dorset, 1948.
Gordon. Peter E. *Migrants of the Profane: Critical Theory and the Question of Secularization*. New Haven, CT: Yale University Press, 2020.
Grayling, A. C. *Against All Gods*. London: Oberon Books, 2007.
Greenblatt, Stephen. *The Swerve: How the World Became Modern*. New York: W. W. Norton, 2012.
Haar, Michel. *Nietzsche and Metaphysics*. Translated by Michael Gendre. Albany: State University of New York Press, 1996.
Habermas, Jürgen, et al. *An Awareness of What Is Missing: Faith and Reason in a Postsecular Age*. Malden, MA: Polity Press, 2010.
———. *Auch eine Geschichte der Philosophie*. Vol. 1, *Die oxzidentale Konstellation von Glauben und Wissen*; vol. 2, *Vernünftige Freiheit: Spuren des Diskurses über Glauben und Wissen*. Berlin: Suhrkamp, 2010.
Hägglund, Martin. *This Life: Secular Faith and Spiritual Freedom*. New York: Pantheon Books, 2019.
Hammer, Espen. *Adorno's Modernism: Art, Experience, and Catastrophe*. Cambridge: Cambridge University Press, 2015.
———. "Epistemology and Self-Reflection in the Young Marx." In *Debates in Nineteenth-Century European Philosophy: Essential Readings and Contemporary Responses*, edited by Kristin Gjesdal. New York: Routledge, 2016.
———. *Philosophy and Temporality from Kant to Critical Theory*. Cambridge: Cambridge University Press, 2011.
Harris, H. S. *Hegel's Development: Toward the Sunlight, 1770–1801*. Oxford: Clarendon Press, 1972.
Harris, Sam. *The End of Faith: Religion, Terror, and the Future of Reason*. New York: W. W. Norton, 2004.
Hegel, G. W. F. *Aesthetics: Lectures on Fine Arts*. Translated by T. M. Knox. 2 vols. Oxford: Oxford University Press, 1999.
———. *Elements of the Philosophy of Right*. Translated by H. B. Nisbet. Cambridge: Cambridge University Press, 1991.
———. *Faith and Knowledge*. Translated by W. Cerf and H. S. Harris. Albany: State University of New York Press, 1977.
———. *Grundlinen der Philosophie des Rechts*. Frankfurt: Ullstein, 1972.
———. *Hegel's Logic*. Translated by William Wallace. Oxford: Oxford University Press, 1975.

———. *Lectures on the Philosophy of Religion: One-Volume Edition, The Lectures of 1827*. Edited by Peter C. Hodgson, translated by R. F. Brown, P. C. Hodgson, J. M. Stewart, and H. S. Harris. Berkeley: University of California Press, 1988.

———. *Lectures on the Philosophy of World History: Introduction, Reason in History*. Translated by H. B. Nisbet. Cambridge: Cambridge University Press, 1975.

———. *Phänomenologie des Geistes*. Frankfurt: Suhrkamp, 1986.

———. *The Phenomenology of Spirit*. Translated by Terry Pinkard. Cambridge: Cambridge University Press, 2018.

———. *Philosophy of Mind (Hegel's Encyclopedia of the Philosophical Sciences)*. Translated by A. V. Miller. Oxford: Clarendon Press, 1971.

———. *A System of Ethical Life* and *First Philosophy of Spirit*. Translated by H. S. Harris and T. M. Knox. Albany: State University of New York Press, 1979.

———. *Three Essays, 1793–1795*. Edited and translated by Peter Fuss and John Dobbins. Notre Dame, IN: University of Notre Dame Press, 1984.

———. *Vorlesungen über die Philosophie der Religion*. Hamburg: Felix Meiner, 1983.

Heidegger, Martin. *Kant and the Problem of Metaphysics*. 5th ed. Translated by Richard Taft. Bloomington: Indiana University Press, 1997.

Hitchens, Christopher. *God Is Not Great: How Religion Poisons Everything*. New York: Twelve Books, 2007.

Hodgson, Peter C., ed. *G. W. F. Hegel: Theologian of Spirit*. Minneapolis: Fortress Press, 1997.

———. *Hegel and Christian Theology: A Reading of the Lectures on the Philosophy of Religion*. Oxford: Oxford University Press, 2005.

Huddleston, Andrew. *Nietzsche on the Decadence and Flourishing of Culture*. Oxford: Oxford University Press, 2019.

Hume, David. *Dialogues concerning Natural Religion and Other Writings*. Cambridge: Cambridge University Press, 2007.

Jaeschke, Walter. "Philosophical Theology and Philosophy of Religion." In *New Perspectives on Hegel's Philosophy of Religion*, edited by D. Kolb. Albany: State University of New York Press, 1992.

———. *Reason in Religion: The Foundations of Hegel's Philosophy of Religion*. Translated by J. M. Stewart and Peter C. Hodgson. Berkeley: University of California Press, 1990.

James, William. *The Varieties of Religious Experience*. New York: Longmans, Green, 1902.

Kant, Immanuel. "An Answer to the Question: 'What Is Enlightenment?'" In *Kant: Political Writings*, edited by H. S. Reiss. Cambridge: Cambridge University Press, 2005.

———. *Critique of Practical Reason*. Translated by Mary Gregor. Cambridge: Cambridge University Press, 2015.

———. *Critique of Pure Reason*. Translated by Paul Guyer and Allen W. Wood. New York: Cambridge University Press, 1998.

———. *Critique of the Power of Judgment*. Translated by Paul Guyer and Eric Matthews. New York: Cambridge University Press, 2002.

———. "Ideas for a Universal History with a Cosmopolitan Purpose." In *Kant: Political Writings*, edited by H. S. Reiss. Cambridge: Cambridge University Press, 2005.

———. *Kritik der reinen Vernunft*. 2 vols. Frankfurt: Suhrkamp, 1988.

———. *Religion within the Boundaries of Mere Reason*. Translated by Allen Wood and George Di Giovanni. Cambridge: Cambridge University Press, 2018.

———. *Werke*. Vol. 8. Edited by G. Hartenstein. Leipzig: Modes und Baumann, 1838.

Kierkegaard, Sören. *The Book of Adler*. Translated by Howard V. Hong and Edna H. Hong. Princeton, NJ: Princeton University Press, 1998.

Kippenberg, Hans. "Dialectics of Disenchantment: The Devaluation of the Objective World and the Revaluation of Subjective Religiosity." In *Narratives of Disenchantment and Secularization: Critiquing Max Weber's Idea of Modernity*, edited by Robert A. Yelle and Lorenz Trein. London: Bloomsbury Academic, 2021.

Kolakowski, Leszek. *The Main Currents of Marxism*. Translated by P. S. Falla. London: W. W. Norton, 2005.

Kolb, David. *New Perspectives on Hegel's Philosophy of Religion*. Albany: State University of New York Press, 1992.

Lewis, Thomas A. *Religion, Modernity, and Politics in Hegel*. Oxford: Oxford University Press, 2011.

Löwith, Karl. *From Hegel to Nietzsche: The Revolution in Nineteenth-Century Thought*. Translated by David E. Green. New York: Columbia University Press, 1964.

———. *Meaning in History*. Chicago: University of Chicago Press, 1949.

Lübbe, Hermann. *Säkularisierung: Geschichte eines ideenpolitischen Begriffs*. Freiburg: Karl Alber, 1965.

Lukács, Georg. *The Theory of the Novel*. Translated by Anna Bostock. London: Merlin, 1978.

Luther, Martin. *The Essential Luther*. Edited and translated by Tryntje Helfferich. Indianapolis: Hackett, 2018.

MacIntyre, Alasdair. *Marxism and Christianity*. Notre Dame, IN: Notre Dame University Press, 1984.

Martin, David. *On Secularization: Toward a Revised General Theory*. Aldershot: Ashgate, 2005.

Marx, Karl. *Early Political Writings*. Edited and translated by Joseph O'Malley. Cambridge: Cambridge University Press, 1994.

———. *Later Political Writings*. Edited and translated by Terrell Carver. Cambridge: Cambridge University Press, 1996.

———. *Ökonomisch-philosophische Manuskripte*. Frankfurt: Suhrkamp.

Michalson, Gordon E. *Kant and the Problem of God*. Oxford: Blackwell, 1999.

Monod, Jean-Claude. *La querelle de la sécularisation de la Hegel à Blumenberg*. Paris: Libraire philosophique J. Vrin, 2016.

Nietzsche, Friedrich. *"The Anti-Christ," "Ecce Homo," "Twilight of the Idols" and Other Writings*. Translated by Judith Norman. Cambridge: Cambridge University Press, 2005.

———. *The Birth of Tragedy and Other Writings*. Translated by Ronald Speirs. Cambridge: Cambridge University Press, 1999.

———. *Friedrich Nietzsche: Sämtliche Werke. Kritische Studienausgabe in 15 Bänden*. Ed. Giorgio Colli and Mazzino Montinari. Berlin: De Gruyter, 2014.

———. *The Gay Science*. Translated by Josefine Nauckhoff. Cambridge: Cambridge University Press, 2001.

———. *On the Genealogy of Morality*. Translated by Carol Diethe. Cambridge: Cambridge University Press, 2007.

———. *Philosophy and Truth: Selections from Nietzsche's Notebooks of the Early 1870's.* Edited and translated by Daniel Breazeale. Amherst, NY: Humanity Books, 1979.
———. *Thus Spoke Zarathustra: A Book for All and None.* Translated by Adrian del Caro. Cambridge: Cambridge University Press, 2006.
———. *Writings from the Late Notebooks.* Translated by Kate Sturge. Edited by Rüdiger Bittner. Cambridge: Cambridge University Press, 2003.
Otto, Rudolf. *The Idea of the Holy: An Inquiry into the Non-rational Factor in the Idea of the Divine and Its Relation to the Rational.* Translated by John W. Harvey. Oxford: Oxford University Press, 1958.
Pasternack, Lawrence R. *The Routledge Philosophy Guidebook to Kant on Religion within the Boundaries of Mere Reason: An Interpretation and Defense.* London: Routledge, 2014.
Phillips. D. Z. *Wittgenstein and Religion.* London: St. Martin's Press, 1993.
Pinkard, Terry. *Hegel: A Biography.* Cambridge: Cambridge University Press, 2000.
———. *Hegel's Phenomenology: The Sociality of Reason.* New York: Cambridge University Press, 1996.
Pippin, Robert B. *Interanimations: Receiving Modern German Philosophy.* Chicago: University of Chicago Press, 2015.
———. *The Persistence of Subjectivity: On the Kantian Aftermath.* Cambridge: Cambridge University Press, 2005.
Rawls, John. *A Brief Inquiry into the Meaning of Sin and Faith.* Cambridge, MA: Harvard University Press, 2009.
Reginster, Bernard. *The Affirmation of Life: Nietzsche on Overcoming Nihilism.* Cambridge, MA: Harvard University Press, 2006.
Reichelt, Helmut, ed. *Texte zur materialistischen Geschichtsauffassung.* Frankfurt: Ullstein, 1975.
Robertson, Ritchie. *The Enlightenment: The Pursuit of Happiness, 1680–1790.* New York: Harper, 2021.
Rorty, Richard. *Contingency, Irony, and Solidarity.* Cambridge: Cambridge University Press, 1989.
Rorty, Richard, and Gianni Vattimo. *The Future of Religion.* Edited by Santiago Zabala. New York: Columbia University Press, 2005.
Rosa, Hartmut. *Resonance: A Sociology of Our Relationship to the World.* Translated by James C. Wagner. Cambridge: Polity Press, 2021.
———. *Social Acceleration: A New Theory of Modernity.* Translated by Jonathan Trejo-Mathys. New York: Columbia University Press, 2015.
Rosen, Michael. *The Shadow of God: Kant, Hegel, and the Passage from Heaven to History.* Cambridge, MA: Harvard University Press, 2022.
Rousseau, Jean-Jacques. *Émile, or On Education.* Translated by Allan Bloom. New York: Basic Books, 1979.
Rutter, Benjamin. *Hegel on the Modern Arts.* Cambridge: Cambridge University Press, 2015.
Scharff, Robert C. "Why Was Comte an Epistemologist?" In *Debates in Nineteenth-Century European Philosophy: Essential Readings and Contemporary Responses,* edited by Kristin Gjesdal, 171–81. New York: Routledge, 2016.
Schelling, F. W. J. *The Grounding of Positive Philosophy: The Berlin Lectures.* Translated by B. Matthews. Albany: SUNY Press, 2007.
Schopenhauer, Arthur. *The World as Will and Representation.* 2 vols. Translated by E. F. J. Payne. New York: Dover, 1969.

Schumpeter, Joseph A. *Capitalism, Socialism, and Democracy*. 3rd ed. New York: Harper, 2008.
Shklar, Judith N. *After Utopia: The Decline of Political Faith*. Princeton, NJ: Princeton University Press, 2020.
Shuster, Martin. *Autonomy After Auschwitz: Adorno, German Idealism, and Modernity*. Chicago: University of Chicago Press, 2014.
Taylor, Charles. "The Opening Arguments of the *Phenomenology*." In *Hegel: A Collection of Critical Essays*, edited by Alasdair MacIntyre, 151–87. New York: Doubleday, 1972.
———. *A Secular Age*. Cambridge, MA: Harvard University Press, 2007.
Taylor, Charles, and Hubert Dreyfus. *Retrieving Realism*. Cambridge, MA: Harvard University Press, 2015.
Vries, Hent de. *Minimal Theologies: Critiques of Secular Reason in Adorno and Levinas*. Baltimore: Johns Hopkins University Press, 2005.
Wartofsky, Marx W. *Feuerbach*. Cambridge: Cambridge University Press, 1977.
Weber, Max. *The Protestant Ethic and the "Spirit" of Capitalism*. Translated by Peter Baehr and Gordon C. Wells. New York: Penguin Books, 2002.
———. *The Vocation Lectures*. Translated by Rodney Livingstone. Indianapolis: Hackett, 2004.
Wood, Allen W. *Kant's Rational Theology*. Ithaca, NY: Cornell University Press, 1978.
———. *Kant's Religion*. Ithaca, NY: Cornell University Press, 1970.
———. *Karl Marx*. 2nd ed. New York: Routledge, 2004.
Young, Julian. *Nietzsche's Philosophy of Religion*. Cambridge: Cambridge University Press, 2006.

Index

Adorno, Theodor W., x, xii, 2, 119; *Dialectic of Enlightenment*, 40–41, 44–46; *Negative Dialectics*, 45, 46, 75–78
Aesthetics: Lectures on Fine Art (Hegel), 102, 110
alienation, xi, 34, 164; Feuerbach on, 6, 113–114, 121, 130, 191; Hegel on, 90, 97, 103, 104–6, 115, 129; Marx on, 4, 114, 135, 141, 143–45, 148
anomie, 24, 26, 83, 190
Anselm of Canterbury, 94
Anti-Christ, The (Nietzsche), 152–56, 164, 167, 180–81, 183
Apollo, 167, 170, 172–74, 178, 184, 186
Aquinas, 89, 94
Aristotle, 37, 97, 145
Armstrong, Karen, 16
asceticism, 20, 43, 162–63, 192
Assorted Opinions and Maxims (Nietzsche), 179
Augustine, 26, 39, 51, 139, 147

Bacon, Francis, 40, 131
beauty: Adorno on, 45; Kant on, 50, 61, 74; Nietzsche on, 170, 172, 173, 178, 184; of religion (Hegel), 103, 107, 109
Bellah, Robert, 18–19
Berger, Peter, 23–27
Birth of Tragedy, The (Nietzsche), 5, 152, 158, 163, 167–80, 184–86, 194. *See also* Apollo; Dionysus
Bloch, Ernst, 128, 147
Blumenberg, Hans, ix, 35–41, 146
Böhme, Jacob, 98, 115
Burke, Edmund, 11

Capital (Marx), 135
capital, 84, 133, 136, 141, 149. *See also* capitalism
capitalism, 1, 26, 39–43, 48; Marx on, 136, 141–43, 148–49
Casanova, Josè, 9
categorical imperative, 50, 60, 73
ceremony, vii, 87–88, 105, 110
Civilization and Its Discontents (Freud), 162
Clark, T. J., 43–44, 148
collective conscience, 21, 26
Comte, Auguste, 10–15, 20, 112
conformity, 19, 21
Crane, Tim, 16–20
creature-feeling, 23
critique and rescue, x–xi, 2–3, 151, 164, 167, 188–89; Feuerbach's approach to, 113, 127–28; Hegel's approach to, 81, 97, 111; Kant's approach to, 48, 54, 79; Marx's approach to, 145; Nietzsche's approach to, 166, 187
Critique of Hegel's Philosophy of Right (Marx), 115, 125, 130, 135
Critique of Practical Reason (Kant), 58–60, 63–64, 67, 70
Critique of Pure Reason (Kant), 47, 52–53, 56, 60–67, 82, 155
Critique of the Power of Judgment (Kant), 49–50, 61, 65–67

Dawkins, Richard, iix–ix, 3, 15
Daybreak (Nietzsche), 179
death, vii, 175–77, 180; of Christ, 123; and suffering, 29, 43, 66, 76, 168, 171, 172

death of God, 1, 10, 188; Hegel on, 80–81, 91, 98–99; Kant on, 74; Nietzsche on, 150, 160, 180, 187, 192
Democritus, 130–32, 138
Derrida, Jacques, 73–74
Descartes, Rene, 32, 52, 74, 89, 124
Dialectic of Enlightenment (Adorno/Horkheimer), 40–41, 44–46
dignity, 3, 11, 36, 47, 66, 192
Dionysus, 152, 164–68, 171–73, 175–78, 180, 183–87
disenchantment: Blumenburg on, 36, 40; Comte on, 14; Hegel on, 81, 82, 94, 108, 164, 190; Kant on, 50, 74, 77; Marx on, 130; Nietzsche on, 165; Taylor on, 31, 33; Weber on, 26, 41–45, 170
dogma, 11, 29, 125; religious, 9, 51, 72, 100, 108, 153, 162
Durkheim, Èmile: and Hegel, 83, 89, 189; and Marx, 149; and Nietzsche, 161, 177; social mode of authorization, 21–26, 34. See also neo-Durkheimian
duty, 49–50, 54, 58–69, 162

Ecce Homo (Nietzsche), 153–56, 167, 179–81, 183
Eckhart, Meister, 115
Elements of the Philosophy of Right (Hegel), 81, 91–92, 100–101, 135–37
Eliade, Mircea, 176
Encyclopedia of Philosophical Sciences (Hegel), 92, 95, 97
Epicurus, 59, 112, 124, 130–32, 138
essence, 16; Feuerbach on, 113–14, 120–22, 125–29, 133, 134, 191; Marx on, 129, 132, 144–45; Nietzsche on, 154–55
Essence of Christianity, The (Feuerbach), 120–21, 125, 127, 129
Euripides, 165, 168, 174
evil, 17, 26, 32, 39, 77–78; Kant on, 54, 58, 61, 64, 66, 71, 77–79; Marx on, 131, 146; Nietzsche on, 158, 174, 179, 180
existentialism, 57
existential solace, 8, 18, 169, 173–74, 177–78, 184
existential void, 25, 28, 45, 102, 165, 168–69
exploitation, 129–30, 138, 142–44, 146, 149, 159

Fackenheim, Emil, 78
Faith and Knowledge (Hegel), 91
fascism, 44, 194
Feuerbach, Ludwig: Christianity, 113, 128, 193; on God, 122–25, 128–29; and Hegel, 113–21, 123–27, 129, 191; and Marx, 113–15, 121, 125, 128–29, 133–34, 139–40; and Nietzsche, 121, 164, 193. See also essence; projection
Fichte, J. G., 6, 38, 74, 116, 141
final judgment, 75, 153
Frank, Manfred, 169, 174
Freud, Sigmund, 34, 75, 96, 114, 121; *Civilization and Its Discontents*, 162; *On Narcissism*, 125; superego, 161

Garve, Christian, 88
Gauchet, Marcel, 29, 34, 103
Gay Science, The (Nietzsche), 150, 152, 160, 179, 181
German Ideology, The (Marx), 134–35, 140, 142
Gillespie, Michael, 36, 38, 165
gnosticism, 39
Goethe, Johann Wolfgang von, 2, 88, 110
grace, 8, 20, 38, 57, 76, 153
Groundwork for the Metaphysics of Morals (Kant), 59, 63–64
guilt, 34, 75, 160–64

Haar, Michel, 164–65, 177, 182
Habermas, Jürgen, ix, 3, 10, 31, 147
harmony, 19, 68, 70, 170
heart, 71, 82, 84–85, 106, 189; matter of, 55–56
heaven, 147, 149
Hegel, G. W. F.: on Christianity, 80–111; and Feuerbach, 113–21, 123–27, 129, 191; on God, 80–111; and Kant, 81–83, 85–86, 88–89, 101, 111, and Marx, 114–15, 129, 131, 133, 135–45, 149; and Nietzsche, 109, 111, 164; on Spirit, 80–116
Heidegger, Martin, 2, 31–32, 34, 41, 160, 192
Herder, Johann Gottfried, 83, 88
highest good, the, 54, 58–78, 189
Hitchens, Christopher, viii, ix, 3, 15
Hodgson, Peter C., 93, 102, 108, 104

Hölderlin, Friedrich, xi, 2, 82, 84, 87–88, 109
Horkheimer, Max, 40, 41, 44–46, 77
Human, All Too Human (Nietzsche), 179
humanism: Feuerbach on, 113, 127–29, 164, 191; Marx on, 128–29, 132, 144–45, 149, 164, 191; Nietzsche on, 161; Taylor on, 29, 32
Hume, David, 11, 19, 38, 51, 84, 112, 154–55

imagination, 122, 125; Berger on, 23, 27; Hegel on, 87; Marx on, 143; Nietzsche on, 153–56, 158, 184
immanence, 20, 45, 81; Hegel on, 98, 158 (*see also* immanent criticism); Kant on, 48, 54, 61, 73, 77–79; Nietzsche on, 4, 166, 187
immanent criticism, 114, 127
immanent frame, 2, 29, 33–34
immaterialism, 116, 119
immortality of the soul, 48, 57, 64, 69–70, 76, 189
individualism, 1, 9–10, 148, 169, 179, 195
Islam, 19, 71, 100

Jacobi, Friedrich, 48, 55, 107–8, 147
Jaeschke, Walter, 62, 93–95, 106, 110
James, William, 16, 19
Jesus Christ: Feuerbach on, 122–23, 128; Hegel on, 81, 90, 98–99, 109, 123; Kant on, 71–72; Nietzsche on, 159, 161, 165, 186
Judaism, 71, 100, 102–5, 158–59
judgment, 28, 119, 154, 193; Kant on, 47, 49–50, 52–53, 56, 75, 77, 89. See also *Critique of the Power of Judgment*; final judgment

Kant, Immanuel: on faith, 53–57, 64, 66–73, 77; on God, 52, 54–55, 57, 64–65, 69, 71–79; on morality, 48, 50, 54–55, 58–72, 85; on religion, 48, 51–56, 58, 66–67, 70–75. *See also* categorical imperative; practical reason; pure reason; *summum bonum*; transcendental idealism
kenosis, 80, 100, 123

Kierkegaard, Sören, vii, 2, 6, 20, 57, 149
Kolakowski, Leszek, 132, 146

language games, 25, 35
Late Notebooks, The (Nietzsche), 151–53, 164, 166, 182, 186, 187
Lectures on the Philosophy of Religion (Hegel), 91–93, 96, 98–99, 102–5, 107–9
Lectures on the Philosophy of World History (Hegel), 92, 99, 101
Leibniz, Gottfried, 52, 74, 89, 107, 124, 180
Lessing, Gotthold, 82–83
Lewis, Thomas A., 82, 88, 93
liberalism, 1, 3, 9, 33, 39, 160; democracy, xi–xii; in society, 48, 136, 142, 144, 148, 194–95
Life of Jesus, The (Hegel), 90
Locke, John, 141
Longinus, Cassius, 175, 183–84
love, 85, 121–22, 125–26, 171; God's, 128; interpersonal, 20, 109, 157; self-, 54
Löwith, Karl, 35–36, 40, 146, 147
Luhmann, Niklas, 9
Lukács, George, 28
Luther, Martin, 38, 55. *See also* Reformation

magic, 27, 32, 102, 107, 170, 176
Marx, Karl: on Christianity, 113, 146, 147–48; and Feuerbach, 113–15, 121, 125, 128–29, 133–34, 139–40; and Hegel, 114–15, 129, 131, 133, 135–45, 149; on history, 134–35, 139–47; and Nietzsche, 149, 164
materialism: Marx on, 129, 131–32, 134, 138–45, 191–92; and secularization, 45, 52, 113. *See also* immaterialism
Metaphysics of Morals (Kant), 54, 59
Michalson, Gordon E., 72–73
Middle Ages, 31, 37, 80
Mill, John Stuart, xii, 9, 101
Milton, John, 26
miracle, 26, 50, 72
money, 23. *See also* capital
music, 9, 162, 167, 176–78
mythology, 87, 107, 165–69

Negative Dialectics (Adorno), 45, 46, 75–78
neo-Durkheimian, 10, 27–29
neo-Platonism, 26, 115, 136
New Atheists, 3, 19, 20
Nietzsche: on Christianity, 150–53, 155–68, 173, 177–79, 186; and Feuerbach, 121, 164, 193; and Hegel, 109, 111, 164; and Kant, 155, 160, 162, 164, 175, 178, 183–84; and Marx, 149, 164; on value, 155–60, 163, 165–67, 169. *See also* Apollo; Dionysus; slave morality; will to power
nihilism: of modernity, xii, 42, 108, 190; Nietzsche on, xi, 4–5, 157–68, 182, 185, 187, 192–94
nominalism, 13, 37–38, 76, 144
Novalis, xi, 11, 79

Ockham, William, 37
On Feuerbach (Marx), 126, 133–35
On Narcissism (Freud), 125
On the Genealogy of Morality (Nietzsche), 152, 156–63, 192
On the Jewish Question (Marx), 135
Otto, Rudolf, 22–23, 187

paganism, 88, 157–70, 178, 180, 186, 193–94
Paris Manuscripts (Marx), 132, 140, 144–45, 149
Parsons, Talcott, 9
Pasternack, Lawrence, 59–60, 63, 67, 72, 74
Phenomenology of Spirit, The (Hegel), 81, 92, 95, 103–7, 114–19, 123, 127, 190
Philosophenbuch (Nietzsche), 151, 153
Pietism, 38, 87–89, 108–9
Pinkard, Terry, 86, 88, 95, 106, 115
Pippin, Robert, 110, 115, 137, 180
Plato, 90, 136. *See also* neo-Platonism
Positivity of the Christian Religion, The (Hegel), 90
practical reason, 47–48, 53–54, 57–59, 64–77, 85, 111. See also *Critique of Pure Reason*
pragmatism, 18–19, 151, 153
projection, 4, 51; Feuerbach on, 6, 113–14, 117, 122–26, 191; Marx on, 113–14, 135

Protestantism, vii, xi, 38; Hegel on, 94, 107, 189; Kant on, 47, 55, 76; Weber on, 26–27, 42–43, 107
psychoanalysis, 75, 125, 161, 174
punishment, 28, 36, 63–65, 75, 112, 161
pure reason, 6, 58, 61–67, 70, 89. See also *Critique of Pure Reason*

Rawls, John, xii, 9, 22, 101
Reformation, 27, 33, 38–39, 80, 107, 160. *See also* Luther, Martin; Protestantism
Religion within the Boundaries of Mere Reason (Kant), 47, 54–55, 57, 60–61, 67–74
ressentiment, 4, 158, 159, 186
revelation, 47–48, 57, 72, 74; self-, 110, 112
ritual, 22, 43, 78, 87, 93, 103, 185
Roman Empire, 33, 80, 102–6, 157, 160
Romanticism, xi, 2, 11; German, 11, 79, 82, 88, 174; Nietzsche's, 176, 179
Rorty, Richard, 139, 151
Rousseau, Jean-Jacques, 78, 88

sacred, the: authority of, 15; and Dionysus, xi, 5, 164–65, 172, 175–76, 184; in modernity, 6, 8–9, 26, 34, 81, 111–12, 168–69, 190; in religion, 21–22, 24–24, 27–28, 39; texts, 17
sacrifice, 64, 86, 87, 161
salvation, 28, 39, 86, 113; in Christianity, 19, 38, 55, 71, 73, 111; Marx on, 135, 145, 147, 193
Schelling, F. W. J., 169, 174; and Christianity, 6, 26; and Feuerbach, 115–16; and Hegel, 82, 87–88, 90, 92, 149; and Marx, 131
Schiller, Friedrich, 2, 178, 183–84
Schlegel brothers, 11
Schleiermacher, Friedrich, 23, 27, 108
Schmitt, Carl, ix, xii, 41
scholasticism, 37, 72, 107
Schopenhauer, Arthur, 156, 162, 166–80
Science of Logic, The (Hegel), 92, 99–100, 123, 137
Scotus, Duns, 37, 116
self-actualization, 25; Feuerbach on, xi, 6, 114, 191; Hegel on, 86, 90, 93, 101, 111, 127–28, 193; Kant on, 50, 189;

Marx on, xi, 132, 141, 143–46, 148, 192; Nietzsche on, 160
self-determination, 118; of the Enlightenment, 10, 39, 40, 112; Kant on, 47–51, 69, 76
self-understanding, 173, 189; Hegel on, 4, 80, 82, 92–96, 114, 190; and secularization, x, 9, 40, 43
slave morality, 157–61, 192
social construction, 23–24, 130
socialism, 148, 160
Socrates, 168–69, 171, 174
Spinoza, Baruch, 99, 115, 124, 182
Spirit of Christianity and Its Fate, The (Hegel), 90
Stoicism, 44, 58–59, 104, 183
summum bonum, 54, 58–78, 189
System of Ethical Life, A (Hegel), 106, 107

Taylor, Charles, 10, 74, 102, 104–6, 145; secularization narrative, ix, 1, 2, 8, 29–35
technocracy, 14, 42
technology: and control of nature, 27, 32, 48, 169; and Nietzsche, 168–71, 194; and science, vii–viii, 10, 36, 39–40, 50
Thus Spoke Zarathustra (Nietzsche), 5, 152, 164–65, 167, 179–87, 192, 194
Tillich, Paul, 74
"Towards a Critique of Hegel's Philosophy" (Feuerbach), 116, 118, 120, 124
transcendental idealism, 51, 53, 55, 61, 78–79

Tübingen Essay (Hegel), 80–83, 86–90
Twilight of the Idols (Nietzsche), 152–56, 167, 180, 181, 183

Übermensch, 158, 165
Untimely Meditations (Nietzsche), 163, 185
utility, 40, 104, 105

virtue: Feuerbach on, 129; Hegel on, 86–87, 91; Kant on, 50, 58–60, 65, 72, 189; Nietzsche on 158–60, 162
Volksreligion, 83, 86, 88, 103, 189, 190
Voltaire, 5, 11, 82, 112, 152, 179
Vorstellung, 95–96, 123, 168

Wagner, Richard, 162, 166, 168–69, 178, 194
Wanderer and His Shadow, The (Nietzsche), 179
Wartofsky, Mark W., 120, 127, 140
Weber, Max, ix, xii, 160, 168; on disenchantment, 26, 31, 41–46, 170; and Hegel, 82–83, 87, 89, 107
Weltalter (Feuerbach), 116
will to power, 156, 159, 163
Will to Power, The (Nietzsche), 152, 163
Winckelmann, Johann, 88
Wittgenstein, Ludwig, 5, 25
Wolff, Christian, 52, 74
Wood, Allen W., 72–74

Young, Julian, 164, 185–86